ReFocus: The Films of Elaine May

ReFocus: The American Directors Series

Series Editors: Robert Singer and Gary D. Rhodes
Editorial Board: Kelly Basilio, Donna Campbell, Claire Perkins, Christopher Sharrett, and Yannis Tzioumakis

ReFocus is a series of contemporary methodological and theoretical approaches to the interdisciplinary analyses and interpretations of neglected American directors, from the once-famous to the ignored, in direct relationship to American culture—its myths, values, and historical precepts. The series ignores no director who created a historical space—either in or out of the studio system—beginning from the origins of American cinema and continuing up to the present. These directors produced film titles that appear in university film history and genre courses across international boundaries, and their work is often seen on television or available to download or purchase, but each suffers from a form of "canon envy"; directors such as these, among other important figures in the general history of American cinema, are underrepresented in the critical dialogue, yet each has created American narratives, works of film art, that warrant attention. *ReFocus* brings these American film directors to a new audience of scholars and general readers of both American and Film Studies.

Titles in the series include:

ReFocus: The Films of Preston Sturges
Edited by Jeff Jaeckle and Sarah Kozloff

ReFocus: The Films of Delmer Daves
Edited by Matthew Carter and Andrew Nelson

ReFocus: The Films of Amy Heckerling
Edited by Frances Smith and Timothy Shary

ReFocus: The Films of Budd Boetticher
Edited by Gary D. Rhodes and Robert Singer

ReFocus: The Films of Kelly Reichardt
E. Dawn Hall

ReFocus: The Films of William Castle
Edited by Murray Leeder

ReFocus: The Films of Barbara Kopple
Edited by Jeff Jaeckle and Susan Ryan

ReFocus: The Films of Elaine May
Edited by Alexandra Heller-Nicholas and Dean Brandum

edinburghuniversitypress.com/series/refoc

ReFocus:
The Films of Elaine May

Edited by Alexandra Heller-Nicholas and Dean Brandum

Edinburgh University Press is one of the leading university presses in the UK. We publish academic books and journals in our selected subject areas across the humanities and social sciences, combining cutting-edge scholarship with high editorial and production values to produce academic works of lasting importance. For more information visit our website: edinburghuniversitypress.com

© editorial matter and organization Alexandra Heller-Nicholas and Dean Brandum, 2019, 2021
© the chapters their several authors, 2019, 2021

First published in hardback by Edinburgh University Press 2019

Edinburgh University Press Ltd
The Tun—Holyrood Road
12 (2f) Jackson's Entry
Edinburgh EH8 8PJ

Typeset in 11/13 Monotype Ehrhardt by
Servis Filmsetting Ltd, Stockport, Cheshire

A CIP record for this book is available from the British Library

ISBN 978 1 4744 4018 9 (hardback)
ISBN 978 1 4744 4019 6 (paperback)
ISBN 978 1 4744 4020 2 (webready PDF)
ISBN 978 1 4744 4021 9 (epub)

The right of the contributors to be identified as authors of this work has been asserted in accordance with the Copyright, Designs and Patents Act 1988 and the Copyright and Related Rights Regulations 2003 (SI No. 2498).

Contents

List of Figures and Tables   vii
Notes on Contributors   viii
Acknowledgments   xi

Introduction: Who's Kidding?—Approaching Elaine May   1
Alexandra Heller-Nicholas

Part 1 Beginnings

1 Teenagers on Stage—The Comedy of Elaine May and Mike Nichols   23
   Mark Freeman

Part 2 Critically Situating Elaine May

2 Hollywood Can't Wait: Elaine May and the Delusions of 1970s
   American Cinema   41
   Maya Montañez Smukler

3 Dangerous Business—Elaine May as Existential Improviser   63
   Jake Wilson

Part 3 Elaine May's Films as Director

4 Kneeling on Glass—Elaine May's *A New Leaf* (1971) as Screwball
   Black Comedy   85
   Samm Deighan

5 "Don't Put A Milky Way in Someone's Mouth When They Don't Want It": A Contemporary Feminist Rereading of Elaine May's *The Heartbreak Kid* (1972)   104
   Clem Bastow

6 *Mikey and Nicky* (1976)—Elaine May and the Cassavetes Connection   119
   Jeremy Carr

7 Cartographies of Catastrophe—Elaine May's *Ishtar* (1987)   139
   Dean Brandum

Part 4 Collaborations/Revelations

8 In/Significant Gestures—Elaine May, Screen Performance, and Embodied Collaboration   165
   Alexandra Heller-Nicholas

9 Otto É. May(zo)—Elaine May's Screenplay of Otto Preminger's *Such Good Friends* (1971) as Affirmation that Hell is Other People   181
   Paul Jeffery

10 Spectral Elaine May—The Later Mike Nichols Collaborations and the Myth of the Recluse   202
    Tim O'Farrell

Conclusion

11 *When in Doubt, Seduce*: An Interview with Screenwriter Allie Hagan   221
    Alexandra Heller-Nicholas and Dean Brandum

Bibliography   234
Index   244

Figures and Tables

Figures

I.1	Director Elaine May, *A New Leaf* (1971) Aries Productions (PictureLux/The Hollywood Archive/Alamy Stock Photo)	9
1.1	Elaine May and Mike Nichols 1960 (Historic Collection/Alamy Stock Photo)	24
5.1	We see what Lenny refuses to see (from *The Heartbreak Kid*, 1972)	112
5.2	The claustrophobic May mid-shot (from *The Heartbreak Kid*, 1972)	113
5.3–5.4	Female onlookers gazing at the gaze (from *The Heartbreak Kid*, 1972)	114
5.5	One last gaze at the gazer (from *The Heartbreak Kid*, 1972)	116
6.1	From *Mikey and Nicky* (Elaine May, 1976)	124
6.2	From *Mikey and Nicky* (Elaine May, 1976)	132
6.3	From *Mikey and Nicky* (Elaine May, 1976)	134
6.4	From *Mikey and Nicky* (Elaine May, 1976)	135
11.1	Screenwriter Allie Hagan	221

Tables

7.1	Box-office takings in *Ishtar*'s opening week	154
7.2	Box-office takings in *Ishtar*'s second week	156
7.3	Takings in the first seven weeks of *Ishtar*'s U.S. cinema release	157

Notes on Contributors

Clem Bastow is a screenwriter and award-winning cultural critic from Melbourne, Australia. Her work appears regularly in *The Saturday Paper* and *The Guardian*. She has written about film for journals including *The Lifted Brow*, *Kill Your Darlings* and *Filmme Fatales*, and books including *Copyfight* (2015), *Fury: Women Write About Sex, Power and Violence* (2015); she has also worked as a film critic for various publications including *The Guardian* since 2009. In 2017 she wrote and co-presented the ABC First Run podcast *Behind the Belt*, a documentary "deep dive" into professional wrestling. She holds a Master of Screenwriting from VCA, and teaches screenwriting at the University of Melbourne.

Dean Brandum gained his PhD at Deakin University (Australia) in 2016 for analysis of historical box office takings. He has taught at a number of universities in Melbourne and has written for various publications, generally on the topic of film distribution. His first book, *Technicolouryawn: Melbourne Drive-ins in 1970*, is forthcoming.

Jeremy Carr teaches film studies at Arizona State University and writes for the publications *Film International, Cineaste, Senses of Cinema, MUBI/Notebook, Cinema Retro, Vague Visages, The Moving Image, Diabolique Magazine*, and *Fandor*.

Samm Deighan is Associate Editor of *Diabolique Magazine* and co-host of the Daughters of Darkness podcast. Her book on Fritz Lang's *M* is due for a 2019 release and she is the editor of *Lost Girls: The Phantasmagorical Cinema of Jean Rollin* (2017), an edited collection written by women critics published by Spectacular Optical.

Mark Freeman is a lecturer in the Department of Film and Animation at Swinburne University, where he teaches and convenes a range of film theory classes. He has published widely in film journals such as *Senses of Cinema*, *Metro*, and *Screening the Past*, and published commissioned articles through publications such as *If Magazine*, *Metro Screen Education* and *Insight*. He also published a chapter entitled "An Uploadable Cinema: Digital Horror and the Postnational Image" for the anthology *Digital Horror: Haunted Technologies, Network Panic and the Found Footage Phenomenon* edited by Linnie Baker and Xavier Aldana Reyes.

Alexandra Heller-Nicholas is an Australian film critic. She has written five books on cult film with a focus on gender politics, and has published for fifteen years in many magazines, journals, edited collections, and home entertainment releases, including a booklet essay on Elaine May's *A New Leaf* on the 2017 Blu-Ray release by Olive Films. Her forthcoming books *1000 Women in Horror* and *Eyes Without Faces: Masks in Horror Film* are scheduled for an upcoming release. She has recently co-authored two other books: *Wonderland* for Thames & Hudson and the Australian Centre for the Moving Image to coincide with the latter's 2017 *Alice in Wonderland* in film exhibition, and another on the work of filmmakers Hélène Cattet and Bruno Forzani to accompany the 2017 Queensland Film Festival retrospective of their work. In 2017 she co-curated the "Pioneering Women" program at the 2017 Melbourne International Film Festival, which celebrated Australian women's filmmaking in the 1980s and 1990s. Alexandra is also a member of the Alliance of Women Film Journalists.

Paul Jeffery trained as an actor before transitioning to writing and directing: first in theater and then in his two independent features, *Adam and Eve* (2001) and *In the Moment* (2004). He is now an independent researcher with a particular focus on acting and cinema.

Tim O'Farrell teaches in the Film & Television program at the Victorian College of the Arts, selects films for the Melbourne International Film Festival, has a PhD in Cinema Studies focusing on documentary, and works as a lawyer.

Maya Montañez Smukler manages the UCLA Film & Television Archive's Research & Study Center. Her book, *Liberating Hollywood: Women Directors and the Feminist Reform of 1970s American Cinema*, was published in 2018. Her audio commentary is featured on Olive Films' Blu-ray of Elaine May's film *A New Leaf*.

Jake Wilson is a freelance writer, a film reviewer for Fairfax Media, and the author of *Mad Dog Morgan* (2015). He lives in Melbourne, Australia.

Acknowledgments

The editors would like to thank all the authors for their enthusiasm and hard work, the *ReFocus* series editors Gary D. Rhodes and Robert Singer for their support and kindness, the staff at the University of Edinburgh Press who have been so helpful, and of course to Elaine May herself for inspiring the responses contained within this volume. We would also like to thank our families: Amanda, Casper, Christian, and Georgia.

Introduction: Who's Kidding?— Approaching Elaine May

Alexandra Heller-Nicholas[1]

Q. Which words or phrases do you most overuse?
A. "You're kidding" and "Oh, fuck" and "Oh, fuck, you're kidding"
—Elaine May, interviewed in *Vanity Fair*, March 2009

She's such a genius of comedy that one never really knows when she's only kidding"
—Ally Acker on Elaine May[2]

"Even in context, Elaine May seems to be out of context," wrote Ally Acker in her 1991 book *Reel Women: Pioneers of the Cinema, 1896 to the Present*.[3] Not merely as a writer, comic, actor and filmmaker but as a member of that amorphous category "celebrity" there is something perpetually out-of-view about May, despite her visibility: the hackneyed phrase "hidden in plain sight" applies to her perhaps more than any other pioneering artist of her generation. This has resulted in a mythic quality to May, an aspect of her public persona that she herself has played a part in creating through her renowned aversion to press attention. As demonstrated in Sam Kashner's famous 2013 *Vanity Fair* "reunion" interview with May and her one-time comedy partner Mike Nichols—with whom she first came to the public's attention in the late 1950s— May seems almost intuitively driven to cast attention away from herself.[4] That she is simultaneously one of the twentieth century's greatest comic writers, performers, and screenwriters demonstrates the tensions and contradictions typical of Elaine May, rendering her an enduring and fascinating icon.

Even a pedestrian attempt at the obligatory biographical background that accompanies profiles such as this finds itself eventually mired in May's sticky enigmas. While there are no hard-and-fast facts that allow a confident statement of year of birth or other such data, according to multiple summaries of her childhood and early years,[5] May—born Elaine Berlin—began her show business career in Philadelphia with her father Jack, a Yiddish stage director, and her mother Ida, a comic and actor herself. Travelling to perform with her parents (she often played a little boy character called Benny), she had attended up to fifty different schools by the time she was ten years old. When she was eleven, her father died and she moved to Los Angeles with her mother. Dropping out of school altogether at fifteen, she worked a number of jobs (waitressing, selling roofing and being a private investigator). She married her first husband, Marvin May, at sixteen and had a child, but the marriage would last only one year. Lacking a high school qualification, she moved to Chicago to take "audit classes" so she could enroll in university. She never bothered doing the latter but still attended classes, and it was here—on the University of Chicago campus—where she met Nichols and her career proper began.

Or so, at least, the story goes. As Sam Wasson noted in his 2017 book *Improv Nation: How We Made a Great American Art*, even by 1951 the mythbuilding around May was in full swing. She was, for starters, exceedingly fashionable: "drop her name and your coolness quotient doubled. Get her to talk to you, or better still, respect you, and you were hip for life."[6] Wasson quotes an anecdote from Nichols about May relating to this period where she was said to have attended a philosophy tutorial and convinced both the professor and students alike that everyone in Plato's *Symposium* was drunk. Rumors of her background conflicted even then, with many believing she was from Philadelphia, Los Angles or even Argentina.[7] These conflicting biographical details would permeate May's career, in large part due to her own doing. In a small footnote to his 1997 description of encountering May, film critic Jonathan Rosenbaum discreetly notes that:

> May told me at our June 27 meeting that much of the biographical information that circulates about her is false, mainly due to her own idle inventions to the press over the years. She said that she was actually born in Chicago, and further suggested that the story about her growing up in the Yiddish theater was not strictly accurate.[8]

The only thing we know for sure about Elaine May's early years, then, is that the construction of popular memory was understood by her even as a young woman as fodder for a profoundly inventive and playful creative mind. She was, as Wasson notes, first and foremost "a shape-shifter, an improviser."[9]

While she's not exactly unknown, we have found anecdotally that Elaine May's work as a director is that which one tends to "discover"—as Chuck Stephens rightly observes, she has been "overlooked in virtually every New Hollywood hagiography."[10] Many come to her through her association with her higher-profile collaborators such as Mike Nichols, Peter Falk and John Cassavetes. My journey towards May was slightly different, yet it was also through her collaborative work with another cinematic icon: Isabelle Adjani. Adjani had long been my favorite actor since the moment I saw her in *La Reine Margot* (Patrice Chéreau, 1994), from which point I worked my way back through her diverse, lengthy filmography. I discovered Elaine May when she and Adjani joined forces on the critically maligned 1987 comedy *Ishtar*. While it famously resulted in what was effectively the end of May's directorial career, it was not a happy ending in terms of Adjani's ambitions at Hollywood either—a superstar in France, her efforts to break into mainstream American cinema evaporated with the *Ishtar* fiasco.

Like Adjani, however, there is certainly no lack of praise for May's work— *The New Yorker*'s Richard Brody having once described her as no less than "the greatest American woman director and simply one of the great modern filmmakers",[11] and she has been compared to filmmaking greats of the caliber of Billy Wilder[12] and Erich von Stroheim.[13] As screenwriter, actor, comic and director, May made only four films: *A New Leaf* (1971), *The Heartbreak Kid* (1972), *Mikey and Nicky* (1976) and *Ishtar* (1987), or, as Jessica Kiang refers to them in shorthand, "The Compromised Debut; The Bittersweet Hit; The Neglected Classic; and The Notorious Flop."[14] But, borrowing a phrase Vincent Canby used to describe her debut feature, all of May's work is "touched by a fine and knowing madness."[15]

Yet until recent years, even watching May's directorial work has itself been a challenge. When *A New Leaf* was finally released on Blu-ray in 2013, *The Village Voice*'s Calum Marsh observed that *The Heartbreak Kid* had been so hard to find that rare, out-of-print DVDs were being sold on Amazon for anywhere between $100 to $1998 a pop.[16] The obscurity of May's work does, admittedly, fit a longer trajectory of desired anonymity on her own part: Ryan Gilbey provides a laundry list of examples, including her requesting an interviewer not to mention her name in a feature article, her bio reading "Miss May does not exist" on her and Nichols' 1959 *Improvisations to Music* album, and—perhaps best of all—*LIFE* magazine publishing a "Where is she now?" article about her in 1967.[17] Over fifty years later, for the editors of this book and its contributors, the answer rings louder than it ever has: Elaine May is here (currently starring in the play *The Waverly Gallery* on Broadway as we write), and her presence as a multitalented writer, performer, and creator is today still as felt, recognized and cherished as ever.

APPROACHING ELAINE MAY

As discussed throughout this book in much further detail, Nichols is of course May's most significant professional collaborator, and her story is impossible to tell without him. As noted, they met at the University of Chicago, and became involved in a performance group called The Compass who, in the mid-1950s, were focused on improvisational sketch comedy.[18] Identified as the first improvisational theater in the United States, Kyle Stevens credits The Compass with "cultivating America's ear for realistic dialogue on stage, record and screen," typified in the later work of May and Nichols.[19] Forming a comedy duo in 1957, they became familiar faces on stage and television, their success on Broadway in particular launching a lucrative career that also included the release of successful comedy records.

When their partnership ended in the early 1960s, both had their eyes on Hollywood. May would appear in two films in 1967—Clive Donner's *Luv* (alongside future *Mickey and Nicky* star Peter Falk) and Carl Reiner's *Enter Laughing*. Nichols would go on to win a Best Director Oscar for 1967's *The Graduate* (in which May makes a brief yet memorable cameo in silhouette as the shadowy roommate of Katherine Ross's character, also called Elaine) and a BAFTA for Best Film the year before for *Who's Afraid of Virginia Woolf?*. May would again collaborate with Nichols on some of his most successful films of the 1990s: *Wolf* (1994), *The Birdcage* (1996), and *Primary Colors* (1998), although she was uncredited on *Wolf*. May's passion for the stage continued, with her successful one-act Off-Broadway play *Adaptation* in 1969, and despite her disappointment with her first screenplay, *Such Good Friends* (Otto Preminger, 1971) leading to that film being released with a screenwriter pseudonym, Esther Dale, May built a strong reputation as a screenwriter, earning an Oscar nomination for 1978's *Heaven Can Wait* (with co-writer Warren Beatty). May received both a National Medal of Arts in 2012 from President Obama and a Laurel Award for Screenwriting Achievement from the Writer's Guild of America in January 2016. As an actor, she later also appeared in films including *California Suite* (Herbert Ross, 1978), *In the Spirit* (Sandra Seacat, 1990), and *Small Time Crooks* (2000) and *Crisis in Six Scenes* (2016), both directed by Woody Allen, the former garnering her the Best Supporting Actress award from the National Society of Film Critics.

But it was as a director that May arguably did her best work and—according to some, at least—her worst. *Ishtar* has, in recent years, been granted a long-overdue reassessment, as many film critics and curators (Richard Brody and Miriam Bale in particular) have gone to extraordinary lengths to allow the film the serious critical reconsideration it deserves. At the time of its original release, however, *Ishtar* was unquestioningly in vogue as the-film-you-love-to-hate, and it destroyed May's directorial career. In retrospect, it's difficult to describe the scale with which *Ishtar*-bashing was so heartily embraced. That Gene Siskel and Roger Ebert christened it 1987's worst film and it won May a "Worst Director" at that year's Golden Raspberry Awards may begin to illustrate the intensity and scale of the critical derision it faced.

Which is a shame. *Ishtar* might not be May's masterpiece, but it is warm, funny and fundamentally joyful. For Richard Brody, it is an "ingenious microspectacle", "a grand-scale riot of a scenario realized with a precise and intimate mechanism."[20] A number of critics shrewdly drew parallels between Dustin Hoffman and Warren Beatty's bumbling, failed musicians who somehow fall on the wrong side of a CIA plot in the imaginary eponymous Middle Eastern country with the classic road movie comedies made famous by Bing Crosby and Bob Hope. Now that the hate-buzz has long died down, for the *Ishtar* defenders among us (whom we suspect are more numerous than you might imagine) it is nothing less than a vindication to have highly regarded critics coming out in the film's defence. What is fascinating about the most succinct of these arguments is how much they agree: aside from its notorious production history, the problem with *Ishtar* wasn't that it was necessarily a "bad" film, but that it cast Beatty and Hoffman—the former in particular—in roles so dramatically against type. Audiences and critics alike were not comfortable with Beatty as anything less than his signature smooth ladies' man. As Brody rightly noted, "critics reacted badly to May's reconfiguration of its stars . . . as somewhat ridiculous characters (exemplary members of May's gallery of the vain and the self-deluding), as if the deglamorization of icons were a sort of crime against cinema."[21] For Julian Myers, the heart of what audiences and critics found so uncomfortable about *Ishtar* went even further: "This is the existential dilemma of the film: Why should you go on if you are totally mediocre? Well, at least we can be mediocre together."[22] Who knows, maybe film critics are just professionally inclined to be a little sensitive about mediocrity.

It would be disingenuous to claim that *Ishtar*'s problems were limited to debates around plot and characterization, however. As *The New York Times*' Janet Maslin observed in her review of the film at the time, "it's impossible to discuss *Ishtar* . . . without noting the extravagant rumor-mongering that has surrounded its making."[23] Apocryphally at least, May's perfectionism reached almost mythic levels of pedantry, with elaborate stories circulating about her involvement in the casting of camels and the correct sculpting of sand dunes. These director-out-of-control anecdotes are not limited to *Ishtar*, but perhaps the film's large budget and high-caliber cast brought them the most attention. This construction of May as a director with an unruly filmmaking methodology forms the core of *Mikey and Nicky* in particular: supposedly she shot 1.4 million feet of film, and would leave numerous cameras running for hours on end, even when stars Peter Falk and John Cassavetes had left the set (her reasoning for this, in her own words, was that "they might come back.") So awful an experience was *Mikey and Nicky* that May took a decade before she returned again to directing,[24] and that it was then the ill-fated *Ishtar* suggests her instinct that the film industry was not in tune with her creative instincts was a correct one.

This spirit of improvisation is not difficult to trace back to May's earlier work as a performer with Nichols. In some respects, the overt theatricality of *A New Leaf* in particular renders it very much part of the stage traditions upon which May's career was initially founded. At the same time, within her improvisational approach to filming—incomprehensible to studio executives in the era of celluloid, but perhaps not totally absurd in a world now dominated by digital filmmaking—May's direction contains something profoundly contemporary in both tone and shape. Reviewing *The Heartbreak Kid* in January 1973, *Time Magazine* prophetically looked back on May's earlier career with an insight that would apply just as much to considerations of her work after the *Ishtar* dust had settled:

> Elaine May, both as a film maker . . . and a performer, is someone from whom we have come to expect a kind of carefree inconsistency. By now it is part of her appeal. She veers effectively, if not exactly smoothly, through wild changes of mood and attitude, from very human comedy to sharp satire to a sort of urchin wistfulness. Her reactions to her characters are so complex and abrupt that the audience is always kept lagging a little behind and slightly off-balance. It is an odd sensation, but pleasant.[25]

The production circuses of *Mikey and Nicky* and *Ishtar* were not new to May, and in fact threatened to derail her directorial career before it had even begun. After an epic ten months of editing, her debut film, *A New Leaf*, was submitted to Paramount (then headed by the iconic Robert Evans) at a whopping three hours. May was so outraged when the task of further reducing the film's length was taken out of her hands that she took legal action in an attempt to have her name removed from the film's credits. Dismissing the 102-minute cut as "cliché-ridden [and] banal",[26] May argued in court that the film would be a disaster if released in its edited version. Paramount retaliated, accusing May of failing "to perform her duties as a director in a timely, workmanlike and professional manner, resulting in substantially increased production costs." New York Supreme Court Justice Irving H. Saypol decided to watch the edited version himself, and he liked it: the shorter version of *A New Leaf* was released and, against May's better judgement, it is this cut that even today enthralls audiences around the world.

Whether the original version will ever come to light remains to be seen,[27] but the script involves a blackmail plot and a substantially increased body count. What was deemed to be May's problematic penchant for darker themes had previously been an issue in what was her first Hollywood job, penning a script version of an earlier version of Evelyn Waugh's 1948 funeral house satire *The Loved One* (itself sharing notable parallels with May and Nichols' classic budget funerals sketch) that the studio rejected for being "overly focused on death."[28] While May's vision of the film was thwarted in a manner far beyond the romanticized notion of authorial control, it is admittedly difficult to imagine how this extra material could build on what feels almost close to perfect (certainly Matthau himself preferred the final cut).[29] The question of whether this scene was in fact shot remains a key subject of debate amongst admirers of Elaine May's film work, and even for other authors in this book. But—as argued throughout this collection—May's status as an artist and performer is as much about the myth as it is hard factuality. These contradictions have themselves become a part of the Elaine May legacy.

A New Leaf follows mean-spirited bachelor Henry Graham (Walter Matthau) as he discovers his entire fortune has dwindled away, forcing him to either accept a life of looming poverty or marry a wealthy woman. Given a time limit by his uncle, desperation leads him to nervous, clumsy botanist Henrietta Lowell—played by May herself. Plotting to murder her soon after their wedding, Henry—against his own will—begins to develop a protective affection for Henrietta as they unify against a number of external threats, from larcenous domestic staff to recalcitrant Grecian-style nightgowns. As Kate Stables wrote in *Sight & Sound* in February 2016, *A New Leaf* "sharply skewers the narcissism of a male hero bent on severing himself from a new bride. But May's portrayal of appealing, soft-voiced helplessness, set against Matthau's deadpan slow burn, is what humanizes the film until its eventual change of tone feels credible rather than contrived."[30]

May had originally intended the role of Henry for Christopher Plummer (then in his early forties), to play alongside herself, taking the role to prevent the studio from imposing their first choice for Henrietta, Carol Channing.[31] Matthau was already in his early fifties when he appeared in *A New Leaf*, but in many ways his performance feels more youthful than the roles he was achieving success with at the time. His Henry is riffing on both Matthau's stingy millionaire from Gene Kelly's *Hello Dolly!* (1969) and the deceitful playboy with a penchant for elaborate romantic schemes in Gene Saks' *Cactus Flower* (1969). And there is something inescapably sad about Henry: May homes in on his hollowness without fetishizing it, capturing perhaps nowhere better that which Roger Ebert pinpointed as the secret of Matthau's most famous roles: "In comedy he never tried to be funny, and in tragedy he never tried to be sad. He was just this big . . . shambling, sardonic guy whose dialogue had the ease and persuasion of overheard truth."[32] Compared to the by-then firmly established Matthau, May in contrast was extraordinarily green when it came to filmmaking when she was given the task of directing *A New Leaf*. By her own account, so limited was her knowledge of how a film set worked in practical terms that she "wouldn't be hired as a PA." Paramount's then-chief Charles Bludhorn refused to allow May approval of either a director or lead actress, but as a compromise offered her the chance to do both herself. Sensing it was an opportunity to protect her film from studio interference, she agreed.[33] On their part, Paramount felt that—perhaps in the charged cultural climate of second wave feminism—having a woman write, star and direct a Hollywood film was good for business, and on the flip side, they also (unwisely) believed "a woman . . . would be easy to control."[34] To state the obvious, this was not the case.

As concrete a connection to the Hollywood establishment and as crucial to the film as Matthau is, *A New Leaf* very much belongs to Elaine May—not only as a director and writer, but as its star. In the wrong hands, her Henrietta could easily collapse into a kind of toothless, overly-cute geek girl parody, or—at the other extreme—a frumpy, fumbling monstrous feminine. May's ability to hit the exact middle ground with Henrietta is extraordinary: watching the film almost fifty years after its first release, Henrietta's embarrassment is contagious—we cringe as we laugh, we blush for her as much as we laugh at her. We shamefully understand on an intuitive level why Henry considers her disposable, yet—like him—we can't help but fall in love with her, too. For better or for worse, *A New Leaf* is arguably Elaine May's greatest work as actor, writer and director (lawsuits aside), and as such forms the basis of chapters in this book that will be outlined further shortly.

The year after the fiasco surrounding *A New Leaf*, May released *The Heartbreak Kid*. If she felt that she had lost her bearings with her debut film, the success of her second no doubt restored her faith in the potential of cinema as an outlet for her numerous talents. Oscar-nominated (including one for actor Jeannie Berlin, May's daughter), it was also remade, with Ben Stiller, by the Farrelly brothers in 2007. Again, however, May struggled with production issues: with a $1.8 million budget, the film's release was delayed after its costs blew out to well over double. Based on a script by Neil Simon, the film follows Lenny Cantrow (Charles Grodin), who marries the simple Lila Kolodny (Jeannie Berlin) in a small Jewish family wedding ceremony—only to find his patience with her beginning to fray mere days into their Miami honeymoon. With Lila quarantined in their hotel room after getting badly sunburned, Lenny turns his romantic attentions to the cold but attractive Kelly Corcoran (Cybill Shepherd). He successfully courts her—despite her father's protestations—after brutally leaving Lila. Although tonally quite different from *A New Leaf*, both films are in darkly comic ways scathing attacks on the hypocrisy and cruelty of marriage as an institution—they are films that seek to humiliate and reveal the impotence of these selfish, arrogant men.

Much has been made by critics of the parallels between *The Heartbreak Kid* and Nichols' *The Graduate*. As Saul Austerlitz notes, the points of comparison

Figure I.1 Director Elaine May, *A New Leaf* (1971). Aries Productions (PictureLux/The Hollywood Archive/Alamy Stock Photo)

are hard to miss: "The mismatched Jewish–WASP romance, the confused antihero, the generational bloodshed." But Austerlitz also observes the influence of another key May collaborator on *The Heartbreak Kid*, identifying that "something of the coarse, oafish intensity of Cassavetes's *Husbands* and *Faces* is carried over into this unlikeliest of scenarios."[35] Calum Marsh also detected further similarities between May and Cassavetes, in terms of the shared "vitality and raw energy" of their comic styles.[36] And the similarities don't stop there: as noted in *Time Magazine*'s review of *The Heartbreak Kid* in 1973, May also fundamentally "shares with John Cassavetes a consuming affection for people, foibles and all."[37] (As discussed further shortly, the relationship between May and Cassavetes will be the subject of Jeremy Carr's chapter).

May's career would intersect most explicitly with Cassavetes' in the drama *Mikey and Nicky* (1976), in which he would act for her alongside Peter Falk. Based around the interpersonal dynamic of its eponymous characters—as Cassavetes' Nicky faces imminent death at the hands of mobsters he has double-crossed—it's the most somber of her films, yet its focus on potentially dysfunctional male relationships foreshadows *Ishtar*. While they're very different films, both are marked by profoundly moving moments of gentle physical intimacy where men in crisis simply hug it out. It is difficult to watch *Mikey and Nicky* and not try to imagine May's directorial career in a parallel universe, one where the festival of eye-rolling surrounding *Ishtar* never happened. The final scene of Mikey and Nicky, in particular, is like nothing May achieved elsewhere in her brief but fascinating career as director, going down as one of the great final scenes of any American film from the 1970s. Its intensity is also astonishingly modern: recalling *The Sopranos* in its tone, form and execution more than *The Godfather*, *Mikey and Nicky* alone earns May the right to a place in critical discussions well beyond the domain of comedy.

Watching her four films today, Austerlitz echoes that inevitable sense of mourning we experience at the realization that there are no more Elaine May-directed films to come: "One wonders if May might have worked more had she been a young male wunderkind and not a middle-aged woman."[38] Elaine May's directing career may have been short, but it was diverse, passionate, experimental, and captivating. If there were failures, they were not hers. As Julian Myers noted in 2009, "It seems like the studio system betrayed her at almost every turn."[39] The reasons for this are often gesticulated towards in broad terms, with sexism rating high on the list of likely explanations. Accordingly, the relationship between discourse surrounding Elaine May's career and her gender are worthy of much deeper consideration.

FUNNY GIRL: ELAINE MAY AND THE GENDER QUESTION

As her collaborations with figures like Cassavetes and Nichols indicate, May by no means sought the all-women filmmaking networks that were on the rise in New York City during the ascent of Second Wave feminism. Her films resist any easy pigeonholing into discourse around what are recognizably understood as "feminist" filmmaking traditions, less because of ideology as such but simply time. As contemporary art curator Jill Dawsey observed, "May is the perhaps the wrong generation for feminism: she comes of age in the '50s."[40] And yet, on a gender front, Dawsey champions May:

> What is amazing is that she was on such equal footing with Nichols—and they both deserve credit for that. It's this moment before second wave feminism, when one might imagine that femininity, with all its tics, might simply be dropped, or turned into comedy.[41]

Certainly, it is difficult not to see the downward spiral of May's reputation as director being the result of some kind of bias resultant of her gender. As May herself has said, "There's always some idiot who'll come up to you and say, 'You're a great gal, you think exactly like a man!' For Chrissake, I always thought intelligence was neuter."[42] While the issue of gender is by no means the only or most important factor to consider in Elaine May's career, it is, regardless, still one that cannot be ignored, as much for how it has influenced her treatment by other women as well as men.

While today there is a broad widespread assumption that women's filmmaking is a practice that allows diverse voices to be heard, as Gwendolyn Audrey Foster has noted, self-identifying feminist women critics and academics have, historically at least, not all been May's allies.[43] If, as Stephens noted earlier, May has been widely omitted from New Hollywood history, similarly she is strikingly absent from a number of monographs on women's filmmaking: for example, while Alison Butler laments as recently as 2002 that "as few as 14 film were directed by only seven women in mainstream Hollywood between 1949 and 1979,"[44] her book includes no mention of Elaine May. Partially, perhaps, this is due to a historical tendency to blur "women's filmmaking" and "feminist filmmaking" into the same category, and on this front a number of self-identifying feminist film scholars have barely disguised their derision of May. Most notable here is Barbara Koenig Quart's analysis of May's career in her 1988 monograph, *Women Directors: The Emergence of a New Cinema*. Arguing, like Alison Butler twelve years later, for gender parity, Koenig Quart seeks to shock her reader from the outset with the appalling statistic that "one-fifth of one per cent of all films released by American major studios" between 1949 and 1970 were directed by women.[45]

And yet, of essential women filmmakers like Lina Wertmüller (the first woman ever nominated for a Best Director Oscar) and May, Koenig Quart is dismissive to the point of vindictiveness. Bewilderingly concluding some kind of in-built self-hating misogyny from their "focus principally, even exclusively, on male protagonists" and stating that their women characters are treated "largely with contempt or sexist stereotyping," Koenig Quart's ageist dismissal ("These women tend to be women over 50, shaped well before feminism"[46]) results in the offensive conclusion that "one must suspect . . . that both May and Wertmüller reflect the wounds of an earlier lonely generation of women directors."[47] Using what she considers May's failed attempt to "sell out" to big business (male-dominated) Hollywood as evidence to support her broader claim that "only low-budget independent filmmaking . . .[was] the most promising route" for successful, meaningful women's filmmaking[48]—a claim that today at least falls flat in the face of movies such as *Wonder Woman* (Patty Jenkins, 2017) and *A Wrinkle in Time* (Ava DuVernay, 2018)—there is inherent in Koenig Quart's suggestion a worrying implication that mirrors much of the criticism lobbed at May and *Ishtar:* that women simply cannot cope with large film production budgets.

Demonstrating a clear disdain for lowbrow and popular films in favor of highbrow, low-budget art and independent cinema,[49] Koenig Quart's dismissal of *A New Leaf* is particularly disheartening: on a simple film analysis level, she fails completely to identify Henry as a deliberately unlikeable protagonist, opting consistently throughout her reading instead to use the word "hero"[50] (likewise, she repeatedly refers to Charles Grodin's pathetically flawed protagonist Lenny Cantrow in *The Heartbreak Kid* in the same way[51]). Consequently, her unsophisticated analysis of the film's morality assumes that May is *championing* Henry's actions, misreading the grotesquery which precisely underscores the mechanics of May's masterful comedy and the plot itself: Henry is *awful*, but he comes around in the end. As for Henrietta, while Koenig Quart considers her somehow emblematic of what she interprets as May's broader disgust with women who "fail" at femininity in general, what is missed here is that Henrietta carves her *own* path towards success, both professionally and—ultimately and hilariously—in her marriage. Koenig Quart *almost* understands the complexity of characterization beyond overly simplistic models of identification when she notes that "May makes her likeable in a curious way, like the old sweet dumb blondes with empty heads; though this one has the head, she has the same sound of dim-witted ineptitude," but of course what is missed here is that Henrietta is a highly successful scientist: in contemporary parlance, Henrietta is a nerd. If Koenig Quart's diatribe against May is already difficult enough to comprehend, the final nail is when she yearns for Henrietta to demonstrate "the positive associations with bookish types in the writing of [Philip] Roth . . . who make[s] university teachers into attractive characters."[52] Although recently such debates were notably absent in the rush of obituaries following his death in 2018, Roth—whose work is frequently accused of sexism and misogyny—is one of the most debated and controversial figures in contemporary literature,[53] and an off-the-cuff suggestion that making a woman character more Roth-like to ensure a more progressive reading is today a curious suggestion at best.

Today, however, while even some of May's women fans acknowledge traces of a "murky misogyny" in *A New Leaf*,[54] for other self-identifying feminists May is an unequivocal ground breaker. For Mac Pogue at feminist website *Bitch Media*, May "broke barriers . . . for women in film" and has "worked against the grain as a writer and director, pushing against systems that normally value women only for their looks and not their wit." [55] Likewise, for Ally Acker in 1991, May "nearly single-handedly opened the doors to directing for women again."[56] At issue here perhaps is the definitional volatility of the word "feminism" itself: as an ideological tool, the meaning and power bestowed within the term can be contorted and corrupted to adhere to the intentions, motivations and biases of those who employ it across a range of different contexts. In this sense, to debate whether Elaine May "is" or "is not" a feminist filmmaker seems beside the point, as the answer will always depend on how that terms is understood. In 2012, art theorist Peggy Phelan offered a useful, deliberately broad definition to use as a starting place to think about issues relating to gender difference and power, positing that "feminism is the conviction that gender has been, and continues to be, a fundamental category for the organization of culture. Moreover the pattern of that organization usually favors men over women."[57] From this perspective, feminism offers a useful framework to rethink Elaine May's work, despite the historical inconsistency of her lived experience and its lack of overlap with second wave feminism. Again, however, this must be considered a separate approach from declaring "Elaine May is a feminist": we argue that no such claim need be made to think through the role of gender difference and power in her career. Certainly, May has spoken articulately on her awareness of the role her gender played when making *A New Leaf* in particular:

> I didn't want to frighten anyone, and people would leave me saying, she's a nice girl. What is this big thing about? She's a nice girl, and the thing is, of course, I wasn't. A nice girl. And when they found it out, they hated me all the more. And I think that's what really happens. It's not that they're women. It's that as women they think I want to show that I'm a nice person . . . I think the real trick for women is they should start out tough. They don't start out tough. They start by saying, "Don't be afraid of me. I'm only a woman." And they're not *only* women, they're just as tough as guys. In that way I think I did have trouble. But only because I seemed so pleasant.[58]

Whether consciously "feminist" or not, then, May's professional practice as a director at least was strongly governed by a strength of will to act against what was expected of her as a woman. What is so radical about her perspective on gender is her determination to not toe the line, to stay in her place, to do what she was told. In 1972, she argued simply against the biological essentialism that marked feminist discourse at the time, countering that "directing is a way of looking at something and then communicating it . . . It would be hideous to think that either sex took a script and in any way pushed it toward any point of view other than the author's. I don't think it's important whether you're a man, a woman or a chair."[59]

Of course, if there's another element of May's career that comes into play when considering gender, it's the clichéd assumption that women aren't funny, an argument that Morwenna Banks and Amanda Swift address directly in their 1987 monograph, *The Joke's on Us: Women in Comedy from Music Hall to the Present Day*. In their attempt to historicize women in comedy, the authors noted that they were impeded by a "lack of documentation about women in comedy," noting that in fields such as music hall commentators "all too frequently gloss over the female contributors."[60] This, they argue, is representative of a broader male bias: "It cannot be denied that the recording of historical fact has for centuries mainly been done by men, and has inevitably represented history from a male viewpoint. Thus it is not surprising that women have played a minor part in historical consciousness."[61] Likewise, Regina Barreca challenges the assumption that "women aren't funny" in the introduction to her 1988 edited collection *Last Laughs: Perspectives on Women and Comedy*. For Barreca, the historical bias against women in comedy has also come from within the feminist ranks; she notes somewhat flippantly that "feminist criticism has generally avoided the discussion of comedy, perhaps in order to be accepted by conservative critics who found feminist theory comic in and of itself,"[62] but adds, "women writers have traditionally used comedy to subvert existing conventional structures."[63] Again, while we are hesitant to haphazardly apply the label "feminist" to Elaine May for reasons already outlined, this is a useful observation to perhaps reframe the traditions with which May critiques institutions such as marriage (*A New Leaf*, *The Heartbreak Kid*) and undermines for both comic (*Ishtar*) and tragic effects (*Mikey and Nicky*) clichés surrounding male friendship.

Yet, as with her observations on directing, it would be erroneous, offensive and overly-simplistic to critically reduce May's unique brand of comedy to being fundamentally tied to her gender. As Gwendolyn Audrey Foster correctly asserts, the strongest influence is perhaps Yiddish humor, and her comedy functions actively to "expose . . . societal falseness, the bleakness of relationships, and the humor of day-to-day life struggles."[64] Importantly for Foster, recalling May's (alleged) origins in theater with her father, her humour is linked closely to the stage rather than to the screen, "a leveller and an anarchic weapon that has more to do with traditional Yiddish theater than traditional Hollywood cinema."[65] Eric L. Goldstein also emphasises the centrality of her heritage to her unique comic perspective, arguing that "as a comic, writer, and director, May is distinguished by the intellectual sophistication of her satire and the independence and artistic integrity of her work." For Goldstein, "Jewishness has often provided the material for her comedy, as well as being a source for some of the identity conflicts of her characters." Importantly, however, May expands this beyond a traditionally niche audience: "even when employing this ethnic framework, May has been able to explore essentially human experiences, an approach that has ensured her wide influence as a creative artist."[66]

INSIDE THIS BOOK

Part 1 starts perhaps unavoidably at the beginning, with Mark Freeman's in-depth exploration of the early days of May's career and her legendary work with her famous collaborator Mike Nichols, both in the early days through their work as a comedy duo, and later on in film, with May often taking screenwriting duties on many of his most famous and celebrated works. Part 2 then turns to the act of "Critically Situating Elaine May," a challenge presented to all the writers in this book as her career bleeds well beyond the lines of one clear, singular career trajectory. As writer, director, actor, and comic, this act of "critically situating" May as one of the most significant and yet broadly unheralded creative forces of twentieth-century American popular art has presented itself to all the writers in this book, and these two preliminary chapters provide different angles "into" May, her work, and her broader creative philosophies or drives. Maya Montañez Smukler locates May's work in the context of a woman making mainstream films in the United States during the 1970s in particular. Jake Wilson articulates what he identifies as a persistent existential drumbeat throughout May's work, underscoring the improvisational nature of her directorial and performance approaches in particular.

Part 3 takes a much closer look at May's work as film director, with a chapter dedicated to each of her four feature films, approaching them from a range of positions. Samm Deighan reconsiders May's debut feature film *A New Leaf* in the tradition of the screwball black comedy, convincingly moving through ancestors in Pre-Code cinema and similarly themed films focused on death, violence and romance from the 1970s. Clem Bastow then reconsiders *The Heartbreak Kid* from the perspective of contemporary feminism, rethinking Laura Mulvey's foundational notion of the male gaze through more contemporary configurations to argue that feminist dismissals in the past unfairly mischaracterized the significance of male critique as a specific kind of toxic masculinity. Jeremy Carr's chapter on *Mikey and Nicky* focuses specifically on her collaborative relationship with one of that film's two main actors, John Cassavetes, and explores the relationship between these two filmmakers' creative practices in relation to the film. Finally, Dean Brandum concludes this section with a deep dive into the highly publicized commercial and critical response to what would be May's final film, *Ishtar*, presenting a compelling argument as to precisely why and how the cards were so stacked against the film's succeeding and unpacking much of the politics—both within the film industry itself and more globally—that saw the film so broadly derided.

In Part 4, we take a step back from May's "pure" directorial work and look at the alternate ways that her authorship can be considered. Titled "Collaborations/Revelations," the title here underscores the way that May's creative practice has been so intensively driven through collaborative projects with others, for better and for worse. On this front, Alexandra Heller-Nicholas looks closely at May as a performer, with a particular emphasis on her physical presence and focus on gesture throughout her work as a screen performer in feature or series television, from *Luv* (Clive Donner, 1967) to *Crisis in Six Scenes* (Woody Allen, 2016). In terms of the "revelation" part of the equation, as Paul Jeffery in particular notes, much of May's screenwriting work was either uncredited or written under an alias if she was unhappy with the project. Of these, he takes a close look at Otto Preminger's *Such Good Friends* (1971), whose screenplay is credited to one "Esther Dale," an alias May chose to use for the project. In the final critical chapter of the book, Tim O'Farrell returns to May's close association with Mike Nichols to look at her documentary *American Masters: Mike Nichols* (2016), a memorial of sorts made after his passing in 2014. As O'Farrell notes, the notion of a "spectral Elaine May"—someone both present and absent—permeates her career, and on the flip side to Jeffery's examination of her uncredited screenplay writing work, O'Farrell looks at two she was happy with where she was credited as screenwriter: *The Birdcage* (1996) and *Primary Colors* (1998), both notably directed by Nichols.

In conclusion, the book wraps up with an interview with screenwriter Allie Hagan, who in late 2017 found her screenplay *When in Doubt, Seduce* short-listed on the influential Blacklist of as-yet unproduced scripts circulating in Hollywood. Based on the early relationship between May and Nichols, Hagan discussed how she discovered their work and the relevance of their story in the present day, as well as broadly touching on many of the themes that permeate this book: gender, comedy, fame, and the mystique of celebrity. For well over sixty years the diverse work of Elaine May has endured, despite a system—and, at times, her own decisions—that has kept so much of what she has accomplished hidden from view. But these works, regardless of how seemingly fractured they may be, collectively construct the story of one of the most enduring and important creative minds of contemporary screen culture and speak in enduring, multilayered ways; as May herself said in discussion with Nichols at a public screening of *Ishtar* in 2006, "From any small thing you can make a million truths."[67]

NOTES

1. Portions of this chapter are republished with permission, from Alexandra Heller-Nicholas, "Mainstream Obscurity: The Films of Elaine May," *4:3 Film*, 6 August 2016 <https://fourthreefilm.com/2016/08/mainstream-obscurity-the-films-of-elaine-may/> (accessed January 2019).
2. Ally Acker, *Reel Women: Pioneers of the Cinema, 1896 to the Present* (New York: Continuum, 1991), p. 83.
3. Ibid. p. 83.
4. Sam Kashner, "Who's Afraid of Nichols & May?," *Vanity Fair*, January 2013 <https://www.vanityfair.com/hollywood/2013/01/nichols-and-may-reunion-exclusive> (accessed January 2019).
5. See Kashner; Gwendolyn Audrey Foster, *Women Film Directors: An International Bio-Critical Dictionary* (Westport: Greenwood Press 1995); Chuck Stephens, "Chronicle of a Disappearance," *Film Comment* March–April 2006: 46–48, 50–53; Eric L. Goldstein, "Elaine May," *Jewish Women's Archive* (no date) <https://jwa.org/encyclopedia/article/may-elaine> (accessed January 2019).
6. Sam Wasson, *Improv Nation: How We Made a Great American Art* (New York: Houghton Mifflin Harcourt, 2017), p. 18.
7. Ibid. p. 18.
8. Jonathan Rosenbaum, "The Mysterious Elaine May: Hiding in Plain Sight," *JonathanRosenbaum.net*, 8 August 1997 <https://www.jonathanrosenbaum.net/1997/08/21700/> (accessed January 2019).
9. Wasson, p. 151.
10. Stephens, p. 46. Says Stephens: "May has a penchant for loading Cupid's bow with poisoned arrows, and her absence from most Seventies film histories no doubt has as much to do with her wilful rejection of proper courting procedures as her rather cavalier disregard for many of the medium's most cherished specificities. Rarely has a major modern director seemed so indifferent to the inherent visual virtues of image composition, or to place so little value on the selection of her cinematographers." (p. 51).
11. Richard Brody, "May Flowers: Ishtar Tonight," *The New Yorker* (no date) <https://www.newyorker.com/culture/richard-brody/may-flowers-ishtar-tonight> (accessed January 2019).
12. Acker, p. 82.
13. Rosenbaum (1997).
14. Jessica Kiang, "Retrospective: The Directorial Career of Elaine May," *IndieWire*, 8 August 2013 <www.indiewire.com/2013/08/retrospective-the-directorial-career-of-elaine-may-95011/> (accessed January 2019).
15. Vincent Canby, "A New Leaf (1971): Love Turns 'New Leaf' at Music Hall," *New York Times*, 12 March 1971.
16. Calum Marsh, "Track Down this Film: A New Leaf, Elaine May's Unfinished Jewel," *The Village Voice*, 22 July 2013 <https://www.villagevoice.com/2013/07/22/track-down-this-film-a-new-leaf-elaine-mays-unfinished-jewel/> (accessed January 2019).
17. Ryan Gilbey, "Gilbey on Film: Shady Elaine," *New Statesman*, 15 February 2011 <https://www.newstatesman.com/blogs/cultural-capital/2011/02/elaine-may-film-hollywood> (accessed January 2019).
18. Again, the rumors surrounding May's background make this hard to lock down. One account suggests that before her duo with Nichols the two formed a comedy trio with Shelly Berman that May called "Two Cocksuckers and Elaine" (Stephens, p. 52).

19. Kyle Stevens, "Tossing Truths: Improvisation and the Performative Utterances of Nichols and May," *Critical Quarterly* 52.3 (2010): 23.
20. Brody.
21. Ibid.
22. Julian Myers, "Four Dialogues 4: On Elaine May," *Open Space*, August 2009 <https://openspace.sfmoma.org/2009/08/four-dialogues-4-on-elaine-may/> (accessed January 2019).
23. Janet Maslin, "Film: Hoffman and Beatty in Elaine May's *Ishtar*," *New York Times*, 15 May 1987 <https://www.nytimes.com/1987/05/15/movies/film-hoffman-and-beatty-in-elaine-may-s-ishtar.html> (accessed January 2019).
24. Kiang.
25. Jay Cocks, "Cinema: Impossible Dream," *Time Magazine*, 1 January 1973 <https://content.time.com/time/magazine/article/0,9171,903651,00.html> (accessed January 2019).
26. Barbara Koenig Quart, *Women Directors: The Emergence of a New Cinema*. (New York: Prager, 1988), p. 39.
27. May says: "I shot the murder. It exists. It was a wonderful scene." See: "Elaine May in conversation with Mike Nichols," *Film Comment*, July/August, 2006 <https://www.filmcomment.com/article/elaine-may-in-conversation-with-mike-nichols/> (accessed January 2019). Despite this, as discussed in Chapter 3, there is still much debate over whether this scene was in fact shot.
28. Stephens, p. 52.
29. Kiang.
30. Ryan Gilbey, "Lost and found: A New Leaf," *Sight & Sound*, 14 January 2016 <https://www.bfi.org.uk/news-opinion/sight-sound-magazine/comment/lost-found-new-leaf> (accessed January 2019).
31. Rosenbaum (1997).
32. Roger Ebert, "Heartbreak Kid," *Chicago Sun-Times*, 1 January 1972.
33. Stephen Saito, "Elaine May On Almost Getting Away With Murder in 'A New Leaf'," *MoveableFest*, 1 January 2014 <http://moveablefest.com/elaine-may-new-leaf/> (accessed January 2019).
34. Wasson, p. 150.
35. Saul Austerlitz, *Another Fine Mess: A History of American Film Comedy* (Chicago Review Press, 2010) p. 436.
36. Marsh.
37. Cocks.
38. Austerlitz, p. 437.
39. Myers.
40. Jill Dawsey in Julian Myers, "Four Dialogues 4: On Elaine May," *Open Space* <https://openspace.sfmoma.org/2009/08/four-dialogues-4-on-elaine-may/> (accessed January 2019).
41. Ibid.
42. Acker, p. 81.
43. Foster, pp. 40–1.
44. Alison Butler, *Women's Cinema: The Contested Screen* (London: Wallflower, 2002) p. 26.
45. Koenig Quart, p. 1.
46. Ibid., p. 9.
47. Ibid., p. 43.
48. Ibid., p. 38.

49. Ibid., p. 41.
50. See ibid., p. 41 in particular.
51. Ibid., p. 43.
52. Ibid., p. 41.
53. See: Sarah Seltzer, "Let's Stop Telling Women They Can't Love Misogynist Art," *Flavorwire*, 12 March 2015 <http://flavorwire.com/509157/lets-stop-telling-women-they-cant-love-misogynist-art> (accessed January 2019); William Skidelsky and Alex Clark, "Why does Philip Roth provoke such strong reaction?," *The Guardian*, 22 May 2011 <https://www.theguardian.com/commentisfree/2011/may/22/philip-roth-carmen-callil-booker> (accessed January 2019); Elissa Strauss, "10 Misogynistic Novels Every Woman Should Read," *Elle Magazine*, 21 November 2015 <https://www.elle.com/culture/books/a32033/10-mysoginistic-novels-every-woman-should-read/> (accessed January 2019); Jonathan McAloon, "Can male writers avoid misogyny?," *The Guardian*, 4 May 2017 <https://www.theguardian.com/books/booksblog/2017/may/04/can-male-writers-avoid-misogyny> (accessed January 2019); Amanda Marcotte, "If Philip Roth Hates Women, Why Does He Want To Have Sex With Them, Hmmm?," *Slate*, 26 February 2013 <www.slate.com/blogs/xx_factor/2013/02/26/is_philip_roth_a_misogynist_keith_gessen_says_no.html> (accessed January 2019).
54. Kiang.
55. Mac Pogue, "Adventures in Feministory: Elaine May," *Bitch Media*, 20 December 2011 <http://www.bitchmedia.org/post/adventures-in-feministory-elaine-may-feminist-film-history> (accessed January 2019).
56. Acker, p. 81.
57. Peggy Phelan, "Survey: Art and Feminism," in Helena Reckitt (ed.), *Art and Feminism* (London: Phaidon, 2012), p. 18.
58. "Elaine May in conversation with Mike Nichols."
59. Goldstein.
60. Morwenna Banks and Amanda Swift, *The Joke's On Us: Women in Comedy from Music Hall to the Present Day* (London: Pandora, 1987), viii.
61. Ibid., p. ix.
62. Regina Barreca (ed.), *Last Laughs: Perspectives on Women and Comedy* (New York: Gordon and Breach, 1988), p. 4.
63. Ibid., p. 5.
64. Foster, p. 246.
65. Ibid., p. 246.
66. Goldstein.
67. "Elaine May in conversation with Mike Nichols."

PART I

Beginnings

CHAPTER 1

Teenagers on Stage—The Comedy of Elaine May and Mike Nichols

Mark Freeman

The prevailing perception of Elaine May is that of the isolate and recluse; one who shuns attention and is suspicious of the entertainment industry, a woman who is fueled by a singularity that has placed her beyond the cossetted glad-handing of popular celebrity. And although there may be an argument that that is indeed how the idea of "Elaine May" has developed over time, it's worth remembering that she began her career not as an isolationist, but as one half of one of the most popular comedic duos of the late 1950s and early 1960s. Her work with Mike Nichols shot them both into the spotlight almost overnight, garnering them incredible success in theater, television and audio recordings. Their ascent was spectacularly fast, the duration of their sketch-based career relatively brief, and their dissolution as instantaneous as their rise.

But the influence of their improvisational approach to comedy has persisted well beyond the few years of their success. Framing the full breadth of May's career with her partnerships with Nichols works against the almost mythologized vision of her aloof iconoclasm. Rather than affirming the image of May as a loner operating to the exclusion of others, the truth is that she and Nichols charted similar career trajectories, coming together, parting ways, reconnecting and intertwining their skills, separating and exploring individual projects before circling back again with multiple collaborations. After their early comedy partnership collapsed in the early 1960s, Nichols of course went on to direct films such as *Who's Afraid of Virginia Woolf* (1966), *The Graduate* (1967), and *Carnal Knowledge* (1971), right through to his twenty-second and final film, *Charlie Wilson's War*, in 2007. May directed four features, but wrote scripts on and off the record for Nichols throughout their careers. Of these two career paths, the former is public and celebrated, while the latter is alternately respected and scorned, both highly visible and obscured. May and Nichols

Figure 1.1 Elaine May and Mike Nichols 1960. (Historic Collection/Alamy Stock Photo)

were the greatest comedy duo of their time, "the Rudolf Nuryevev and Margot Fontaine of exquisitely turned-out neuroses",[1] and their experiences coming up through Chicago improv shaped their careers—and the careers of others—for decades to come.

THE COMPASS PLAYERS

That May and Nichols became such a strong comedic team seems to have emerged out of the distinctive, idiosyncratic personae they modelled as teenagers in a theater group called The Compass, a precursor to the now well-lauded Second City in Chicago. As individuals within The Compass they stood out as awkward, eccentric figures; talented, but in many ways separate from the other performers. As a team they worked with such synchronicity that their position within The Compass Players became increasingly untenable. These two performers came from radically different backgrounds before they were grafted together to form the great Nichols/May partnership. Nichols and his family fled Nazism, with Mike leaving Berlin with his brother Robert in 1939 for the U.S. "each with ten marks in a purse around his neck."[2] His father arrived in Manhattan a year earlier, established a medical practice and changed the family name from Peschowsky to Nichols, after the Russian Nikolaevitch, a name passed down from his Russian father. Nichols' mother arrived a year later—her passage had been delayed by illness—and she established a writing service for other German refugees. This early hardship as the Nichols family worked to establish a new life in a new land away from the immediate threat of Nazi Germany was compounded by the death of Nichols' father in 1942, an event which placed increasing financial strain on the family. Janet Coleman, in her book on The Compass, notes that since the age of four, Nichols had been rendered bald by an extreme reaction to a whooping cough injection, and as finances ran dry, he was left to rely on a "cheap ratty wig" to cover his affliction.[3] His success at school, however, meant that he had a number of colleges open to him upon graduation. He initially chose New York University, lasted exactly one day, and then headed to the University of Chicago—a decision which led him to the formative years of The Compass, and his fated meeting with Elaine May.

If Nichols' path to the Chicago theater was somewhat circuitous, May's was more assured. May began as a child touring with her family, and was included in their performances in Yiddish theater. Her father was a writer, a director, and an actor and he specifically shaped performances around his daughter. Like Nichols, May demonstrated a profound intelligence in her early years, described by a colleague as "the smartest woman I ever met. Like Samuel Beckett. Really a brain."[4] Her schooling consisted of a short stint at Hollywood High School, until she refused to attend by the age of fourteen ("I sat around the house reading, mostly mythology and fairy tales").[5] She married Marvin May at sixteen and gave birth to a daughter, Jeannie, who adopted Elaine's maiden name of Berlin. Elaine then divorced Marvin and, leaving Jeannie in Los Angeles with her mother, headed to Chicago to pursue her primary interest in the theater. This early history says much about May in her youth. There is a strand of headstrong stubbornness, but it is not the futile rebelliousness of the disaffected teenager. What seems to propel her in this period is a drive to find her place, to stake a claim in an arena that offered her creative avenues, career opportunities. May arrived in Chicago with a stronger history in performance than Nichols—she had studied acting with Maria Ouspenskaya in Los Angeles[6]—and had a history of performance stretching from her days in the Yiddish theater through to a stint as "Elly May", an act she performed in Hollywood. Significantly, May had also shown interest in writing and she had begun to write advertising copy, and considered writing treatments for films she could sell to producers.

It is through these divergent paths that Nichols and May made their way to the University of Chicago: Nichols as a student, May as someone who just sat in on classes for pleasure. By the time the student-focused theater at the University of Chicago emerged in the late 1950s, Nichols had already dropped out of his psychotherapy degree. Both May and Nichols were considered oddities upon their arrival within the troupe of student actors, which in the early years was known as *Tonight at 8.30*.[7] If Nichols' later on-stage persona with May is that of the naïve, socially awkward numbskull, those who worked with him in these early years saw a different attitude in reality. Described as "insufferable," "insecure," and "ambitious,"[8] Nichols appears to have been received as a witty, intelligent performer, but as colleague Heyward Ehrlich claimed, Nichols "was like the abused child who turns the abuse on others. He always seemed to be vying with others for power and authority . . . I liked him in those days, but he was a pain in the ass."[9] May and Nichols first met at a *Tonight at 8.30* production of August Strindberg's *Miss Julie*. Nichols recalled performing on stage and looking out into the audience, where he saw "this evil, hostile girl staring from the front row. I was about 4 feet away from her, and she stared at me all the way through it, and I knew she knew it was shit."[10] It would be several years until May and Nichols truly met and worked together, but once the relationship was forged, the bond between them was incredibly powerful. Nichols has described them both as "dangerous-to-vicious depending on the stimulus"[11] which seemed to drive them together out of a shared estimation of their own reputations and forged what he claimed was a bond which kept them "safe from everyone else when we were with each other. And also safe from each other. I knew somehow that she would not do to me the things she'd done to other guys . . . I knew instantly that everything that happened to us was ours."[12] The students that initially fueled *Tonight at 8.30* had segued into the Playwright's Theatre Club, and then, under the direction of David Shepherd and Paul Sills, The Compass was formed in 1955.

The Compass had a very specific remit: it was fueled by a desire to replicate the Italian *commedia dell'arte* and their traditions of improvisation, song and pantomime, and to rely on sketches and scenes written by the actors themselves. And, as with the Renaissance theater, The Compass saw improvisation and sketch comedy as a way to interrogate and satirize social and cultural norms, as well as political structures. This improvisational tradition took shape under The Compass founder Paul Sills' mother, Viola Spolin, who had long taught improvisational acting and theater to teenagers. Her early belief in improvisation saw her at odds with the Stanislavsky School that gained popular currency during the 1940s and 1950s. She artfully delineated the difference between these two approaches to performance: Stanislavsky believed that the "work is in the head, but mine is in the space . . . they were in the past, I was in present time."[13] Spolin came to have enormous influence on May and Nichols—although it must be noted that at the beginning of The Compass only May was present, as Nichols returned to New York to study acting on his own. Workshops became a staple for the actors in The Compass from the very beginning. Spolin taught through games, demanding the actors play repeatedly to maintain an awareness of the cues and opportunities from their scene partners and develop strong instinctive responses, an intense acting acuity. Spolin argued that on stage "you have to be present in the moment. And that's what a game does for you . . . if you're not present to the ball coming, you ain't playing. Behind the bat, you can't be thinking about how you hit it last month, or how you felt when you didn't hit it. You are there in the moment having to hit that ball. And you have to be in waiting for the ball to come to you."[14] It was a process that fostered generosity and equality, with actors finely tuned to the demands of their fellow actors and aware that anything too showy or self-serving would overbalance the scene and create discord. Amy Seham's investigation into improv notes that Spolin's position was that the improvised scene must "have no starts, nor may anyone impose any intentional message or political agenda on the organic truth that must emerge through group agreement."[15]

The approach involved finding a balance between the individual and the group; the expression of a singular position, but an awareness of that position within a larger dynamic. This environment proves supremely important in relation to the comedic style that was to emerge with Nichols and May only a few years after the beginning of The Compass. These improvisational exercises under the guidance of Spolin place such emphasis on an awareness of space, and an awareness of the other actors, that it is patently evident when interrogating the comedic teamwork of Nichols and May. The constant drum beat of the actor being in the present, and not enmeshed in the interior backstory of a Method process, cast a significant imprint on the future work of both performers. One game Spolin taught involved the actors filling a space one by one with an object through pantomime, demanding recall and spatial awareness as each person stepped through the area. Barbara Harris, who went on to achieve success with directors such as Hitchcock and Altman, was also a member of The Compass Players in these early years and argues that Spolin encouraged a capacity to help the actors "understand what it feels like not to be attached to a script or to know what's coming next . . . the exercises gave you a point of concentration outside of yourself."[16]

On stage, following the *commedia dell'arte* tradition, the sketches and scenes performed leant into exaggeration and stereotype, with both Barbara Harris and Elaine May clearly proving adept at flaky teenage daughters and pushy mothers respectively.[17] Co-founder of The Compass David Shepherd recalls how distinctive May was during her years with the group. He recalled: "In her improvisations she rarely chose traditional female roles. She played challenging, sophisticated, worldly women. She was the doctor, the psychiatrist, the employer, the wicked witch."[18] Off stage, May became the director of the workshops. She relied on her training in Stanislavsky before the move to Chicago, but now also integrated improvisation through Viola Spolin, making her workshops stretch the actors further with both exercises in the present and in sense memory. In practice, The Compass explored the socio-political concerns of the time, delivering long, sometimes unfocused improvisational routines to a somewhat startled audience. By 1955, Nichols had returned to Chicago and joined The Compass after a lengthy stint studying with Method acting coach Lee Strasberg in New York. It's worth recognizing that, again through divergent paths, both Nichols and May found themselves in improvisational theater after studying the Method under two of the leading proponents of that process. As Spolin had observed, these are two radically different approaches to the craft of acting. Amy Seham argued that the Chicago iteration of improvised theater "sometimes meshed, sometimes clashed productively to create exciting performances, and sometimes strained and pulled apart,"[19] and Nichols recalls that his early performances with The Compass were a struggle, except those he did with Elaine. "I was a disaster! For a month I cried in scenes because that's what I thought I'd learned from Strasberg,"[20] he claimed, but soon with May as a scene partner, this transformed to "almost arrogance. A feeling (towards the audience) that 'I can handle you guys'."[21] May's improvisational style moved towards characters that were the controlling, the domineering, or the vacantly idiotic. Nichols, in an exaggeration of his own personality, found aptitude in clumsy, awkward fools, or dry academic blowhards. Nichols describes the experience as having "a group of people who were not actors, really, and didn't have a lot of theatrical experience, but who were very intelligent and in some cases, highly educated. And they were thrown in front of an audience with very little help."[22] By sheer good fortune, the natural impulses of both May and Nichols found a perfect complement in each other—the dominant and the submissive, the idiot and the sophisticate, the confident and the shy. It became clear from very early on that their partnership was something exceptional. The intensity of this connection saw May and Nichols apply some very simple rules to their comedy—Nichols himself called them "vulgar."[23] Nichols had a natural affinity for words—he loved the rhythm, the sound of them, the structure of wordplay. May explored character, was inventive, led a scene in unexpected directions. Nichols described it this way:

What she's interested in is character and the moment. What I'm interested in is moving on and giving it shape. I was always very concerned with beginning, middle and end, and when it's time for the next point to be made and when it's time to move because, after all, we're telling a story. She could go on and on in character. I could not. I could make my few points, I had my two or three characteristics, then I had to move on to the next point because I was out. I couldn't do it anymore.[24]

THE RHYTHM OF IMPROVISATION

One of Nichols and May's first scenes together at The Compass was the basis for one of their most famous routines later in their careers, *Teenagers in a Car*. Geoff King argues that comedy is frequently predicated on an in-between space, where we forge an emotional commitment to the characters, and a "more distanced perspective from which we can sit back without emotional consequence to enjoy the comedy of their incapacities and set-backs as well as their unlikely triumphs."[25] This early improv from May and Nichols endures simply because of its capacity to do exactly that—it fosters a level of intense emotional investment (and recognition), while also allowing us to stand back and enjoy the fumbling attempts of two teenagers to make out in a car parked by a lake. Raymond Durgnat noted that inherent in comedy is an understanding that the weaknesses we laugh at in a comedic character are also weaknesses of our own: it's the recognition of the failure that fosters the comedic outcome.[26] *Teenagers in a Car* works because of the capacity for May and Nichols to riff on the horny, frustrated teenager trope without taking the comedy so far as to be absurd; their behavior always remains—often painfully—identifiable. The sequence as it came to be features both actors studiously looking at their hands—May picking nervously at her nails, Nichols awkwardly attempting to light two cigarettes at once, but with a clumsy, two-handed process that undermines the skill and maturity he thinks the action implies. If Paul Henreid manages to make the move appear masterful and controlled, with a restrained eroticism as he passes the second cigarette to Bette Davis in *Now, Voyager* (Irving Rapper, 1942), Nichols telegraphs his teenage posturing with the awkwardness of his arms, the undignified plume of smoke that erupts from his lips. The look that passes between Nichols and May as he hands the cigarette to her is telling—May is gracious, demonstrating a level of emotional control; Nichols juts out his jaw in a clumsy forced smile, the epitome of failed nerve and adolescent male bravado. The rhythm of this delivery is incredibly important—as Nichols regains some level of control over his face, his demeanor, it is May who suddenly veers into a mugging, exaggerated representation of forced cool. It's representative of a lot of their comedic genius—they recognize and adjust performance as an ebb and flow: one moves aggressively, the other withdraws; one becomes confident, the other reticent. It's a rhythm that May and Nichols mine continuously throughout their comedic partnership. That their characters are never at the same position in confidence or awareness draws out the comedy from the shifting states of incompatibility. May waves the cigarette carelessly, somewhat uncertainly drags on it, her eyes wide. The scene then pauses for a moment, both actors holding the tension between the previous action, and what must come next. The comic exaggeration of Nichols' yawn-and-embrace move, and the stolid, frozen expression on May's face serve as perfect comic symmetry. Keeping in mind May's intense training under Spolin, and the significance of space as part of improvisational comedy, Nichols' act results not in May's movement toward the embrace, but a sudden false interest in something in her line of vision off to her right: she directs the action away from the intimacy. The pantomimed rolling down of the window, the stretch of her neck outwards from the invisible space of the car brings into sharper relief the space within, and the world outside the car these teenagers inhabit.

It's a full minute before the first words are spoken in this sketch—May comments on the beauty of the lake that is evoked just beside their car. "It's suicidally beautiful tonight," she declares, and the synthesis between the aspirant poetry of the nervous teenager and an awkward attempt at first date small talk is met by Nichols, his voice awkwardly squeaky, his chin thrusting his bottom lip skyward: "It's OK." The second attempt at intellectual depth also falls flat: "You look at that lake out there, you know and you think, like, what is it? . . . It's a lot of . . . little water. And you put it together and it's an entire lake!" Nichols, confounded by the attempted profundity, remains silent. These opening moments establish character with great precision and economy—the young girl, desperate to be taken seriously, stretching for profundity beyond her intellectual capacity; the young man desperate to appear cool, unconcerned with the scenery, and only driven by his own desire for the young woman beside him. It is truly an exercise in control: hers intellectual, his sexual. This breaks after an awkward pause, when May, her lungs filled with smoke is suddenly kissed passionately by the uncontrolled Nichols. After a beat, her exhalation of the cigarette smoke exposes the failure of his attempt, his hopeless lack of self-control producing a kiss devoid of desire and intimacy. It's a bit of comedic business that Nichols returned to later in his career where Benjamin (Dustin Hoffman) kisses Mrs. Robinson (Anne Bancroft) in *The Graduate* (1966). The lack of responsiveness from May—demonstrated by Nichols shaking her shoulder to see if she has dozed off mid-kiss—is reinforced by her question about college as soon as Nichols comes up for air. What follows is a quite melodic, rhythmic sequence where Nichols' voice breaks in sexual frustration, May's voice becomes calm and assured, and a second attempt at a kiss sees the two teenagers trying to maintain their kiss while maneuvering their cigarettes into a more suitable position, Nichols carefully eyeing the lit cigarette of May which is mere centimeters from his face. It's a moment that works in perfect synchronicity with the dialogue—both May and Nichols find the rhythms of strength and weakness, control and powerlessness in an orchestration of verbal and physical interaction. The following pantomime of Nichols, dropping his hand towards her breast, and May struggling to force his hand over her shoulder works both as an astute understanding of the expectations for women in conservative 1950s America, and just as pure physical comedy. This sketch plays out with the desire of both characters unspoken—Nichols, desperate to make out with his girl, May determined not to allow the boy to go too far with her, but also to impress him with her understanding of the world. The scene concludes with a switch, where everything that's hidden is stated openly. Nichols claims that if May submitted to his advances "I would respect you like CRAZY!," while May, understanding her role in Nichols' plans asks "Are you sure you wouldn't just be grateful?" Yet Nichols' position inverts at the end, with his own overt nervousness as May's desire becomes evident. His clumsy attempt to divert the action, "Do you think you will go to college when you get out of high school?" closes off a symmetrical sketch of sexual power and repression, advancement and retreat, aggression and diversion.

Teenagers in a Car plays as a perfect representation of how May and Nichols found a rhythm and a structure to their improvised comedy at The Compass. It is an orchestrated symmetry, a movement of attempted control and stuttering collapses expressed verbally, spatially, physically; beats of hesitation that generate comedic tension, clumsily innocent statements that deflate expectations. Steve Martin, in the documentary *Nichols and May: Take Two*, described their act as "like music . . . it was something like a song; you could hear it over and over and over".[27] The rhythm that they found at The Compass drew the attention of the other players, but also the crowds in Chicago. The success of The Compass proved shortlived, however, as the troupe increasingly splintered—with May and Nichols for a time relocating with new performers to St. Louis, before they left The Compass altogether in 1957. As the sketches performed by May and Nichols pervaded the culture, requests came to repeat the same sketches over and over. Nichols notes that as this occurred, May "got bored with the old pieces and I kept wanting to do them. This always remained true, even when we had our own act."[28] Seham explains the collapse of The Compass by suggesting: ". . . despite Spolin's original insistence on mutual support and shared focus, improvisation could be manipulated to give some performers star status at the expense of others, male and female. After many defections, firings and recriminations, the group finally disbanded in the winter of 1957."[29] The implication is, perhaps, that as the "star" duo, May and

Nichols had created a disequilibrium within the group: this may have been one of the factors that contributed, but it is clear that as an organization, The Compass had unraveled as Nichols, May and Barbara Harris all sought new opportunities. Nichols suggested that that the separation of Nichols and May emerged out of a recognition that in terms of their integration with members of The Compass ". . . we began to have a body of material with each other, and not that much with the other members of the group."[30] The next step, from well-respected members of an improv comedy troupe to comedic icons, occurred alarmingly quickly, with a meeting with an agent which Nichols describes in typically droll fashion: ". . . this strange audition came up with Jack Rollins. I called [Elaine May] and said, 'Do you want to audition for this guy?' and she said sure and we were famous three weeks later. It took no time at all."[31] December 1957 marked two important events for the duo—they began a live show at the Blue Angel in New York and they appeared on *The Steve Allen Show* performing a sketch that had been perfected on stage at The Compass. As Nichols suggests, a month later, in January 1958, they had become nationally recognized as an exciting new comedy duo sought out by a range of television variety and comedy shows, with reviews and articles emerging out of publications like *Variety*, *Time Magazine* and *The New Yorker*.

The ascent was almost brutally rapid. Lawrence Christon described their immediate success as ". . . a defining moment. They caught the urban tempo, like Woody Allen did".[32] They released an album of their sketches in December 1958 titled *Improvisations to Music*, with their comedy set against a classic piano played by Marty Rubenstein, the music swelling as May lovingly declares in *The Dentist*: "I know more about oral prophylactics now than I've ever known about anything!" Their appearance at the eleventh Emmy Awards in 1959 demonstrates several critical truths—their confidence on a large stage so quickly after their appearance beyond the boundaries of The Compass is remarkable, and their incisive, biting attacks on American culture was in no way lessened by their popular appeal. On her introduction, May walks confidently to the podium and assumes the expression and reverent demeanor of an awards presenter. With the careful, measured tones of someone who has rehearsed this introduction a thousand times, May, with downcast eyes in front of the leaders of the television industry states: "There will be a lot said here tonight . . . about excellence, and the creative, the artistic, the skillful will all be recognized and awarded." May pauses for the tiniest beat, the audience having relaxed into a conventional, earnest introductory speech. "But what of the others in this industry?" she asks, her face deadpan, and the laughter in the room erupts. "Seriously, there are men in the industry who go on, year in, year out, quietly and unassumingly producing garbage." The response from the audience is rapturous—May even breaks character for a short second—before she introduces Nichols, the man who has been awarded the Total Mediocrity

Award. Nichols bounds onto the stage and fixes May with a long, passionate kiss. The skill of the beginning of this skit is the reliance on the traditional markers of the awards ceremony: the earnest speech, the passionate declaration for the power of the creative industry, the self-congratulatory nature of the event itself. But the May/Nichols take on this selects specific elements to invert, creating tension in the dichotomies of the serious and the absurd, the reputable and disreputable, decorum and extravagance. May and Nichols remain lip-locked for more than is remotely appropriate, but they emerge from the kiss beaming, as if their overly demonstrative and passionate behavior still conformed to the expectations of their situation.

Nichols begins his acceptance speech with a series of platitudes and clichés, declaring he has achieved his success by "sticking to my one ideal: money." If May appeared to have operated within the confines of socially accepted behavior, despite her absurd take on those structures, Nichols abandons the protocols, engaging with gusto in the disreputable approaches to creativity, delivered to an audience ostensibly present in celebration of its opposite. "No matter what suggestions the sponsor makes, I take 'em" Nichols declares, his head wobbling in an awkwardly youthful pantomime of naïvety. "I disregard talent in order to hire only swell guys. And lastly and most important of all, I think, I've tried to offend no one anywhere on earth . . . and I think the measure of my success is that in ten years of producing, we have received not one letter of any kind." In these brief minutes, May and Nichols not only transgress the boundaries of social and cultural value, but also expose the ethical, moral, and creative pitfalls of television. Nichols swiftly identifies the boys-club mentality of television, the subjugation of creativity to sponsorship, the flattening out of anything dangerous or controversial that could push for change or analysis: it's a wide-ranging spray at a creative industry in front of those who work within it. Seham describes comedy of this nature as "using tactics of irony and observations of incongruity to challenge the status quo, if only temporarily"[33] and although certainly this performance at the Emmy Awards in 1959 did not bring an end to the practices they were criticizing, May and Nichols boldly paraded these criticisms in front of an industry that endorsed these practices, and a home audience that consumed them. It is worth remembering this occurred only a year after their abandonment of The Compass and their first booking on *The Steve Allen Show*. This sketch is remarkable for its courageous satire of the television industry, when they themselves had been a part of it for not even twelve months.

In 1959, The Compass re-emerged in a new form as Second City, an improvisational comedy troupe still in operation today, while the two breakout stars from The Compass debuted their 1960 Broadway stage show *An Evening with Mike Nichols and Elaine May*. The show read like complete improvisation to those new to Nichols and May, but in truth there was generally only one true improv per night—the rest were a series of tried and tested sketches. This single truly improvised sketch saw the duo asking for a first and last line and a thematic style, and they took those parameters to construct something new. Even if these routines were less successful than those that had been worked and reworked over time, the energy in the room and the freshness of the approach demonstrated the mental alacrity and the creative flexibility of their act. The truth was that the styles from performance to performance were frequently the same—audiences called for similar modes repeatedly, and Nichols and May were mostly prepared for whatever came out of this audience participation. But fundamentally, they had forged a process by which to construct those improvisations, each of them fulfilling an essential function within the improvisational structure. Nichols maintained that "Elaine can ... do a million things. She can fill and fill and fill. What I did was push it on. I think I brought a sense of form to us—what points should be made, what kind of conflict and so forth."[34] May also had her own structural methods, famously declaring that if an improvisational routine finds itself backed into a corner "When in doubt, seduce."[35] Their run on Broadway lasted for just over a season, and the recording of that show was released in 1960, also named *An Evening with Mike Nichols and Elaine May*; it was a recording that would be awarded a Grammy in 1961 for Best Comedy Performance, Single or Album. This too relied on some of their most beloved routines, including both *Telephone* and the sketch Nichols claims was inspired by one of his own mother's "lethal phone calls,"[36] *Mother and Son*.

Mother and Son perfectly typifies the way both May and Nichols had found their rhythms, the differences in cadences, the reliance on repetitions, the gradual reversals and discovery of new avenues for comedy. At the beginning, May is all slow drawls, caustically delivering an ode to the long-suffering, neglected mother. "Arthur, I sat by that phone all day Friday ... and all day Friday night ... and all day Saturday ... and all day Sunday ... until your father finally said to me 'Phyllis, eat something, you'll faint.' And I said 'No, Harry, no. I don't want my mouth to be full when my son calls me.'" The carefully measured tones of her delivery sit in direct juxtaposition with Nichols, whose Arthur babbles rapidly, reassuring her, calling her "honey," offering excuses, but the control May's mother exerts, the measured strength of her delivery, quickly renders the son powerless. Yet that understanding of tempo forces the next shift, where, beaten, Arthur asks after his mother's health, and she becomes instantly animated, while Arthur sinks into low monosyllabic response. The routine concludes with a monologue from May, as the mother Phyllis, insisting that her son Arthur will always be her baby. Arthur is rendered speechless, his excuses forgotten, his token reassurances dissolved into silence, his potential power as a rocket scientist lost. "Oh please, baby please," the mother begs, desperate for more attention from her son. The infantile, soft surrender from Nichols as the son, "I will, I promise," signals his capitulation, and the clear reinforcement of their power structure. Adopting a baby voice herself, May finishes with "And Mommy wants to wish you lots of luck with your rockets." Nichols' Arthur, now completely infantilized, replies in a melodic, childlike voice "Thank you Mommy." It's a perfect May/Nichols sketch, playing its way through power, control, and the gender roles we adopt or have forced upon us. *Telephone* operates along similar lines. In a clear antecedent to Lily Tomlin's Ernestina, May becomes the operator, the controlling pedant ("Kaplin? That's K for knife, A for aardvark, P for pneumonia?"), while Nichols is the frantic man with car trouble, desperately late for an appointment. The escalation of the emotion, with May's character again the one in control, Nichols' again the one who is forced to collapse under the weight of the intractable force of her will, hits the beats that their collaboration was based on. May's flat refutation of Nichols' increasingly desperate plea for a return of his last dime, "Information cannot argue with a closed mind," on the live recording leads to one of the features the May/Nichols partnership was known for: the live break in character as one—or both—collapse into laughter. May noticeably begins to giggle as she assumes the role of the information supervisor, the absurd voice she has adopted wavering and wobbling as she attempts to drop a register to distinguish herself from the previous character. By the time she assumes the role of the managing supervisor, May becomes the assured, seductive voice of reason. Immediately, Nichols falters, weakens, sobs, the routine concluding with May's triumph over Nichols, whose character is once again proven to be way out of his depth when confronted with the strength of May's character's control over every situation.

But the significant success of the Broadway show proved shortlived. May quickly grew dissatisfied, the repetition of the same sketches night after night solidified what was intended to be vibrant, new, dangerous. Nichols suggested that he became "more and more afraid of our improvisational material . . . We found ourselves doing the same material over and over, especially in our Broadway show. This took a great toll on Elaine."[37] May had sought greater challenges by writing a play called *A Matter of Position*, which Nichols had starred in. Conflict erupted over the play, and its swift failure fractured the partnership, even as the success of their latest album *Mike Nichols and Elaine May Examine Doctors* proved successful. Their ascent into the cultural landscape began in 1959, but just two years later, after astonishing comedic success as a pair, the partnership between Nichols and May began to unravel. Fred Coe, the director of *A Matter of Position* stated that "he was arrogant, she was nuts" with her determination to recast Nichols, whom May saw as the primary issue while Nichols asserted that the problem in fact was that May's play was too long. The arguments and struggle for control which had formed so much of their comedic power now became the thing that undid Nichols and May.

Nichols himself recognized that "once we'd gone through that experience, of trying to screw the other one, out of panic and discomfort, it was sort of over."[38] The animosity that stemmed from that experience, and the increasingly stultifying environment of their Broadway show, drew their partnership to a close by the end of 1961, and the vibrancy and danger of the Nichols and May experience was over.

The partnership had ended, but their careers of course continued. A few years after the collapse of Nichols and May, May stopped giving interviews and focused on writing, and ultimately directing. Although she has granted some access to journalists late in her career, it is from this earlier period of silence that the almost mythical image of Elaine May as an enigmatic isolationist was cultivated. It is an image at odds with what is apparent in the early stages of her career, which was so intensely focused on partnerships not just with Nichols, but with the entirety of The Compass Players. Nichols moved on to directing theater, and then spent the rest of his career largely as a film director. Their post-Broadway trajectories seem so radically opposed—May's private and removed, Nichols' public and ebullient. But what is completely apparent—especially when their careers again intertwined thirty years later in the 1990s—is how closely their creative output, both separate and apart, demonstrates all that was in evidence in those early years from The Compass through to *An Evening with Mike Nichols and Elaine May*. Their subsequent work always demonstrates a keen eye for the complexities of relationships, expectations of gender and the absurdity of the roles we feel compelled to perform, along with an astute ear for the rhythm and timbre of dialogue between two characters. The improvisational strategies they perfected at The Compass marked them for success when improv was a new approach to theater and to comedy. It is a tradition that became hardwired into the way that they pursued their own individual careers after their fast, bright success in the late 1950s and early 1960s. It is a prism through which so much of their work makes sense. Gerald Nachman, in his analysis of the comedians of the 1950s and 1960s suggests that Nichols was a man who wanted to please, and that May was a woman who needed to invent.[39] Reductive, possibly, but Nichols certainly took his experiences from The Compass and beyond to drive a prolific career filled with numerous popular successes. May's cinematic output is much more modest, but proved to be formally, dramatically and comedically distinct, even if pure box office popularity largely eluded her. The past has its blueprint, and in the careers of May and Nichols, their perspective on character, timing and comedy shaped the way forward for those who stepped into their place on the improv comedy scene. There are few greater influences on comedy today than that which was forged in Chicago through the fateful meeting and subsequent collaboration of Mike Nichols and Elaine May.

NOTES

1. James Wolcott, "Mort the Knife," *Vanity Fair*, August 2007 <https://www.vanityfair.com/culture/2007/08/wolcott200708> (accessed January 2019).
2. John Lahr, "Making it Real," *The New Yorker*, 21 February 2000 <https://www.newyorker.com/magazine/2000/02/21/making-it-real-2> (accessed January 2019).
3. Janet Coleman, *The Compass: The Improvisational Theatre That Revolutionized American Comedy* (Chicago: University of Chicago Press, 1990), p. 21. It is worth acknowledging that Nichols disputed aspects of Coleman's account of his and May's years at The Compass—in particular the circumstances surrounding their transition from The Compass to independent success. Nichols, as cited in Gerald Nachman's account calls Coleman "that awful woman who wrote that awful book"—see Gerald Nachman, *Seriously Funny: The Rebel Comedians of the 1950s and 1960s* (New York: Pantheon Books 2003), p. 339.
4. Ibid., p. 39.
5. Ibid., p. 39.
6. Ouspenskaya had trained under Stanislavsky in Russia, and brought his approach to acting, known as The Method, to America, where she in turn trained actors in this technique. She, along with Lee Strasberg, who taught Mike Nichols, were the two most significant proponents of Stanislavsky's Method in the U.S.A.
7. Coleman, p. 17.
8. Ibid., p. 18.
9. Ibid., p. 18.
10. Ibid., p. 39.
11. Jeffrey Sweet, *Something Wonderful Right Away: An Oral History of Second City and The Compass Players* (New York: Limelight Editions, 2003), p. 74.
12. Amy Seham, *Whose Improv Is It, Anyway?* (Jackson: University Press of Mississippi, 2001), p. 342.
13. Coleman, p. 31.
14. Ibid., p. 32.
15. Seham, p. 8.
16. Coleman, p. 94.
17. Ibid., p. 105.
18. Ibid., p. 120.
19. Seham, p. xvii.
20. Sweet, p. 76.
21. Ibid., p. 77.
22. Ibid., p. 75.
23. Ibid., p. 75.
24. Ibid., p. 83.
25. Geoff King, *Film Comedy* (London: Wallflower, 2002), p. 9.
26. Ibid., p. 10.
27. *American Masters: Take Two: Nichols and May*, film, dir. Phillip Schopper, Eagle Rock Entertainment, 1996.
28. Sweet, p. 80.
29. Seham, p. 15.
30. Nachman, p. 388.
31. Seham, p. 356.
32. Nachman, p. 343.

33. Seham, p. xxi.
34. Nachman, p. 348.
35. Ibid., p. 349.
36. Lahr.
37. Nachman, p. 354.
38. Ibid., p. 355.
39. Ibid., p. 353.

PART 2

Critically Situating Elaine May

CHAPTER 2

Hollywood Can't Wait: Elaine May and the Delusions of 1970s American Cinema

Maya Montañez Smukler

Elaine May began her career as a filmmaker during the 1970s at a unique moment when the mythology of the New Hollywood male auteur defined the decade; and the number of women directors, boosted by second wave feminism, increased for the first time in forty years.[1] In 1968, May signed with Paramount Pictures to write, direct, and star in *A New Leaf* (1971); the following year she joined the Directors Guild of America in the feature film director category.[2] Her membership to the Directors Guild was unusual in 1969: May had only two film credits and they were as an actor in supporting roles; and she was adding her name to a very short list of women feature film directors who had ever been members of the Guild—Dorothy Arzner, Ida Lupino and Shirley Clarke. Well-known to audiences through her creative partnership with Mike Nichols and their wildly successfully comedy team on stage, television, and radio in the late 1950s and into the early 1960s, in 1969 May had only just begun to transition from her collaboration with Nichols, to breaking out on her own. Her early success as a comedian positioned her as an emerging filmmaker in 1970s Hollywood at a time when the film industry was experiencing a financial crisis and cultural disconnect from audiences and was willing to take a risk on new talent with no filmmaking background to direct a major motion picture.

In 1972 May directed Neil Simon's script *The Heartbreak Kid* at 20th Century Fox and in 1976 she returned to Paramount to write and direct *Mikey and Nicky*. Each of the films May directed illustrates her interest in misfit characters as socially awkward as they were delusional, and her ability to seamlessly move them between comedy and drama typified the New Hollywood protagonist who captured America's uneasy transition from the hopeful rebellion of the 1960s into the narcissistic angst of the 1970s. However, the filmmaker's reception, which culminated in the critical lambast of her comeback film *Ishtar* in 1987, to be discussed in subsequent chapters in this collection, was uneven and her battles with studio executives are legendary. Still, in the face of much discord, May was celebrated for her immense talent and given second chances sometimes by those she had been in battle with previously. This chapter investigates Elaine May's career within the lore of 1970s Hollywood to understand the industrial and cultural circumstances that contributed to the emergence of her influential body of work, and the significant contributions to cinema she made in spite of, and perhaps because of, the conflicts with which she was faced.

OLD HOLLYWOOD STRUGGLES TO BE NEW

"The movie industry is financially sick," wrote Paul E. Steiger for the *Los Angeles Times* in the fall of 1969.[3] According to Steiger, already that year MGM, 20th Century Fox, and Paramount, three of the largest film studios, were reported to have lost over $50 million. These doomsday observations reverberated throughout the entertainment press during the late 1960s. The largest film studios were still struggling to adjust to the post-classical studio system, including their relationship with television and the encroachment of conglomerate buyouts. Of significant concern were also the changing tastes and buying power of younger audiences that by the end of the 1960s had begun to dominate box office tallies. In 1968, sixteen to twenty-four year-olds constituted 48 per cent of the ticket-buying public, the majority of whom claimed to go often to the movies and prefer content that had undergone "liberalization" in terms of more explicit depictions of sex and violence.[4]

"Your young audience doesn't care about lavish productions with Elizabeth Taylor and thousands of extras," an experienced executive told Stanley Penn of *The Wall Street Journal*. "They want to identify with people on the screen."[5] Evidence of this was not difficult to come by. *The Graduate*, an independent film made by Embassy Pictures in 1967, directed by Mike Nichols and introducing Dustin Hoffman—both men in their thirties—as the young, wayward, post-grad suburbanite male protagonist and featuring the misadventures of his romantic life. The film's budget was an estimated $3 million; within a year of its release it had grossed close to $40 million in the United States and Canadian markets alone. In 1969, Dennis Hopper's *Easy Rider*, a low-budget biker picture that became the counter-culture emblem, was independently produced for an estimated $400,000 by Peter Fonda, Bob Rafelson and Bert Schneider—all of whom were under forty years old—and distributed by Columbia Pictures, went on to earn $7 million domestically in its first year. The studios limped along, continuing to invest in genres such as the big budget musical that had been sure money-makers in the past, but now proved to be some of the most high-risk ventures. Intended spectaculars such as 20th Century Fox's *Doctor Dolittle* (Richard Fleischer, 1967) and *Hello, Dolly!* (Gene Kelly, 1969), and Universal's *Sweet Charity* (Bob Fosse, 1969) crashed at the box office.

The success of these smaller youth-market films became the benchmark against which the majors were measured. An anonymous industry veteran recommended that, "each of the majors should have at least one bright young guy under thirty on its board, just to help in setting up films for today's youth market."[6] In fact, by the end of the 1960s, the rise of the under-forty, white male studio executive had begun to sweep the industry. Studios began making fewer films each year and there was a focus on pictures with smaller budgets; star salaries were reduced and an interest in up-and-coming talent—performers, writers, directors, and producers—who could capture the changing cultural mores, and could be hired for a lesser fee balanced against a percentage of the film's grosses. It was in this unique moment of industry flux that Elaine May found her entrance, as a first-time writer-director-co-star, on a major motion picture.

Paramount Pictures, faced with the challenges overtaking the industry at this time, was reimagining itself as a motion picture studio. In 1966, Charles Bluhdorn and his company Gulf and Western, a manufacturer of industrial materials, bought the studio. Bluhdorn, who did not have prior experience in film, invested in younger management, hiring independent producer and men's clothing manufacturer Robert Evans and former journalist Peter Bart, both in their thirties, as production executives. Evans and Bart worked to rebrand the company as contemporary and forward-thinking by investing in new talent, with an emphasis on writers. Evans, the new vice-president of production, in 1968 boasted how "We believe that our studio must play a role in encouraging fresh writing talent in our industry, not merely relying on the supposedly 'safe' experienced writers who have already established their reputations."[7] May was listed as one of those "fresh" talents.

Elaine May was born in 1932 in Philadelphia to a theatrical family. Jack Berlin, her father, was an actor in the Yiddish theater and May would sometimes appear with him on stage. The comedian joked, in an interview with *Redbook Magazine* in 1961, that she "was 'somewhat raised' in a string of public schools and Yiddish theaters. 'The despair of my youth was that I didn't wear braces and eyeglasses like the rest of the girls'."[8] May, since the early days of her celebrity, rarely sat for an interview and once told a journalist, "I will tell you something, but I warn you it is a lie,"[9] never revealed much in all sincerity about her creative process or professional experiences. By most accounts, May dropped out of school at the age of fourteen; as she told one journalist, "Frankly, I was tired of it."[10] To another, when asked if she had missed out on high school subjects, May responded, "I never missed French, but Botany was a kick in the heart."[11] In 1949, May had her daughter, Jeannie Berlin, with Marvin May, to whom she was married at the time.

Divorced, and having placed the care of her young daughter with her mother, Ida Berlin, in Los Angeles, May made her way to Chicago in around 1953 and became part of the landmark improvisational comedy group The Compass Players, where she met Mike Nichols. May and her collaboration with Nichols are detailed in other chapters of this collection. What is significant to this discussion of her career as a studio film director in the 1970s is how successful she was as a stage comedian in the preceding years. In less than six months after arriving, Elaine May and Mike Nichols had exploded onto the New York City comedy scene. The story is now the stuff of legend: that after the years honing their craft of improvisational sketch humor as part of The Compass in Chicago, in 1957 the two went to New York to explore their options and signed immediately with theatrical agent Jack Rollins. "I knew they had something odd and wonderful," said Rollins, describing their first meeting, "but I didn't know whether to laugh or cry."[12]

In November of 1957 the two made their first appearance on the New York City club scene. By the next January their first television appearance on NBC's "Suburban Revue" portion of the "Omnibus" had solidified their success. Bob Bernstein, writing for *Billboard* magazine, described the act as "two of the funniest, freshest comics ever to use TV as a stepping stone to national fame" and whose "inspired handling of everyday events gave the revue its only bright moments."[13] Art Murphy in *Variety* followed with: "The hour show's highlights resulted from the fresh and engaging humor put forth by Elaine May and Mike Nichols—especially by Miss May."[14] By October 1958 the pair had cut their first album, "Improvisations to Music" on Mercury Records; and in 1961 their show *An Evening with Mike Nichols and Elaine May* was a hit on Broadway.

May and Nichols had begun to disband their act around 1962. During that time May worked on a screenplay for *The Loved One* (1965), based on the novel by Evelyn Waugh, directed by Tony Richardson. Elizabeth Taylor gushed to Mike Nichols, who directed Taylor and Richard Burton soon after in *Who's Afraid of Virginia Woolf?*, that "Richard and I think it's the best script we ever saw. We want to do the picture."[15] May's involvement in the film went no further and Terry Southern and Christopher Isherwood received the screenwriting credit. It was reported that May, described as "comedienne, screenwriter, playwright and stage director," signed a multi-picture deal with Columbia Pictures in 1966, although it is not clear in the press release what job(s) the studio was considering her for.[16] May would co-star in two films for Columbia, both released in 1967: Carl Reiner's *Enter Laughing*, and the screen adaptation of the Broadway play *Luv*, where she appeared with Peter Falk and Jack Lemmon. She received favorable reviews for both performances, but no other projects materialized with the studio. It was Paramount Pictures where she ultimately landed: first in March of 1968, to write her first screenplay, "One Hundred Dollar Misunderstanding" based on the novel by Robert Gover,[17] a project that did not appear to take shape; and finally, it was announced a few months later that May would write and direct *A New Leaf*.[18]

A NEW LEAF: THE SEEDS OF MAY'S DISCONTENT

A New Leaf starred Walther Matthau as Henry Graham, a lazy New York socialite who has squandered all his money on a lavish and self-serving lifestyle and now must marry beneath himself, in social status, to survive financially. Henry devises a plot to find an unsuspecting millionairess whom he can wed for her money and then murder to get out of the relationship. May co-starred as Henrietta Lowell, a rich, kind-hearted, disheveled botanist without a conniving bone in her body; she is generous and gullible and instantly falls prey to Henry's plotting. May's script was based on the short story "The Green Heart" by Jack Ritchie. The film had a thread of social satire running through it in the way it poked fun at the crisis of a middle-aged trust fund baby in opposition to the scatterbrained scientist who works, not because she has to, but because she loves her job. The story was also a dark comedy on how murder, treated lightly, serves as the main source of narrative conflict and humor. Henry's plot to kill Henrietta is constantly thwarted in the screwball tradition of pratfalls and miscommunication: she misinterprets his scheming as a show of love and adoration, which, ultimately, in the end it turns into when the groom realizes he is content being the husband of a botanist and spares his bride's life.

Matthau was not the traditional romantic male lead. He was not, by industry standards, handsome, and was often described as having "hangdog looks."[19] His brand of charm was in the form of playful yet cantankerous and sarcastic characters, qualities that extended to his public persona. Born in 1920, Matthau was fifty years old to May's thirty-eight when making *A New Leaf*. While it was certainly not unusual for an older male actor to be matched with a much younger actress, in this film the juxtaposition of Harry as the elder and eternal snob paired with Henrietta the innocent and perpetual slob was part of the film's humor and charm.

The casting of Matthau, more than the potential for on-screen chemistry, was necessitated by the star power he brought to May's directorial debut. Matthau had an established career in television and in the 1960s had found considerable success as a leading man in films, especially in comedies; in 1967 he won an Oscar for Best Supporting Actor in Billy Wilder's *The Fortune Cookie*. He was a star on Broadway and won a Tony Award in 1965 for his portrayal of the iconic slob, Oscar Madison, in Neil Simon's *The Odd Couple*, a role that he portrayed to much acclaim in the film adaptation in 1968. Matthau had made *The Odd Couple* at Paramount with Howard Koch, the studio's former vice president of production before he was replaced by Evans and started a producing deal with the company. Talent manager Hillard Elkins had teamed with May to pitch the film to Paramount, and eventually Elkins and Koch packaged the film; Koch and Matthau, who were collaborators and friends, guaranteed the film's delivery to Paramount.[20]

May had come to Paramount as a reputable comedian with dazzling critical reviews and impressive ticket sales; she and Nichols were responsible for original content; she had written and directed for off-Broadway; and she had received good reviews for her co-starring performances in *Enter Laughing* and *Luv*. As common as it was during these years for young filmmakers to helm studio pictures without coming up through the ranks compared to previous generations, it was still expected that these lucky few would be hired with some previous filmmaking skills, such as: having directed television and/or independent films; as a screenwriter of produced work; or having been a lead actor in several feature films. Paramount was attracted to May for her outstanding talent, but as a first-time film director, it would be essential for her to have the participation of industry veterans with current track records as a kind of endorsement and security.

May frequently described her turn at directing in circumstantial terms, claiming that Paramount would not give her the power to choose the director or actress, but they would hire her as the writer, director, and co-star, "And all for the same money."[21] Elkins, her manager at the time, pitched May as a triple threat to Paramount. "I never wanted to be a director," May confessed to an audience in 1975, but Elkins promised he had ". . . set a wonderful deal. I produce. You direct and write."[22] According to Elkins, the producer had attempted to entice the studio executives with the cultural clout of hiring a woman director, but only Bluhdorn seemed remotely moved by the idea.[23]

The last time Paramount had employed a woman for the job was in 1931, when Dorothy Arzner directed *Merrily We Go to Hell* starring Sylvia Sidney and Fredric March. In 1968 when May was signed to direct, Ida Lupino had been the only woman to direct a studio film during the 1960s—*Trouble with Angels*, for Columbia Pictures in 1966. During the silent era, early Hollywood had been much more open to women filmmakers; in a time before the transition to sound and the industry's financial reliance on the masculinized culture of Wall Street and the influence of the craft union's patriarchal hierarchy, filmmakers such as Dorothy Davenport, Frances Marion, and Lois Weber had successful careers that competed with their male peers. Arzner was the only woman director to transition from the silent era and sustain a career, and a successful one, in the classic studio system. She retired in 1943. In 1949 and during the 1950s Lupino, actress turned writer, director, and producer, followed Arzner as the only woman making movies in Hollywood, through her independent production company The Filmmakers.

When it was announced, in 1968, that May would direct *A New Leaf* it was read as the slightest sign of change, the first on the industry's periphery, given the paucity of women directing feature films. Independent art house filmmakers Shirley Clarke and Juleen Compton worked outside Hollywood's financial and distribution networks, Clarke based in New York City and Compton in New York and Europe. Each woman made two features during the early and mid-1960s: Clarke *The Connection* (1961) and *The Cool World* (1963); and Compton *Stranded* (1964) and *The Plastic Dome of Norma Jean* (1966). In Los Angeles, on the margins of cinema, low-budget, independent exploitation filmmaker Stephanie Rothman—who began her career working for Roger Corman—earned her first solo directing credit on *It's a Bikini World* in 1967, and the similarly placed Beverly Sebastian, in collaboration with her husband Ferd, co-directed *I Need a Man* that same year.

Hollywood—and Paramount—in the late 1960s may have been willing to invest in young talent, but including women directors on that roster was in no way seen as part of revitalizing the industry. The New Hollywood "generation" of filmmakers was almost exclusively white men; and in the midst of second wave feminism, Hollywood during the 1970s was not at the forefront of the women's liberation movement. Among major studios, Paramount might have hired the most women directors during the 1970s—two women directors in total during the decade—but the company's upper management did well in maintaining the industry's status quo chauvinism. According to Robert Evans, "Despite Women's Lib, I don't think people want to see a woman in a man's world," he told Marjorie Rosen of *The New York Times* in 1974. "She loses her femininity. The two men in 'The Sting' [Paul Newman and Robert Redford] have something more visual and romantic, something more exciting, than two women would."[24]

May would be the only woman since Lupino in 1966 to have a film produced and distributed by a major studio until 1977, when Paramount would hire Joan Darling to direct *First Love*. In 1978 two women would be hired by major studios: Jane Wagner would write and direct *Moment by Moment* for Universal; and Joan Micklin Silver would write and direct *Chilly Scenes of Winter* (initially released as *Head Over Heels*) for United Artists; that same year Warner Bros. would distribute Claudia Weill's independent feature, *Girlfriends*. In 1980 Weill would make *It's My Turn* for Columbia and Anne Bancroft would write, direct, and co-star in *Fatso* for 20th Century Fox. During the decade, eight films—three directed by May—would be the total number of features directed by women for the major studios.

Perhaps Charles Bluhdorn thought that May's gender was a novelty that could be an added selling point for her film, but the studio did not use this detail beyond a short line in the picture's press release that stated how acting, directing, and writing *A New Leaf* "mark[ed] the first time in film history a woman has handled the three assignments."[25] As the only woman filmmaker in production on a studio film at this time, and as a first-time director with limited industry experience, where the company did exploit May was with her salary. Matthau, as the bankable star, received $375,000, and the two producers were paid $50,000 each. May was paid $50,000 for her services as writer, co-star, and director, plus sharing 35 per cent of the film's grosses with Elkins, Koch, and Matthau.[26]

While May's novice status was a financial bargain during the initial contract signing, almost immediately the executives began to express concern over her inexperience. Paramount exec Peter Bart, writing in 2011 about working with May, was still hostile some forty years later, remembering how even before production on the film started he "didn't like or trust Elaine May and suspected that she didn't know which end of the camera to look through."[27]

Principle photography had gone over schedule, and even May admitted to her flaws as a first-time director who was starring in her own picture. In a humorous interview, conducted a few months after production was completed, May, who was rarely if ever transparent with the press, described, in a moment of near candidness, the challenges of her first film. "I really didn't know anything, but when I told them that, they thought that was my technique. You're supposed to be crisp. People would ask me where to put the camera and I'd say, 'I don't know'."[28] Decades later, in 2006, May continued to be funny and honest in describing how "I knew absolutely nothing, I barely knew what a camera looked like. Really, I struggled through. This story is almost unbelievable. I had written screenplays and I could write great-looking scenes, but I didn't know there was such a thing as coverage."[29]

May's failure to understand "coverage"—shooting a scene from multiple angles in order to have adequate footage to reassemble the material in the edit—did in fact prolong the production schedule when she had to go back and reshoot footage.[30] Anticipating delays due to May's inexperience, during the film's contract stages Paramount outlined, in no uncertain terms, the control the company had if the budget went over, outlining that if "the estimated finish cost exceeds 100% of the approved budget, Paramount shall have the right to take over production of the picture and make any and all changes and substitutions with respect thereto."[31] Koch, who had always planned to leave the production early for his next project, *On a Clear Day You Can See Forever* (1970), was replaced with Paramount's rising-star producer Stanley Jaffe, who would become president of the studio in 1970. Jaffe, who had been able to reign-in the production, which had gone over schedule, was already anticipating that post-production would take a similar turn when shooting came to a close. Preparing for the edit, Jaffe and May already seemed to be irritated with one another. Jaffe, updating the top studio executives on the film's progress, griped that May's "reservations about [first-time editor Eddy Beyer] probably do not reflect on his inexperience, but on the fact that this is the only area left for her to bitch about."[32]

Peter Bart had expressed concerns during the development of the script regarding what he saw as two disconnected storylines—one between Henry and Henrietta and the other about various murders, which he felt were distracting from the narrative. Writing to Robert Evans in February 1969, Bart advised that, "the key objective, I think, is to continue to focus on our two central characters and their odd-ball love story and not let the story run off in too many homicidal directions."[33] May's initial script involved Henry murdering two other characters as he prepares to kill his wife before having a change of heart by the end of the film, sparing his wife's life and giving himself over to the provincial life of university teaching and searching for plant specimens. Bart, Evans, and Jaffe agreed that the murders must be omitted to streamline the story. Encountering resistance from May over this decision, they utilized a clause in the film's contract that allowed Paramount "the sole and exclusive right to cut and edit as we see fit."[34] The studio executives decided that they would hire a new editor, remove May from post-production and finish supervising the edit of the film. Bart admitted that this was "not a course of action we would follow with a respected filmmaker, but none of us respected Elaine May. She had worn out every shred of goodwill."[35]

In January 1971, a few months before the planned release of the picture, May responded by suing Paramount, claiming that she had "suffered interference" on the film and that the final product had been altered so much by the studio "under my name and the film is not mine."[36] Paramount fought back. In a story retold by several of the executives involved, when the judge was shown the studio's version he thought it was hilarious and ruled in favor of Paramount, while complimenting May by predicting that her film would be a success at the box office.

Reviewers responded similarly to the judge, praising the film and in doing so giving credit to each of the battling sides by acknowledging how their differences had come together to create a success. Charles Champlin of the *Los Angeles Times* noticed the creative conflict in the "occasional moments that don't quite hang together" and sensed, in the more earnest and sentimental finale that "Miss May probably intended a sharper ironic thrust to the ending . . ." But ultimately, for Champlin, the film's "level of successful invention is marvelously high, and 'A New Leaf' achieves the nutty and improbable grandeur of the best movie comedies of the past."[37] "May has gotten off some sharp and amusing dialog in her screenplay, which she may or may not have directed," wrote *Variety*, making jest about the lawsuit, while at the same time applauding May's debut work. "The net result is an ingratiating film that will make the winner's circle."[38]

For May, the struggle for creative control was one that would frame her career as a director moving forward, whether she was in conflict with studio heads or perhaps facing her own creative challenges. If she had joked about how being hired to direct, write, and act in her first film was an accident, she also knew that it was an act of self-protection. "It's this," she told an interviewer who was visiting the set of *A New Leaf* one day during filming, "You don't expect just to sit down and write a script, like that. You may never see it again as you wrote it. That's the traditional Hollywood way, you know . . . So I'm directing this because I wondered if it could be kept unchanged."[39]

ROMANTIC COMEDY AND THE 1970S HEARTBREAKING ANTI-HERO

May followed *A New Leaf*, immediately, with *The Heartbreak Kid*, in which she directed Neil Simon's script adaptation of Bruce Jay Friedman's short story, "A Change of Plan," produced by Palomar Pictures for 20th Century Fox. *The Heartbreak Kid* begins with young New York Jewish newlyweds Lenny Cantrow and Lila Kolodny, played by Charles Grodin and Jeannie Berlin, May's twenty-three-year-old daughter. Lenny, who is socially ambitious and emotionally shallow, leaves his bride only days into the couple's Miami Beach honeymoon. For him, Lila's enthusiastic show of affection—her constant talking during sex, the unself-conscious way she eats and how she sings off-key with abandon—is a sudden turn-off in the face of until-death-do-us-part. Lenny meets Kelly, the blonde and bronzed *shiksa*, played to perfection by Cybill Shepherd, who appears on the beach in a ray of sunlight; Lenny promptly breaks it off with Lila over a lobster dinner to then pursue Kelly. For Grodin and Berlin the film was each performer's first major screen role; Berlin would be nominated for an Academy Award for Best Supporting Actress.

If, according to her critics, May had been indecisive, ill-prepared, and difficult on *A New Leaf*, for *The Heartbreak Kid* she curbed those tendencies and the making of the film went smoothly. By her own admission on *A New Leaf*, May had felt the constant struggle to catch up as she learned how to direct a major motion picture on the job. It seemed for her next film, the learning curve she had experienced prepared her for success. In fact, *The Heartbreak Kid* would be the only film that May directed that would go unmarred by studio battles.

Some of the film's stability was attributed to the reduced amount of control May had over the material. Neil Simon, acclaimed playwright and screenwriter, had stipulated in his contract that screenplays he wrote could not be changed without his consent. Furthermore, he was an integral part of production, being present on set everyday, where he was able to rewrite scenes and observe May's approach to directing. Simon was especially impressed with the way she used her expertise in improvisation to rehearse with actors. "The reason it seems improvised is that that's the way Elaine May directs, and that's what was so wonderful about it," recalled Simon in a 1978 interview. "She would rehearse the words [script], then throw out the words, then just have them do the scene the way they wanted to, and then put back the words . . . Not all actors can do that."[40]

Richard Sylbert, who was the production designer on *Heartbreak*, described May's style of control as the tenuous space between the security of personal relationships and borderline delusional behavior. "She operates on trust," observed Sylbert. "If she trusts you, she is the most wonderful person to work with. If she is suspicious, if she doesn't trust you on some bizarre level, you've got a problem. It's a form of paranoia."[41] On *The Heartbreak Kid*, she was surrounded by several important alliances that provided a secure creative environment: Anthea Sylbert (sister-in-law to Richard), who was the costume designer on *A New Leaf* and *Heartbreak*; Grodin, whom May had championed for the role and who would appear in *Heaven Can Wait*, which May would co-write, as well as her fourth film, *Ishtar*; and with her daughter, Berlin. *Heartbreak* would mark the first of many collaborations between mother and daughter.

During the release of the film, Berlin was effusive about the experience of being directed by her mother. "I trust her. Everyone trusts her. She lets you try things, even if they're no good. And she has sense enough to edit it out if it's lousy. Almost everything I know about acting, she taught me."[42] Although it is perhaps unsurprising that she would praise her mother in the press, critics agreed with the actress's assessment of her director and Berlin received outstanding reviews for her performance of Lila, the put-upon bride. In addition to the Oscar nomination, Berlin won the Best Supporting Actress award from the National Society of Film Critics and the New York Film Critics Awards. Alan R. Howard, of the *Hollywood Reporter* described Berlin as "breathtakingly comic, honest and poignant . . . Her performance puts pain and comedy on the line, indicating a big future."[43] *Variety* thought the actress demonstrated "a jewel of understanding her character, a natural comedienne of fine talent."[44] Eddie Albert was also nominated for an Academy Award for Best Supporting Actor, and he won the National Society of Film Critics for his supporting role (in a tie with Joel Grey for *Cabaret*). Grodin and Shepherd received enthusiastic praise in the press, as did Audra Lindley, for her supporting role. Made for under $3 million,[45] *The Heartbreak Kid* grossed an estimated $5.6 million, in the U.S. and Canadian market, during its first year in theaters.[46]

The film was a success by all accounts and part of its success was how it polarized critics and audiences alike. Joe Gelmis of *Newsday*, Vincent Canby of *The New York Times*, and *Time Magazine* ranked the picture on each of their "Best of the Year" film lists. Canby delighted in how "the film succeeds in being equally merciless to the unfortunate Lila . . . and to the magnificent-looking Kelly [Shepherd] . . .,"[47] promising viewers that "it's very, very funny, totally unsentimental and just a bit cruel."[48] Where critics applauded May's inaugural effort as a filmmaker on *A New Leaf*, in light of the studio fracas, on *Heartbreak* many reviewers felt that she had come into her own as a director. "Elaine May's deft direction," wrote *Variety*, "catches all the possibilities of young romance and its tribulations in light strokes and cleverly accents characterization of the various principles."[49] Howard Kissel of *Women's Wear Daily* agreed: "'The Heartbreak Kid' is one of the best comedies in years and a sign of Ms. May's arrival as an important director."[50]

Some critics were torn about the film, finding themselves caught between the appealing performances and May's influence, and a narrative execution that felt weak. Diane Jacobs acknowledged May's "directorial expertise" and thought "the cast is superb," but ultimately the film to her was shallow and flat. "What is missing," Jacobs explained, "is any kind of real affection for the characters. Grotin [*sic*] and Berlin are not even anti-hero and heroine, but personalities, like all the rest, to be uncompromisingly analyzed and laughed at and then all too easily dismissed."[51] In a similar way, Charles Champlin adored the actors and cited May's skill as a director in bringing out good performances, but he too thought the characters lacked depth in the way they "arise in a kind of limbo between farce and black humor."[52]

But where some found poignancy and humor in the story of humiliation, heartbreak, and ill-fitted romance, others experienced the narrative's cruelty not as clever, but as just plain mean. In his article entitled "'Blume' and 'Heartbreak Kid'—What Kind of Jews Are They?" Robert F. Moss, writing for New York Times, lambasted Hollywood's attempts at depicting Jewish characters, citing *Blume in Love* (1973), and what Moss considered the industry's worst offender, *The Heartbreak Kid*. For this critic the film exploited the most offensive stereotypes in Berlin's portrayal of Lila, depicting her as "noisy, vulgar, demanding, insanely possessive, impossibly overbearing . . . In short, a Jewish princess of unmistakably lower middleclass origins."[53] Moss's article sparked a letter to the editor from a self-identified "16-year-old Jewish-American woman," Diana K. Bletter, who was appalled that the creators of the film—Friedman, Simon, May—who were all Jewish, had "[taken] the worst aspects of human nature and tried to dump them on Jewish women."[54] Viewer Larry Bone wrote a letter to the *Los Angeles Times* voicing similar issues with the film, but this time pointing his ire at Simon specifically. In his letter, titled "Outraged at Simon," Bone took the writer to task for the film's misuse of humor at the expense of human sadness. "What is funny about a wife being emotionally tormented and abused by a husband leaving her for another woman?," demanded Bone. "Does Neil Simon have any sensitivity?"[55]

Simon's work defines a dominant strain of comedy, with attention to romantic comedy, in the 1960s and 1970s. His style of humor focused on white middle-class, and frequently middle-aged, malaise. Linda Lavin, who appeared in the stage performance of Simon's "Last of the Red Hot Lovers" in the early 1970s, identified the playwright's audience as "the tired businessman and his wife, not young people, not blacks ... They come to the theater to see their lives verified and they go home saying 'We're all human. We're all in the same boat.' They haven't been offended. The life they lead hasn't been challenged—it's been reaffirmed."[56] The characters in Simon's scripts—for the theater and screen—during these years are often in the throes of a midlife crisis, turmoil sparked by or leading to romantic conflict, but his characters always resolve their troubles through interpersonal harmony that reassures the human experience. Where Simon observed the pain of the modern condition, he did so as a conformist and in conventional, frequently sentimental, terms.

May, in contrast, is not committed to tidy resolutions for her characters and any display of affectionate reconciliation at the film's conclusion is wrapped in satire; for her the punchline of the joke is delivered in the "happily ever after". In *A New Leaf* the couple is united in the final scene as an act of failure: after so much nefarious plotting, Henry experiences that, against all odds, he does have a heart and cannot resist a feeling of fondness for Henrietta and her lowly way of life as a botanist and teacher. In a similar way, *Ishtar* ends with wannabe night-club singers Lyle (Warren Beatty) and Chuck (Dustin Hoffman), like Henrietta unaware that their perception of reality is out of line with the real world, and having survived being lost in the Sahara desert while under fire, revelling in false heroism as they perform to a packed house on the eve of their album's release. Worse than the fact that they remain painfully talentless is that the crowd and their record deal are staged. For May, the joke reaches a crescendo in how Lyle and Chuck remain delusional by being unable to distinguish what they see as their success from the bewilderment and anguish on the audience's faces.

The Heartbreak Kid does something similar to May's other films by ending with a bittersweet laugh at a protagonist celebrating flawed achievements, in this case Lenny's illusion of social ascendency through romantic triumph, or vice versa. The film's final scene closes on Lenny, at his wedding party to Kelly, sitting alone, seeming even more aimless now that he has conquered his supposed ideal woman. He has experienced no self-discovery during this process, which is surprising and therefore pathetic, and has not endeared himself to the audience, which allows viewers to find his situation funny. "[M]aybe only Elaine May and the author of the screenplay, Neil Simon, could make such a hurtful situation funny, and still somewhat true," offered Roger

Ebert of the film's predicaments.[57] Even Simon found the characterization unsettling, acknowledging that he had stepped outside familiar territory. In a 1978 interview he explained how his approach to adapting the story was to write like Friedman in order to capture the author's "oblique and unique sense of humor." Simon confessed that, "when I got halfway through, I got nervous. It seemed very bizarre, and very heavy to me . . . The character is a hero, but he's an anti-hero. You like him one minute, and you hate him the next minute. It's exactly what happened with audiences."[58]

The Heartbreak Kid's unsympathetic male anti-hero and the film's disoriented take on love and marriage fit right in with a style of romantic comedies emblematic of the 1970s: love during this decade was funny, but devastating. In 1967 *The Graduate* utilized conventions key to the genre—seemingly incompatible love interests, faced with enormous obstacles and hijinks, but a couple that is finally united in the end. *The Graduate*, however, disrupted the formula of chaos evolving into romantic harmony with a tenuous reunion between a couple, a twist that reviews of *The Heartbreak Kid* identified as a common link between the two films. In *Harold and Maude* (Hal Ashby, 1971), the lovers are separated in the end by age and life experience. At the end of *Annie Hall* (Woody Allen, 1977), the couple part on eventually amicable terms, but the Woody Allen character is nostalgic for his old love, Diane Keaton. *Shampoo* (Hal Ashby, 1975) follows Warren Beatty's character as he jumps in and out of multiple women's beds under every false pretense imaginable. In the final scene all hilarity has disappeared and the handsome Hollywood lead is reduced to a lonely man who has alienated all those who once swooned over his charming ways. This is love in the 1970s, and it is depressing.

FRIENDS AND ENEMIES: *MIKEY AND NICKY* AND ELAINE AND PARAMOUNT

Hollywood has historically relished flawed male leads and in the late 1960s and into the 1970s men in movies flourished in new ways under the changing cultural and industrial conditions. In addition to the take on romantic comedies centered on male missteps came the era's male-centric buddy films. In 1969 Dennis Hopper and Peter Fonda's *Easy Rider* introduced the counterculture outlaw buddies, and that same year Dustin Hoffman and Jon Voight, in *Midnight Cowboy*, were scrappy yet sentimental social pariahs bonded together. Paul Newman and Robert Redford reigned as the heartthrob outlaws in period pieces such as George Roy Hill's *Butch Cassidy and the Sundance Kid* (1969) and *The Sting* (1973); and race and ethnicity were brought to attention in pairing white/Jewish Gene Wilder with African-American co-stars Cleavon

Little in *Blazing Saddles* (Mel Brooks, 1974) and Richard Pryor in *Silver Streak* (Arthur Hillier, 1976).

In 1976 May made her first buddy picture, following *The Heartbreak Kid* with *Mikey and Nicky*, the story of two childhood best friends who are now adult gangsters the night before Mikey (Peter Falk), who has been hired to help orchestrate Nicky's (John Cassavetes) assignation, must fulfill the mark. Cassavetes and Falk had an existing rapport, the two were close friends and would work together several times, including a few years prior on the 1970 film *Husbands*, written and directed by Cassavetes in which he and Falk co-starred. As Mikey and Nicky, the two tramp around Philadelphia on a dark and rainy night, disheveled and combative, while still feeling the intimate bonds of friendship. Cassavetes' character falls deeper into paranoia and anxiety over his correct suspicions that the mob boss is out to get him, and Falk tries to reassure his friend while, with great guilt, helping the mob's hitman follow the target. The film was not a comedy.

Andrew Tobias, writing for *New West* in December 1976, painted a condemning picture of May as an unruly filmmaker gone wild on a production gone awry. "With only a simple, first-rate script (her own), and not so much as a single mechanical monster to malfunction, or even George C. Scott (or an actor of similar temperament) to contend with," wrote Tobias, "Ms. May managed nonetheless to direct a truly monumental behind-the-scenes disaster."[59] May had been working on *Mikey and Nicky* for years. In 1968 Peter Falk, who had co-starred with May in the screen adaption of *Luv*, told the press that he and Cassavetes were scheduled to appear in the picture.[60] May's original script, initially conceived as a one-act play, was reported to have been sold to United Artists in 1969.[61] In 1972, Palomar Pictures signed a deal with 20th Century Fox to produce seven small feature films, to be made for around $1.5–2.5 million each. May, *The Heartbreak Kid*, and *Mikey and Nicky* were part of the line-up.[62] Tom Miller, the studio publicist for *Mikey and Nicky*, noted that May had made *Heartbreak* for Palomar so that the company would in turn make *Mikey and Nicky*.[63] By 1973, *Heartbreak* had experienced a successful release, and *Mikey and Nicky* had been dropped from the Palomar-Fox agreement due to an escalating projected budget ($1.6 million, moving closer to $2.2 million).

In a startling turn of events, May returned, in March of 1973, to Paramount, where she would make *Mikey and Nicky* just two years after battling the studio in court over authorship issues on *A New Leaf*. New executives appeared to present a protective layer between her and those she had fought with previously. *Broadcasting* reported that Bud Austin, who at the time had just been hired as Paramount's vice president of creative services and marketing, "a friend of Elaine May, who wrote 'Mickey [sic] and Nicky' at his home in New York several years ago," had been convinced by the filmmaker to executive produce the film, which he was responsible for selling to the studio.[64] Frank Yablans, who was president of the studio, got along well with May, who even cast him in a small part as a gangster before Charles Bluhdorn stepped in to remind the executive of his true role overseeing the film as a representative for the studio that was bankrolling it.[65]

In an effort to protect itself from revisiting past trauma with May, Paramount drew up a thirty-three-page, single-spaced contract that reinforced the company's control and May's accountability. The filmmaker would be responsible for any costs that exceeded 15 per cent of the budget; and the film would be delivered by 1 June 1974. In return May was afforded final cut and the provision that the only studio executive she would have to work with was Yablans, thus keeping her and Robert Evans apart.[66]

By the time she was working on *Mikey and Nicky*, May had the experience of two feature films and more leeway, even with the detailed contract, than on her previous features; she was now directing her own script based on original content and working with a cast and principle crew that she knew well. May found kindred spirits working with Cassavetes, who was known for his love of actors and his belief in giving them the creative space to interpret their characters, and with Falk, who had already collaborated with Cassavetes in this kind of environment. "It's easy enough for a director to say 'Faster' or 'Slower' or 'I don't believe you're doing it right,'" said Falk of the difficulties a performer could face, "but to hit that precise phrase an actor will respond to . . . that's tough." For Falk, working with May was a positive experience in terms of method. "The thing about Elaine is that if she can't find the phrase, she won't say anything. For that, I love her."[67] Cassavetes was equally effusive in his praise for May's approach to filmmaking and when asked what it was like to be directed by a woman he claimed that, "It's better. Being a woman, Elaine can be more objective about the relationship between Mikey and Nicky. She can bring more insight to it . . . but I wouldn't call Elaine May a 'woman Director.' She is a director who happens to be a woman and one of the best in the business."[68]

May's approach, however, to directing her actors and allowing them the freedom to develop their characters over multiple takes and work-shopping on set, while the crew stood by idle, or rebuilding sets to accommodate last-minute scene changes, became a detriment to production logistics. Tom Miller, the publicist assigned by the studio and who observed production for a few weeks in May and June 1973 described the way ". . . Elaine May shoots reel after reel of film. There are no camera rehearsals. What would be a camera rehearsal for another director, Miss May films. She films in segments of sometimes ten minutes, without calling cut. And she might call for such scenes to be done fifteen times."[69]

As a director, May is frequently described as vacillating between a profound ineptitude for the technical skills and organizational systems inherent in studio filmmaking and a unique, almost profound, understanding of the creative process/drive to fulfill the artist's vision at any cost. Together, these two qualities have created dynamic films, but with much distress. Sid Gecker, the script coordinator on *Mikey and Nicky*, described "her problem [as] she's too much of a perfectionist. She won't compromise on anything."[70] Michael Hausman, the film's producer and a self-described "director's producer," who first met May on *The Heartbreak Kid* as an associate producer, felt that although "Elaine demands a lot," her high expectations were justified. "She demands a good crew to carry out her demands," he explained to Dan Rottenberg of the *Chicago Tribune* in one of the only articles done on the film during its production, "because *she's* good."[71]

But the shoot was a difficult one not only for the cast and crew, whose call time to set was at eight every evening—the film was shot only at night—and on the average, they would work nine to ten hours, and often even more, sometimes until eight the next morning. Falk and Cassavetes would attend dailies with May every evening around five or six before arriving on set. Sometimes May would go straight from the set in the morning to work with her editor for a few hours before finally going to bed.[72] Her assistant at the time, Nola Safro, observed that, "Elaine is tired. [I] can never get through to her. Impossible to get her to anywhere on time . . . never gets enough rest, no time for herself, is getting very tired of it all . . ."[73] If on *A New Leaf* May's tendency towards inefficient work habits can be understood—in part—within the context of a beginner thrown into extraordinary circumstances, the way she ran the set of her third film was *her* process. The film was initially set for a sixty-day shoot (all at night and on location in Philadelphia),[74] which ultimately went over to 120 days;[75] principle photography began in May of 1973 and was completed in March of 1974.

Difficulties manifested themselves even more during post-production, where May supervised the edit of her film at the Sunset Marquis Hotel in West Hollywood, where Paramount had set up her editing and living suites. Again, Tobias's *New West* exposé of the film is the most detailed (and colorful) reporting on the film; it describes the filmmaker as "terribly shy," practically a recluse, who wore dark glasses and could be seen talking only with Cassavetes, Falk and her family. She subsisted on odd "health food" combinations (keffir, yeast, yogurt) and was extremely protective of her film in progress, keeping out housekeeping and Paramount studio executives alike.[76] May's behavior, in combination with technical difficulties that had transpired on set with faulty sound recording and the tremendous amount of film that she had shot, caused the editing to go on for over a year.

A year and a half after *Mikey and Nicky* had completed production May was still editing the film. Paramount finally said no to pouring any more money into it and demanded that she complete the picture. When the filmmaker refused, both sides filed lawsuits. The budget for the film had now increased from an estimated $2 million to $4 million (and eventually would creep to $5 million because of legal fees). Arthur N. Ryan, senior vice president for the studio, told the press that Paramount was reluctant to move forward with a lawsuit. "We offered her all of the support possible to make the film she and we originally wanted. But we were unable to get her to deliver the picture."[77] May, in return, sued the studio for $8 million for damages and breach of contract, claiming Paramount refused to pay an additional $180,000 needed to complete the film, which was days away from being finished. What followed was an episode out of an Elaine May movie: she sold the film, owned by Paramount, to Peter Falk's company, Alyce Film Inc., and in the process a number of film reels disappeared and then reappeared when Paramount's new studio president, Barry Diller, infuriated at being hoodwinked by the filmmaker, demanded that she orchestrate the return of the missing film, which she did.[78]

It was no surprise that when Paramount finally released the film in December of 1976, the studio did so quickly and without any fanfare. Critics, after the success of May's last film, *The Heartbreak Kid*, were confused and put-off by *Mikey and Nicky*. "Elaine May's first two films . . . were comedies of sometimes inspired and often touching lunacy," wrote Vincent Canby. "'Mikey and Nicky' . . . is something else entirely." Canby found the supporting actors appealing, but was unforgiving of the two leads: "It's nearly two hours of being locked in a telephone booth with a couple of method actors who won't stop talking, though they have nothing of interest to say . . ." For Canby, May was a "very intelligent director," but on this effort he felt she had failed.[79] In a similar way, *Variety* praised Cassavetes' and Falk's performances, describing how "the interplay between the stars is excellent," but ultimately the reviewer felt the story to be "like a theatrical project that wandered into the wrong medium." This reviewer predicted that the "stormy and costly production history of the project is the more interesting facet" to the film than anything beyond the worthy performances.[80]

Elaine May's career as a director came to a standstill after *Mikey and Nicky*. The film was re-released, to much better reviews, in 1986, but the experience had not been easy for her. When the Museum of Modern Art in New York City screened the film that year May made a rare appearance, admitting to the crowd that, "It was difficult for me to get directing jobs [afterwards] because I seemed sort of crazy." Where May didn't seem "crazy" is when she was working as a writer only. Following *Mikey and Nicky*, May excelled as a screenwriter—sometimes for credit, as in the case of *Heaven Can Wait* (Warren Beatty and Buck Henry, 1978), which she co-wrote with Warren Beatty and was nominated for an Oscar for Best Screenplay; and in other instances without screen credit, per her discretion, on successful movies such as *Reds* (1980) also co-written with, directed by, and starring Beatty, and *Tootsie* (Sydney Pollack, 1982) for which she is credited with developing Bill Murray's character, Jeff, in the film. With the accolades from *Heaven* . . . and the validation from Beatty, one of the most powerful star/filmmakers at the time, in 1987, May was given one final chance to direct: *Ishtar* is the last feature film (to date) that May wrote and directed, for Columbia Pictures, with Beatty as producer and co-star with Dustin Hoffman. *Ishtar*, which is discussed in detail in Chapter 7, has been named one of the biggest Hollywood flops in history, although in the last decade in particular it has also been reclaimed and newly appreciated by contemporary audiences.

Elaine May's body of work as a director is small—four films—but robust. Her talent is large and legendary, and the movies that she struggled with during the 1970s were small enough in terms of budgets and studio resources, during a time when studios invested in small films and took chances on talent that had not come up through the traditional Hollywood hierarchy. As a woman directing films, May was the first in a "figurative" generation of female filmmakers who, very slowly and in small numbers, began to emerge during the decade against the sexist odds of 1970s Hollywood. When asked in 2011 at a retrospective of her work at Harvard Film Archives how she felt about the making of *Mikey and Nicky*, May, in her typical fashion, joked about a serious situation. "It was really . . . yes, it was awful," she confessed to the crowd. "The movie was hard, but all of it was very difficult." The best advice that she received about the lawsuit came from John Cassavetes, as she told Haden Guest in the interview. He told her:

> "'if you want to avoid the lawsuit—,' he was so smart this way, you wouldn't think it—," she interrupted, "'give a party and invite all the important people you know including the head of the studio.' I said, 'Are you crazy? I'm not giving a party! That's ridiculous! I'm not inviting these people to my house . . . !' But he was right," she laughed thinking back on it. "Had I given a party, they wouldn't have sued me. It's such a tiny community. But I didn't."[81]

NOTES

1. For a detailed history of women directors in 1970s Hollywood, see Maya Montañez Smukler, *Liberating Hollywood: Women Directors and the Feminist Reform of 1970s American Cinema* (New Brunswick, NJ: Rutgers University Press, 2018).
2. *Directory of Members 1969–70* (Directors Guild of America, Inc., 1969): 199.
3. Paul E. Steiger, "Movie Makers No Longer Sure What Sparkle Is," *Los Angeles Times*, 17 November 1969.

4. Lee Beaupre, "Pic Biz Booby-Trap: 'Youth'," *Variety*, 31 July 1968; "Pix Must 'Broaden Market'," *Variety*, 20 March 1968.
5. Stanley Penn, "Focusing on Young: A New Breed of Movie Attracts the Young, Shakes Up Hollywood," *The Wall Street Journal*, 4 November 1969.
6. Beaupre, "Pic Biz Booby-Trap: 'Youth'."
7. "Bob Evans Pays Chips-Service to 'Writer as Star' at Paramount," *Variety*, 1 May 1968: 19.
8. Helen Markel, "Mike Nichols & Elaine May," *Redbook Magazine*, February 1961: 99.
9. Markel, p. 100.
10. Markel, p. 99.
11. Michael Braun, "Mike and Elaine: Veracity-Cum-Boffs," *Esquire*, October 1960: 202.
12. Markel, pp. 99–100.
13. Bob Bernstein, "Review: Omnibus (Net)," *The Billboard*, 20 January 1958: 15.
14. Art Murphy, "Tele Follow-Up Comment: Omnibus," *Variety*, 22 January 1958: 46.
15. Thomas Thompson, "Whatever Happened to Elaine May?" *LIFE* magazine, 28 July 1967: 56.
16. "Columbia Signs Elaine May to Multiple-Picture Deal," *Boxoffice*, 23 May 1966, W-4. Also see "From Columbia Pictures' 'News', Biography: Elaine May," 18 August 1966, Studio Biography for the film *Luv*, Elaine May Clipping Files, Margaret Herrick Library.
17. Syd Cassyd, "Ronald Kahn Buys Rights to 'Return of the Tiger'," *Boxoffice*, 25 March 1968: 17.
18. "Bob Evans Pays Chips-Service to 'Writer as Star' at Paramount": 19.
19. Thomas Meehan, "What the OTB Bettor Can Learn from Walter Matthau: A Lesson From . . .," *New York Times*, 4 July 1971: SM6.
20. "Inter-Office Communication From Bernard Donnenfeld to Charles Bluhdorn and Martin Davis, Re: *A New Leaf*," 26 February 1968. *A New Leaf*, Paramount Pictures Special Collection, Margaret Herrick Library: 1–2.
21. "Elaine May in conversation with Mike Nichols," *Film Comment*, July/August 2006 <https://www.filmcomment.com/article/elaine-may-in-conversation-with-mike-nichols/> (accessed January 2019).
22. Michael Rivlin, "Elaine May: Too Tough for Hollywood?" *Millimeter* 3.10 (1975): 16.
23. Rachel Abramowitz, *Is That a Gun in Your Pocket? Women's Experience of Power in Hollywood* (New York: Random House, 2000), p. 61.
24. Marjorie Rosen, "Isn't it About Time to Bring on The Girls?" *New York Times*, 15 December 1974.
25. "Paramount Pictures Corporation: Production Notes, *A New Leaf*," 20 August 1970. *A New Leaf* Production Files, Margaret Herrick Library: 10.
26. "Inter-Office Communication From A. N. Ryan to Eugene H. Frank, Re: *A New Leaf*," 3 April 1968. *A New Leaf*, Paramount Pictures Special Collection, Margaret Herrick Library: 1–3.
27. Peter Bart, *Infamous Players: A Tale of Movies, the Mob (and Sex)* (New York: Weinstein Books, 2011), p. 145.
28. Dick Lemon, "How to Succeed in Interviewing Elaine May (Try, Really Try)," *New York Times*, 4 January 1970.
29. "Elaine May in conversation with Mike Nichols."
30. Ibid.
31. "Inter-Office Communication From A. N. Ryan to Eugene H. Frank, Re: *A New Leaf*," 3 April 1968: 1.
32. "Letter from Stanley Jaffe to Charles Bluhdorn, Martin Davis, Robert Evans, Bernard

Donnenfeld," 7 October1970. *A New Leaf*, Production Files. Margaret Herrick Library: 2.
33. "Inter-Office Communication from Peter Bart to Robert Evans, Subject: *A New Leaf*," 7 February 1969. *A New Leaf*, Production Files, Margaret Herrick Library: 3.
34. "Letter from Norman Flicker to Stanley Jaffe, Subject: *A New Leaf*," 16 February 1970. *A New Leaf*, Production Files, Margaret Herrick Library: 1.
35. Bart, p. 147.
36. "Evans May Have Been Thinking of Her," *Variety*, 10 February 1971: 13.
37. Charles Champlin, "Critic at Large: Elaine May's 'A New Leaf'," *Los Angeles Times*, 2 April 1971.
38. Gene Moskowitz, "Film Review: A New Leaf," *Variety*, 10 March 1971.
39. Howard Thompson, "Elaine May Spends Her Summer Knee-Deep in Film," *New York Times*, 26 August 1969: 36.
40. James Powers, "Dialogue on Film: Neil Simon," *American Film* 3.5, 1 March 1978: 38.
41. Abramowitz, p. 62.
42. Richard Natale, "Eye View: Please, Mrs. Worthington, DO . . .," *Women's Wear Daily*, 21 December 1972.
43. Alan R. Howard, "Social Satire in 'Heartbreak Kid'," *Hollywood Reporter*, 13 December 1972.
44. "Film Reviews: The Heartbreak Kid," *Variety*, 13 December 1972: 20.
45. Lee Beaupre, "Elaine May's 'Mikey' To Paramount; Palomar In Scratch When Budget Rises," *Variety*, 21 March 1973: 94.
46. "Big Rental Films of 1973," *Variety*, 9 January 1974: 19. Per *Variety*'s explanation, this number does not reflect the film's total box office grosses, which would have to include the theater owner's percentage, but rather accounts for only the distributor's earnings.
47. Vincent Canby, "Which Should You See?" *New York Times*, 24 December 1972, D3.
48. Vincent Canby, "'Heartbreak Kid': Elaine May's 2nd Effort as Director Arrives," *New York Times*, 18 December 1972: 56.
49. "Film Reviews: The Heartbreak Kid."
50. Howard Kissel, "Films: 'The Heartbreak Kid'," *Women's Wear Daily*, 18 December 1972: 18.
51. Diane Jacobs, "The Heartbreak Kid," *Changes in the Arts*, Jan/Feb 1973. *The Heartbreak Kid*, Clipping Files, Margaret Herrick Library.
52. Charles Champlin, "Credible Comedy in 'Heartbreak Kid'," *Los Angeles Times*, 20 December 1972: C1.
53. Robert F. Moss, "'Blume' and 'Heartbreak Kid'—What Kind of Jews Are They?" *New York Times*, 9 September 1973.
54. Diana K. Bletter, "Letter to the Editor: Disgraced," *New York Times*, 30 September 1973: A11.
55. Larry Bone, "Outraged at Simon," *Los Angeles Times*, 7 January 1973: O8.
56. Paul D. Zimmerman, "Neil Simon: Up From Success," *Newsweek*, 2 February1970: 53.
57. Roger Ebert, "Heartbreak Kid," *Chicago Sun-Times*, 1 January 1972.
58. Powers, p. 37.
59. Andrew Tobias, "For Elaine May, a New Film—But Not a New Leaf," *New West*, 6 December 1976: 57.
60. Wayne Warga, "Falk—Many a Sinking Ship's Saving Grace," *Los Angeles Times*, 16 December 1968: G1.
61. "Elaine May's 'Bumpy Ride' on 'Leaf': Manduke Sticks on 'Mickey [sic] & Nicky'," *Variety*, 27 August1969: 6.

62. "Worldwide Rights: Seven Pix Pact For Fox-Palomar," *The Independent Film Journal*, 3 February 1972, 6; Lee Beaupre, "Elaine May's 'Mikey' To Paramount; Palomar In Scratch When Budget Rises," *Variety*, 21 March 1973: 94.
63. Tom Miller's working notebook, *Mikey and Nicky*, Publicity 1973. Tom Miller Papers, Special Collection, Margaret Herrick Library: 41.
64. "Paramount's Bud Austin: turned on to television," *Broadcasting*, 2 December 1974: 57.
65. Tobias, p. 59.
66. Ibid., p. 59.
67. Guy Flatley, "At the Movies: Falk on 'Mikey': 'This is No Romp in the Park'," *New York Times*, 17 December 1976: 62.
68. "Women Calling 'Camera!' Women Calling 'Cut'!" Folder: *Mikey and Nicky*, Tom Miller Papers, Special Collection, Margaret Herrick Library: 5.
69. Tom Miller's working notebook, *Mikey and Nicky*: 6.
70. Dan Rottenberg, "Elaine May . . . or She May Not," *Chicago Tribune*, 21 October 1973: 56.
71. Ibid., p. 56.
72. "Production Notes 'Mikey and Nicky,'" Folder: *Mikey and Nicky*, Tom Miller Papers, Special Collection, Margaret Herrick Library: 5.
73. Miller's working notebook, *Mikey and Nicky*: 42.
74. Ibid., p. 27.
75. Tobias, p. 62.
76. Ibid., p. 62.
77. "Par, Elaine May Sue Each Other; Film Over-Budget And Incomplete," *Variety*, 29 October 1975.
78. Ibid.; and Tobias, p. 66.
79. Vincent Canby, "'Mikey and Nicky,' Film on Amity," *New York Times*, 22 December 1976 <https://www.nytimes.com/1976/12/22/archives/mikey-and-nicky-film-on-amity.html> (accessed January 2019).
80. "Mikey and Nicky," *Variety*, 22 December 1976.
81. Elaine May, interview with Haden Guest, Harvard Film Archive, 13 November 2011.

CHAPTER 3

Dangerous Business—Elaine May as Existential Improviser

Jake Wilson

"Miss May does not exist"
—liner notes from *Improvisations to Music* (1958)

EARLY STAGES: THE YEARS OF NICHOLS AND MAY

Before she was a filmmaker, Elaine May was famous as an improviser, first as a member of Chicago's pioneering Compass Players—under the direction of Paul Sills, who drew inspiration from the "theater games" developed by his mother Viola Spolin—and then in partnership with Mike Nichols, another Compass veteran. By the time May broke up the act in 1962, Nichols and May had made countless appearances on radio and television, released a trio of albums, and starred in a hit Broadway show, introducing a broad public to a brand of improvisational comedy that has been vastly influential ever since.[1] This chapter argues that not only Nichols and May's sketches but May's subsequent films can be understood as examples of improvisation, in an existential sense that entails a blurring of boundaries between life and art.

By her own account, Spolin's vision of improvisation took shape through a series of experiences largely outside the professional theater, including the amateur performances staged by her immigrant family and, most crucially, her time spent teaching drama to both children and adults as part of a Chicago public works project during the Depression.[2] As Kyle Stevens puts it, Spolin saw theatrical play as "a catalyst for self-expression and self-realization," seeking to "blur the line between two senses of acting: the doing and the mimetic."[3] Understood in these terms, improvisation was not merely about putting on a show for an audience, but a means of communication between the performers themselves: a given improvisation was not the creation of any single individual, but came into being through their spontaneous responses to each other.

These principles were echoed in the set of guidelines for improvisers which May developed with Compass director Theodore J. Flicker, later distilled into the single famous rule of "yes, and"—meaning that one performer cannot negate a premise another has established, but must add something of their own which will carry it further.[4] As Nichols and May moved further into the realm of popular entertainment, their definition of "improvisation" shifted: while they did not use written scripts, much of their "act" consisted of sketches repeated and refined from one performance to the next. Even so, by May's account, the principle of spontaneous exchange remained central: the aim was not adherence to a fixed model, but "recreation of the original impulse" with each performance.[5]

The birth of one such "original impulse" was described by Nichols in an account of his first encounter with May, itself a tale told repeatedly in different contexts.[6] After being introduced at the University of Chicago, the pair found themselves sitting next to each other on a railway platform, and spontaneously launched into "a whole long spy mystery improvisation for the benefit of the other people on the bench."[7] This, evidently, was the routine which developed into "Mysterioso," one of the tracks on Nichols and May's first album, *Improvisations to Music* (1958). The pair play spies who meet on a train, exchanging banalities that appear—as delivered in heavy cod-European accents—to contain some hidden, sinister significance:

> NICHOLS: I hev chenged my seat, because it vas . . . too varm.
> MAY: I always travel vith the vindows . . . open.
> NICHOLS: Eet is dangerous to travel vith the vindows open . . . there is alvays flying smut.
> MAY: Eet is not dangerous eef you keep your elbows . . . inside.[8]

As so often in Nichols and May sketches, the characters are speaking in code—here, a code which we as audience members can identify as such but lack the means to decipher. In the context of the Cold War, eavesdroppers on the original exchange described by Nichols might just possibly have believed they had stumbled onto evidence of an actual conspiracy. In the recorded version of the sketch, we understand that the false conspiracy hides a real one, that Nichols and May share not just a sense of humor but an uncanny ability to build on each others' comic impulses. In another sense, the relation between fiction and reality is one of contrast: while the spies' exchange boils down to a series of pre-arranged signals, Nichols and May present themselves as leaving enough leeway within their own pre-arranged scenario for a genuine encounter to occur.

For all the absurdity of the sketch, an edge of ambiguity is maintained, both within the fiction and beyond. Overtly, we are allowed to listen in on a pair of probably subversive foreigners posing as dull Americans, the humor lying in the feebleness of their pretense. It is for us to ponder exactly what these characters might be up to, and how this premise might echo Nichols' and May's own sense of themselves as outsiders: while their shared Jewish background is rarely made explicit in their joint work, it tacitly informs their position as satirists at a wry distance from the American mainstream (and from their own less-assimilated elders, as in a famous sketch with May as a guilt-tripping, implicitly Jewish mother). As John Limon notes, Nichols and May as a duo are drawn to triangular situations, as in their many sketches about adultery: the audience, in effect, is the third party, raising the question of whether the joke might be partly on us.[9]

Emerging on the national scene in the late 1950s, Nichols and May were a nearly unprecedented phenomenon: a male–female comedy team not presenting themselves as a real-life romantic couple, operating as creative equals and scoring a roughly equal number of laughs. Nichols is the less versatile of the pair, most commonly playing variations on fat-headed, muttering complacency; May's range goes from bimbo to virago, with a gallery of self-satisfied housewives and anxious upper-middle-class women in between. For each, the lack of any fixed persona conveys a measure of flip detachment towards the roles being tried on: they might almost be excessively gifted amateurs, or teenagers cynically mocking their elders (not so far from the truth: both were still in their twenties when the act broke up). Their alliance against the world seems to arise from a shared perception that no one is really adult at all, but only pretending to be—conveyed in their habit of slipping from an assumed sophistication to a spluttering or babbling that approaches baby-talk.

Paradoxically, it is Nichols and May's sustained rapport that gives them scope to explore less successful efforts to communicate: the characters they play are constantly performing for each other in turn, revealing themselves through their failures of self-presentation. James Naremore describes their style as reliant on "naturalistic clumsiness—a halting, nervous incoherence, together with little indications of tension and repression."[10] An early *New Yorker* profile characterizing the pair as "trained and convinced Method actors" was not entirely off the mark: May had studied with Maria Ouspenskaya—a pupil of Konstanin Stanislavsky, commonly viewed as the father of modern naturalistic acting—and Nichols with Lee Strasberg, who developed Stanislavsky's teachings into the famous "Method,"[11] with its emphasis on the personal "sense memories" of the performer. This, however, was Method acting turned against itself, put to a satirical purpose that forestalled direct self-revelation: slipping from one role to another, Nichols and May were able to hold the audience at arms' length, their very virtuosity blocking any certainty about who they themselves might be.

A related paradox is inherent in Spolin's notion of the "theater game," whereby the freedom of improvisation is made possible precisely through the imposition of an arbitrary set of rules. To understand a pre-existing form of communication as a "game" in this sense is to see it as available for parody—and all of Nichols and May's sketches can be described as parodies, whether the target is a specific work, an artistic genre, or a brand of conversation that might be overheard in a certain milieu. Ultimately what they seem to be parodying is acting itself—or the notion that acting can or should make visible the "depths" of human nature. A paradigmatic instance is *Bach to Bach*, again on *Improvisations to Music*, which casts them as a pair of pseudo-intellectuals eager to cement their spiritual bond:

> MAY: When I read *Thus Spake Zarathrustra* . . .
> NICHOLS: Yes?
> MAY: . . . a whole world opened for me.
> NICHOLS: I know *exactly* what you mean.
> MAY: Do you know what I mean?
> NICHOLS: *Exactly*.
> MAY: Oh, did that happen to you too?
> NICHOLS: I know *exactly* what you mean.[12]

This is realistically observed, yet close to the defamiliarized clichés which were common currency at the same period in the Theater of the Absurd.[13] Whether each speaker knows "exactly" what the other means is beside the point—which, as in "Mysterioso," lies in the conventionalized signals that identify them to each other as members of an in-group. Name-dropping a laundry list of highbrow cult figures, the speakers notably fail to mention Jean-Paul Sartre, viewed in America from the late 1940s onward as the "quintessential French intellectual."[14] Yet it is Sartre's existentialism above all that provides the philosophical context for Nichols and May's sketches, through his contrast between the bad faith of convention and the quixotic project of authenticity—which, crucially, entails not the straightforward recovery of a pre-existing "true" self, but the assumption of full responsibility for one's actions in the moment. For Sartre, a sharp distinction exists between the two meanings of "act", existential "doing" and inauthentic mimicry (illustrated in his famous account of the café waiter who consciously "plays" his socially assigned role).[15] Nichols and May's work, however, suggests a different perspective: improvised performance can be seen as an authentic activity in its own right, allowing an escape from any identity determined in advance.

Several commentators have identified more specific links between Nichols and May and other intellectuals of the era concerned one way or another with the role played by convention in "ordinary" language and behavior. Some of this activity was happening not far away: sociologist David Riesman, for instance, taught at the University of Chicago at the same period the Compass Players were getting off the ground, and was even said to attend the group's performances from time to time.[16] Riesman's 1951 bestseller *The Lonely Crowd* popularized the notion of the "other-directed personality," ruled not by tradition or by a set of inner values but by the desire for acceptance from peers.[17] While Riesman was no existentialist rebel,[18] his concept of "other-directedness" can plausibly be seen as an extension of Sartre's "bad faith":[19] either label can be applied to many of Nichols and May's sketch characters, including the intellectuals of *Bach to Bach*, whose attempts at "sincerity" remain fatally bound to socially prescribed scripts.

In a different vein, the notion of scripted or ritualized behavior likewise figures in the work of the philosopher J. L. Austin, cited by Kyle Stevens as another thinker whose ideas resonate with the sketches of Nichols and May.[20] Posthumously published in 1959, Austin's *How To Do Things With Words* explored a class of utterances he dubbed "performatives," which do not merely describe an existing reality but alter it through the fact of having been spoken. For the British Austin, these performatives typically relied for their effect on the sanction of tradition, as with the vow "I do" in a marriage ceremony;[21] in a broader sense, the concept of the performative is central to the entire literary mode of drama, in which characters make constant use of language to promise, threaten, reveal, deceive and so forth. Just as common, especially in comedy, are situations where such utterances go awry, one set of conventions about their usage colliding with another. Here again was the idea of dialogue as a game open enough in its rules to allow a degree of potential freedom to the players; tasked with generating dramatic or comic situations at a moment's notice, Nichols and May found themselves formulating their own theories about the dynamic purposes served by language or other techniques of communication. Nichols discovered that "there only were three kinds of scenes in the world—fights, seductions, and negotiations." May boiled this down to a still simpler rule of thumb: "When in doubt, seduce."[22]

Closest of all to Nichols and May (and to Sartre) was another sociologist associated with the University of Chicago: Canadian Erving Goffman, whose work, like Riesman's, was widely read outside academia.[23] Goffman's 1956 book *The Presentation of Self in Everyday Life* is filled with vignettes that could be starting-points for Nichols and May sketches, illustrating the ways in which individuals within society are necessarily performers, albeit the kind regularly forced to improvise to keep up appearances. Goffman dubbed his method "dramaturgical analysis," employing theatrical imagery throughout his book: each sphere of society has its public and backstage realms, its audiences and its stars.[24] Conversely, this implies that to "act" in the narrower, theatrical sense is also to play a role within society, if one more flexible than most: an actor on a stage is licensed to behave unexpectedly, though not to the point of defying the common understanding of what acting consists of.

In Sartre's terms, this implies that the actor, like any other individual, bears full responsibility for his or her choices—whether to stick to a pre-existing script or to venture into the unknown. Much of the allure of improvisation as a theatrical technique lies in this courting of existential danger, an element of Nichols and May's work necessarily lost in the recorded versions of their sketches available to us today. Spolin's favored metaphor for improvisation described performers as "tossing the ball to each other":[25] watching Nichols and May on stage on any given evening, audiences waited to see if either might miss a catch or throw wide. Thus the comedy of any given fictional scenario was underwritten by the drama of a real-life relationship put to the test: was the understanding between the pair as complete as it seemed, or might it collapse under pressure? On this level at least, Nichols and May did present themselves as "characters", if unknowable ones, forcing the audience to ponder how their "act" might continue backstage.

In retrospect, Nichols' and May's reluctance to disclose themselves within their work can be seen as both bold and cautious: if their fluid shifts of role allowed an escape from the fixity of Jewish (and, in Nichols' case, immigrant) identity, this is not the only sense in which their own use of language as action rather than statement allowed awkward realities to be broached yet plausibly denied. The sexual tension that powers the majority of their sketches is conveyed through archly indirect means, partly to evade censorship but also as a matter of comic principle: the less is stated, the more scope exists for the audience to fill in the blanks. Their audio work makes a virtue of the absence of imagery, enabling mental pictures to be conjured up through stray lines of dialogue—as when Nichols, midway through *Bach to Bach*, murmurs "Can you move over a little, I'm falling off the bed." In their televised sketches, the possibility of such daring implication is diminished—and yet the physical side of the performance is ostentatiously minimal, Nichols and May typically standing side by side as they deliver their lines to the camera.

"Nichols and May could afford to play with words," Kay Young suggests, "because their bodies were not at stake."[26] This is apt, but not the whole story. The physical, held at a distance, keeps returning, not least in the qualities of the performers' voices—Nichols' nasality, May's breathiness—which bear traces of a bodily origin. Even the restraint of their TV appearances is not absolute. The awkwardly flirtatious dialogue of *Teenagers in a Car*, broadcast in 1958, is punctuated by moments when Nichols' character switches from staring straight ahead to hurling himself at his date in clumsy lust, rather in the manner of Jean-Pierre Léaud a few years later with his leading ladies of the French New Wave.

Near the end of Nichols' and May's joint career the physical would return with still greater force, suggesting what high stakes they had been playing for all along. This occurred during a performance of one of the team's most significant sketches, never recorded for posterity: *Pirandello*, the first-act finale of their Broadway show, in which the subject was explicitly the riskiness of improvisation itself. After announcing they would be "doing Pirandello"—that is, Luigi Pirandello, author of the meta-fictional *Six Characters in Search of an Author*—the pair would launch into an improvisation that appeared to get out of hand. Starting out as a couple of children imitating their parents, they would transform without warning into the parents themselves, and then into the actual Nichols and May, screaming and tussling, their "real" relationship laid bare at last. Only after causing thorough alarm would they call a halt, explaining they had been "doing Pirandello" all along.[27] Once again, the audience was the butt of the joke, the punchline chiding them for imagining that Nichols and May had the situation under anything less than full control. Until, one night, they didn't. "I had you by the front of your shirt," Nichols recalled to May in 2012. "I had been slapping you back and forth for quite a while, and my chest was pouring blood."[28]

SCREEN TESTS: IMPROVISING BEHIND THE CAMERA

> "Telling the truth can be dangerous business . . ."
> —"Dangerous Business," sung by Lyle Rogers (Warren Beatty) and Chuck Clarke (Dustin Hoffman) in *Ishtar* (1987)

Pinning down the "real" Elaine May remains a challenge, partly due to her recurrent tendency to treat being interviewed (when she has agreed to this at all) as one more improvisational game. Journalists speaking to her in the 1960s tended to emerge dazzled and bewildered, painting her as a brilliant yet ditzy screwball comedy heroine prone to confessions of despair that might be theatrical or candid or both. "In life, you don't decide what you'll do," she told one interviewer. "It just happens. It's all Kafkaesque."[29] Lurking in much writing about her from this period is the sense that she might simply be too gifted, attractive and versatile for her own good. This suspicion arose not only from her failure to fit any accepted showbusiness mold, but from her already evident dedication to process over product: a 1969 *LIFE* magazine profile described her as "constantly revising her works . . . attacking them with a fierce black pencil until no one but she could possibly decipher them."[30]

With her move into film direction, May acquired a new image, which has clung to her ever since: that of a total incompetent. Critics of her films have seldom failed to dwell on her tendency to blow out budgets and run over schedule, and to agonize over details while digging in her heels over perverse artistic choices. Much the same could be said of some of the most revered figures of cinema history, such as Erich von Stroheim or Stanley Kubrick,[31] but where these men have long been acknowledged as rule-breaking geniuses, the consensus on May has tended to be that she simply did not know what she was doing.[32]

Superficially, May's own statements have not done much to put the accusation to rest. By her account, she did not set out to become a filmmaker at all: offered the chance to direct her script for *A New Leaf* (1971) for Paramount, she began, supposedly, by mistaking the camera for one of the lights. Yet even her comments on this apprentice period go against the frequent view of her as uninterested in cinema as a specific artform—suggesting, rather, that she sought to seize control of the image despite an acknowledged lack of expertise:

> I knew how I wanted it to look. And I would say things like I want them to be full-figure but not tiny. Because everyone said you don't have to know about lenses, you know, little girl. And finally someone took me aside and told me that there are long lenses and wide lenses.[33]

Once again, May was thinking on her feet, accepting the rules of the game while inventing her own strategies as a player. Neither *A New Leaf* nor its successors were improvised in any conventional sense, any more than were most of the films directed by John Cassavetes, her friend and sometime collaborator (as discussed at length in Jeremy Carr's chapter in this book).[34] Yet for May, to enter the world of filmmaking was to embark on another kind of existential adventure—this time without the support of Nichols, her most trusted creative ally.

For a writer-performer who had made her name in hip social satire, *A New Leaf* marked a total departure, running aggressively counter to the fashions of 1971. Portrayed satirically but not without sympathy, the anti-hero Henry Graham (Walter Matthau) is a caricature of reactionary misanthropy, living only for the possessions such as his red Ferrari which are symbols of his privilege. The film itself likewise looks backward, to the "classical" tradition of Hollywood comedy: its formalized dialogue immediately announces itself as "written," in contrast to the naturalism of Nichols and May's routines. Yet it remains unmistakably personal, centrally though not solely through May's own scene-stealing performance as Henrietta Lowell, the meek botanist and heiress whom the bankrupted Henry decides to marry and then murder.

While May did not originally intend to play Henrietta herself,[35] it is tempting nonetheless to view the character as an ironic self-portrait, a variant on the eccentric persona her creator had conjured up for journalists. Henrietta's leading traits are her intelligence and her clumsiness, both social and physical: she first appears at a fancy gathering where she spills one cup of tea after another, angering her hostess and giving Henry the chance to sweep in and take her side. Where Henry cherishes order, Henrietta is a force for chaos through her alarming vulgarity and her disabling sensitivity alike—scattering crumbs as she eats, and countering Henry's verbal precision with free-associative monologues delivered in an ingratiating murmur.

If the physical is held at bay in May's routines with Nichols, it returns with a vengeance through Henrietta—and while we have to wait for her first appearance, we might feel in retrospect that someone not unlike her has been behind the camera all along. In contrast to the virtuosity of Nichols and May's recorded sketches, *A New Leaf* makes a defiant feature of its lack of technique: barely motivated zooms, awkward passages of post-dubbed dialogue, jarring scene transitions such as the shot that introduces Henry's uncle (James Coco) as a monstrous apparition guffawing in extreme close-up. While the raw primitivism of this anti-style is not typical of May's subsequent work, it establishes a pattern: her films are some of the most uncomfortably material in American cinema, forcing us to register the effort required to keep images in focus, cut shots smoothly together, and shift actors from A to B.

Another word for this might be modernism, in a sense that can also be applied to Nichols and May's sketches: what these share with May's films is the enrichment of the fiction by the visibility of a secondary drama concerning the risks courted in its creation. The reality of this drama is confirmed by accounts from behind the scenes of *A New Leaf*, which give an almost uncanny impression of life imitating art and vice versa. Viewing May with suspicion as a "tough little lady,"[36] Matthau nicknamed her "Mrs Hitler,"[37] alluding to a dreamlike gag in which Henry is introduced to a society woman of the same name (implying that WASP snobbery and Nazism are somehow one—among the many moments in May's cinema when the glimpse of a specifically Jewish perspective resembles a return of the repressed). Henrietta's dealings with a pack of parasitic and domineering servants were paralleled in May's battle to maintain authority over her crew: lacking a Henry of her own to lay down the law, she took the opposite tack, banking on the sympathy elicited by her "feminine" vulnerability in front of the camera. This was the behavior not of a naïf but of a resourceful manipulator, evident too in her decision to sew herself into her nightgown to enhance the physical comedy of Henry and Henrietta's wedding night: Matthau had no idea what he was up against, at least on the first take.[38]

More traumatic for all concerned was the battle that ensued over *A New Leaf*'s final cut: after May spent ten months in the editing room, the film was taken out of her hands and released in a bowdlerized version which she attempted to have legally suppressed.[39] May's cut, supposedly running three hours, included two murder sequences excised by Paramount; this has led some critics (Chuck Stephens, for instance) to assume that in this version Henry went through with his plan of drowning Henrietta while accompanying her on a field trip to upstate New York.[40] But there is room for doubt, especially as in the finished film it is unmistakably May herself, not a stand-in, we see struggling in the water and being dragged to the bank. Would she really have brought this level of physical commitment to an ending in which she did not believe?

Besides, the ending we have is the one which the whole film moves towards, daring us to imagine that Henry and Henrietta really are the soulmates their twinned names suggest: it is not coincidental that May had thought of filming Plato's *Symposium*, with its famous speech in which each soul is imagined as searching for its mystical counterpart.[41] Each has what the other lacks, Henry's assurance complementing Henrietta's sense of vocation: it is through Henry that Henrietta transcends oppressive social expectations, freeing her to accomplish her dream of discovering a previously unknown fern. What she gives him in turn is a vocation of his own: his existence, we gather, will now be devoted to caring for her, as he previously did for his red Ferrari.

Not all critics have seen this ending as reassuring, even given the fleeting implication that Henrietta may have had the upper hand all along. Stephens, viewing Henry as somehow unmanned, bizarrely but tellingly connects his downfall to the homosexual rape in John Boorman's *Deliverance* (1972).[42] Certainly, the film's vision of how a successful relationship could arise is a provocative one. Henry, in Riesman's terms, is a tradition-directed type—defining himself through obedience to an inherited model of good form, not to an inner set of values nor to the conventions of the society he actually inhabits. While this renders him largely powerless in a modern context, the gap between tradition and convention provides him with a surprising margin of existential freedom: for all his personal disdain for Henrietta, he commits without reserve to the role of her lover and protector, building on her premises according to the rule of "yes, and". When she confesses her desire to discover a new fern, he enters into the dream of immortality; when she spills tea, he doubles down by pouring a full cup onto the carpet. Ultimately, he is unable to deny the now-established premise of their double act: having made the traditional gesture of commitment that is marriage, he finds himself committed in truth, despite his best (or worst) intentions.

In its ultimate affirmation of a heterosexual couple, *A New Leaf* itself remains obedient, however perversely, to Hollywood tradition. This is less true of May's subsequent films, which nonetheless remain concerned with the possibility of communication between soulmates—or, in existentialist terms, with the proposition that the project of authenticity is necessarily a joint one.

This "tossing the ball back and forth" can take many forms, not all of them obvious: *A New Leaf* gradually makes clear that Henrietta's unworldliness is not passive but passive-aggressive, in a positive sense that forces Henry to develop new strengths. This further demonstrates the existential principle that to "act" is not to reveal a pre-existing essence, but to bring new, previously unthinkable possibilities into being: it is through playing the role of a loving husband that Henry becomes one, in defiance of anything we have learned about him earlier.

Many of May's comments on her work imply an understanding of filmmaking itself as a social situation where role-play is necessary—and where a "passive" role can generate desired results as well as an active one, as with her strategic use of her own "femininity" on *A New Leaf*. Thus it is not the paradox it seems that her highly individualistic approach to filmmaking should also rely on collaboration, not only with her actors (often friends) but with others such as production designers or composers who (as she put it) "tell the same story in their own specific voice."[43] Less clear is the question of how far the tensions between May and her studio overseers have themselves been artistically productive: at the least, it can be said that this is the terrain on which her films take shape, and that her frustrations with the Hollywood system parallel those of her characters with the material and social restrictions they encounter.

By comparison with *A New Leaf*, the making of May's follow-up *The Heartbreak Kid* (1972) went relatively smoothly—perhaps precisely because it was the only one of her four features she did not write, and because restrictions were put in place from the outset. The screenwriter Neil Simon went out of his way to curtail May's improvisatory instincts, having it written into his contract that not a word of the script would be changed without his approval. Nonetheless, May found ways to put her stamp on the material, defying Simon's wishes by casting her twenty-three-year-old daughter Jeannie Berlin as one of the two female leads. This could be seen as May again inserting herself into her film, this time by proxy—especially as Berlin's character Lila, the hapless young wife of the go-getting anti-hero Lenny Cantrow (Charles Grodin), resembles Henrietta in being as grotesque as she is sympathetic.

Despite the restraints imposed by Simon, *The Heartbreak Kid* proved as personal to its director as *A New Leaf*, which it both inverts and mirrors in its exploration of how heterosexual relationships are "performed". Both films hinge on weddings as if to illustrate J. L. Austin's famous 1955 conception of marriage vows as performative utterances, while asking what is really established by such acts of commitment. Both, too, show husbands repulsed by the inadequacy and uncouthness of their new brides. But where Henry marries with his eyes open, Lenny races through the rituals of courtship with no pause for thought—and where Henry handles the situation in his own way, Lenny emerges as a pure "other-directed" personality, performing for the imagined audience that is society even when no literal third party is in sight.

Our understanding of this crystallizes in the early scene of Lenny and Lila driving to Miami on their honeymoon: they sing together, first in unison on "Close to You"—Lila nuzzling up to Lenny as he drives—and then in counterpoint. Then Lila sings a climactic note roughly and holds it too long, in a moment of comic, self-deprecating display: enraptured by her own performance, she fails to see Lenny's proud grin giving way to a frozen grimace. "You're a lousy singer," he finally mutters. She laughs it off—but the rhythm of give-and-take between them is broken, and will never be fully restored (this applies, needless to say, to the characters, not the actors, whose inspired performance of disconnection implies connection on another level).

By the time the pair reach their hotel, Lenny is ready to start afresh: while Lila is recovering from horrific sunburn—a chance for May to maximize the character's physical grotesquerie—he ventures out onto the beach where he encounters another young woman, Kelly Corcoran (Cybill Shepherd), on holiday with her family. Immediately, he is smitten by her blonde WASP "perfection," an exotic contrast to his and Lila's Jewish background; after breaking up with Lila in an acutely painful scene in a restaurant, he pursues his new love to wintry Minnesota, where he woos and, inexplicably, wins her.

As with *A New Leaf*, this ending has been varyingly received, critics' judgement of Lenny resting not only on their degree of sympathy for Lila but on their sense of how far Kelly—whose idly flirtatious manner borders on indifference—is a prize worth pursuing. At one extreme, Richard Brody credits Kelly with "a breathless and ruthless romantic intelligence," comparing her, astonishingly, with Katharine Hepburn's madcap Susan Vance in *Bringing Up Baby* (1938).[44] At the other, Julian Myers dismisses her as "just an image, for us and for Lenny—maybe even for herself."[45] To my mind, May's verdict on both Lenny and Kelly is clear in the larger context of her body of work, with its relentless mockery of the "other-directed" for whom identity depends on conventional markers of status: if Lenny departs from his script, as Brody maintains,[46] he surely does so only in order to follow another.

As Jonathan Rosenbaum has noted, May's treatment of Simon's screenplay sets the story in an unspoken but immediately visible social context, allowing us to see Lenny's behavior as expressive of specifically Jewish self-hatred.[47] Simon, speaking to a *Playgirl* interviewer, actively resisted this: "It wasn't the city or the society that was sick. Just the guy."[48] The evidence of off-screen tension once again suggests a fusion of life and art, Simon's distaste at the physical excess of Berlin's performance paralleling the film's depiction of the failure of the sexes to arrive at common ground.[49] The near-impossibility of bridging the gender gap is, in fact, an axiom of May's cinema: while her subsequent films replace heterosexual couples with male platonic duos, this only sharpens the theme, implying a despairing need to look beyond straight "romance" for examples of potential human connection. As Brad Stevens has pointed out, May's first "buddy movie" *Mikey and Nicky* (1976) contains her most unsparing critique of gender roles,[50] though this is mounted from a position less specifically feminist than, again, existential: any fixed role is a prison, in that it limits the potential for the improvisation which constitutes a relationship from moment to moment.

Mikey (Peter Falk) and Nicky (John Cassavetes) are hoodlums, friends since childhood, affiliated with the Philadelphia mob. Late one night, Mikey comes knocking on the door of the apartment where Nicky is holed up. Believing there is a contract out on his life, Nicky is in panic, chain-smoking and waving a gun; Mikey has to talk his way in, first by coaxing, then by threats. This marks the beginning of an encounter between the two men which spans the film, resembling one long theatrical improvisation—as well as a wrestling match, a business meeting, a slapstick routine, a seduction and a dance. As in Nichols and May's *Pirandello* sketch, the characters find themselves slipping helplessly between roles: sometimes they suggest sulky little boys, sometimes parent and child, sometimes estranged lovers.

These transformations are possible because society has, however temporarily, been kept at bay. *Mikey and Nicky* is a night film, moving towards the breaking of dawn, when roles will be frozen. Our knowledge that this reckoning awaits is secured by the revelation, early in the film, that Mikey has sold Nicky out to his bosses, and that a hitman (Ned Beatty) is poised to make his move. In the meantime, the central duo are in constant flight, cast adrift like Beckett characters, moving between the dark noisy streets and various temporary havens. At some points they manage to strengthen their bond by ganging up on a third party, as in a squabble on a bus, or a visit to the apartment of Nicky's disturbed lover (Carol Grace): thrown back on each other once more, they return to their routine of bickering softened with affection.

While the fictional universe of *Mikey and Nicky* is chaotic to the point of nightmare, the film is not formless: anything but. Here, as throughout May's cinema, each scene has a clearly delineated purpose, one character striving to gain something from another; the larger narrative is likewise a game with clear rules, establishing a set of parameters which define a relationship and proceeding to turn them inside out. Taken in themselves, May's narratives have a sketchlike, almost abstract neatness: as *The Heartbreak Kid* moves from one wedding to another, *Mikey and Nicky* is bookended by closed doors, Mikey pleading to be admitted at the outset and Nicky at the end. This diagrammatic symmetry is something May has in common with Roman Polanski, a fellow absurdist whose work shares more with hers than has been generally recognized, including the perception that most relationships boil down to struggles for the upper hand.

But these are the rules of the game, not the game itself. Within a given framework, May and her actors are entitled to use any means available to maintain the film's energy: the more resourceful they are, the less conventional dramatic material is required, leaving the impression that the original premise is willfully being tested and stretched thin. Physically, Mikey and Nicky are constantly shifting in relation to each other, approaching and retreating, getting into scuffles and switching places (a vaudeville bit where they exchange coats recalls both the nightgown scene in *A New Leaf* and the hat-switching routine in *Waiting for Godot*[51]). Likewise, their dialogue is full of repetitions, clichés, pet phrases, rhetorical questions and incomplete statements: enactments of friendship or hostility detached from literal meaning or even psychological subtext. The imperative of "tossing the ball back and forth" is ever-present, for characters and actors alike: whatever larger goal remains to be achieved, the immediate need is for a momentum that will keep the relationship alive in the present tense.

Even more than on *A New Leaf*, May's own desire for spontaneity on *Mikey and Nicky* resulted in what to some looked like chaos behind the scenes as well as on screen. The shoot was delayed by her insistence on filming in strict continuity, overruling the "practical" objections of her crew; further delays in editing led to another legal battle before the film was finally released.[52] Still, the results of her procedures speak for themselves: what might have been taken for artlessness in *A New Leaf* is here fully recognizable as a style in its own right. If May's work with Nichols exploited the potential of verbal disjunctions and lapses in clarity, *Mikey and Nicky* does the same with the language of cinema: unexpected cuts, seemingly erratic camera moves, disruptive direct sound, objects and parts of bodies obtruding themselves or sliding in and out of focus.

As expressive rhetoric, this style functions on multiple levels—corresponding with the agitation of the two main characters and the instability of their relationship, and heightening our awareness of the unpredictable urban environment, with its population of night owls and tired shift workers who drift into the orbit of the leads. At the same time, it renews the modernism of *A New Leaf*, asking us to view filmmaking as a series of necessarily improvised choices, solutions to problems that must be confronted anew each time. This is not in contradiction to May's reported tendency to shoot countless takes of the same scenes, and then to linger in the editing room: this too is a sign of her commitment to process over product, delaying the moment when the elements of the film will be frozen in place. As May herself put it, improvisation is not merely a matter of making things new every time, but of circling back to the "original impulse": as long as this can be recaptured, a given piece of material can be reworked indefinitely, much as Mikey and Nicky continue to renegotiate the terms of their friendship.

With *Ishtar* (1987), May's fourth and final credited feature, the circle in some respects appears complete. Unlike any of her previous duos, the songwriters Lyle Rogers (Warren Beatty) and Chuck Clarke (Dustin Hoffman) are would-be professional performers—already up and running as a team when we first encounter them in the film's opening sequence, improvising possible lyrics to what will become one of their signature numbers. Ultimately, they settle on the opening line "Telling the truth can be dangerous business"—a truth in its own right, as the rest of the film will bear out. What the scene demonstrates is that Rogers and Clarke themselves have the courage to court this danger, opening up to one another in the process of creation: this is again a matter of listening to and building on each others' contributions, and equally of incessant revision, returning each time to the same "original impulse." True, from any outside perspective their songs are terrible—and yet this does not lessen the value they themselves find in their collaboration, which requires no validation from a third party. Significantly, for the first part of this opening sequence they are heard but not seen: bodiless voices echoing and chiming in with each other, like Nichols and May in their recorded work.

It is significant, too, that the film begins at this near-utopian moment, before flashing back to show Rogers and Clarke discovering each other as soulmates (superseding previous relationships with women). This bonding is not accomplished without trauma: a despairing Clarke threatens to commit suicide by leaping from his apartment, and Rogers must venture out on the ledge to talk him down, an image of the risks both have taken in joining forces. When Clarke protests that "I'm not the kind of guy that you thought I was," Rogers responds with a statement of principles: "Hey, it takes a lot of nerve to have nothing at your age . . . Most guys'd be ashamed. But you've got the guts to just say 'to hell with it.' You say that you'd rather have nothing than settle for less, understand?"

The "nothing" Rogers is referring to could be his and Clarke's songwriting process, a squandering of energy yielding little of market value; it could equally be represented by *Ishtar* itself, a throwaway sketch of a movie, a self-indulgent waste of money and, as it turned out, a fabulous failure.[53] Both May's "lightest" work and her most notorious, *Ishtar* is paradoxical in other ways as well. Outwardly it is the most hermetic of her films, full of showbiz jokes so far inside they seem almost private: yet these jokes in themselves hint at larger realities, as with the against-type casting of Hoffman as a ladies' man and Beatty as a "schmuck" (another version of this Jewish–Gentile pairing—both within the fiction and outside it—appears in *Mikey and Nicky*). Moreover, the larger context which these characters are set against bears a political significance far more explicit than anything in May's previous features. After accepting an offer to perform at a Moroccan hotel, Rogers and Clarke are separately approached by an alluring revolutionary (Isabelle Adjani) from the fictional neighboring nation of Ishtar: each is drawn into her plot, forcing them to deceive each other and threatening the integrity of their friendship.

While the theme of international conspiracy had been with May since the start of her career, the direct model for *Ishtar* was the globetrotting *Road* series of comedies made in the 1940s by Bob Hope and Bing Crosby. The joke of these films lay precisely in their winking acknowledgement of themselves as Hollywood product, guaranteeing that the dynamic between the bumbling Hope and the smooth Crosby would never be altered by their experiences in exotic lands (recreated, of course, on the Paramount backlot). In the wake of the Iran–Contra scandal, May brilliantly saw this format as a metaphor for U.S. *realpolitik*, with its refusal to acknowledge non-Americans as more than counters in a global power game. The innocent Rogers and Clarke represent Yankee self-involvement at its most sympathetic, stumbling through the mirage of international politics—and, eventually, through a literal desert—as if this were merely another setting for their "act." But that they come to side with the Islamic rebels against American officialdom bears witness to the scope of May's sympathy for the "foreign," as well as her willingness to buck the conventions of mainstream American entertainment and politics alike: it was not entirely irrational for her to wonder if the onslaught of negative publicity accompanying *Ishtar*—starting well before the film's release—might have been orchestrated by the actual CIA.[54]

May's concerns, in other words, were global, meaning that her satire of imperialist fantasy had to be counterpointed by something approaching actuality: a version of North Africa recreated in a studio would not do. So she and her cast and crew were, as Bob and Bing once punned, Morocco-bound: filmmaking once more as existential adventure, on the largest scale yet. In what was now a pattern for May, accounts from the set of *Ishtar* immediately became part of its legend, renewing the accepted image of her as an over-thinker out of her depth—as Henrietta winds up literally out of her depth when she heads into the wild on her field trip.

Much of this behind-the-scenes lore closely echoes accounts of May's process on earlier films: friction with the studio, extended takes of the actors trying to remember their lines, and a long, fraught editing period, here complicated by the fact that Beatty was also the film's producer. Meanwhile, life yet again threatened to imitate art, with the Moroccan government embroiled in a struggle with Sahrawi guerrillas, and tensions between Israel and the PLO erupting not far off.[55] Some portions of May's screenplay might have been designed to add to the chaos, such as a lengthy gag sequence involving a blind camel, "played" in the finished film by a plainly undirectable beast who serves as not just a symbol but a direct embodiment of the intransigence of the real (like the prop Aztec throne hauled about in Polanski's *Pirates* [1986], another ill-fated absurdist "blockbuster"). "That big, dumb, stupid-ass camel!" says

Clarke. "He'd rather just sit there than move when you ask him! He'd rather get shot!" "Actually I kind of admire that," Rogers admits. Clarke barely hesitates: "Me too."

"Directors control in different ways, and she controlled by creating mass confusion," a crew member on *Ishtar* said of May.[56] In assessing the often-contradictory accounts of her behavior on set, it is difficult to escape the conclusion that her approach had a passive-aggressive intransigence of its own, responding to the double bind faced by a woman stepping into a traditionally male position of power while still being judged by conventional standards of "femininity". Even on *A New Leaf*, she had learned that the trick of using her perceived vulnerability to her advantage was one that could only work up to a point. As she told Nichols, "the thing is, of course, I wasn't a nice girl. And when they found this out, they hated me all the more."[57] Doomed to be seen as either inappropriately domineering or helplessly indecisive, it is as if she resolved to play up to these perceptions in the spirit of "yes, and," embodying the male chauvinist nightmare of what a woman director might be.

Yet it would do May a further injustice to see her gender as the defining fact of her career—which has been consistent only in its inconsistency, its resistance to definitions of any kind. Creativity is necessarily spontaneous, the exact opposite of knowing how to behave in advance: whatever impression we gain of May from her work, it is not that of a "master filmmaker." If her films succeed, it is through their absence of mastery, calling on us to bear witness to their battle to sustain themselves, and to ponder whether success and failure, whatever these might mean, are the only measures of worth. Even her rebelliousness implies a knowledge of its own limits, aiming not at a triumph that would ensure a seamless final product, but an escalation of conflict to the point where the seams necessarily show. Each of her films is thus the record of an encounter: with a specific team of collaborators, with her own artistic shortcomings, with filmmaking as an industry, with the impossibility of life.

May's films are existential acts, gambles in which she placed herself and her reputation on the line (most recklessly with *Ishtar*, a bomb which effectively ended her filmmaking career). But they are also fictions that dramatize the idea of going to the limit, the risks run by May herself paralleled by the suffering she inflicts on her characters: Henrietta floundering in the rapids, Lila burnt to a crisp, Nicky sick with despair, Rogers and Clarke collapsed in the desert with vultures hovering above. What is gained, or proved, by such ordeals? Certainly, they serve to test the bond between potential soulmates, demonstrating just how far one will go out on a ledge for the other. Yet even at best this guarantees nothing about the future, since a relationship is not a goal but a process: it will have to be invented all over again tomorrow, the adventure of doing so being its own reward. What remains, for the moment, is the prospect of further improvisation, movement without a higher object, energy circulating. To toss the ball away is to hope to have it returned. Perhaps May, too, would rather have nothing than settle for less.

NOTES

1. Sam Kashner, "Who's Afraid of Nichols & May?" *Vanity Fair*, January 2013 <https://www.vanityfair.com/hollywood/2013/01/nichols-and-may-reunion-exclusive> (accessed January 2019). At the time of writing, many of Nichols and May's televised sketches can be viewed online on YouTube and other platforms.
2. Viola Spolin, *Improvisation for the Theatre* (Evanston, IL: Northwestern University Press, 1963), pp. xlvii–xlix.
3. Kyle Stevens, "Tossing Truths: Improvisation and the Performative Utterances of Nichols and May," *Critical Quarterly* 52.3 (2010): 27–8.
4. Sam Wasson, *Improv Nation: How We Made a Great American Art* (New York: Houghton Mifflin Harcourt, 2017), p. 51.
5. Kyle Stevens, p. 30.
6. Stephen Galloway, "'Trouble Always Seemed Glamorous'," *The Hollywood Reporter*, 18 May 2012: 92; John Lahr, "Making It Real," *The New Yorker*, 21 February 2000 <https://www.newyorker.com/magazine/2000/02/21/making-it-real-2> (accessed January 2019); Gavin Smith, "Of Metaphors and Purpose," *Film Comment* 35.3 (May–June 1999): 12.
7. Smith, p. 12.
8. Elaine May and Mike Nichols, "Mysterioso," *Improvisations to Music*, with pianist Marty Rubenstein, produced by Jack Tracy, Mercury Records, 1958.
9. John Limon, *Stand-Up Comedy in Theory, or Abjection in America* (Durham NC and London: Duke University Press, 2000), p. 71.
10. James Naremore, *Acting in the Cinema* (Berkeley: University of California Press, 1998), p. 282.
11. Robert Rice, "A Tilted Insight," *The New Yorker*, 15 April 1961 <https://www.newyorker.com/magazine/1961/04/15/a-tilted-insight> (accessed January 2019). David Krasner, "I Hate Strasberg," in David Krasner (ed.), *Method Acting Reconsidered* (New York: St Martins, 2000), pp. 3–39.
12. Nichols and May, "Bach to Bach," *Improvisations to Music* (sound recording), with pianist Marty Rubenstein, produced by Jack Tracy, Mercury Records, 1958.
13. Compare Eugene Ionesco, *The Bald Prima Donna* [1950], in *Plays vol. 1*, trans. Donald Watson (London: Calder, 1958), pp. 85–120.
14. George Cotkin, *Existential America* (Baltimore: The Johns Hopkins University Press, 2003), p. 96. Testifying to his American celebrity at this period, Sartre was spoofed in the Hollywood musical *Funny Face* (1957)—directed by Stanley Donen, who would much later become May's companion. See John Heilpern, "Out to Lunch with Stanley Donen," *Vanity Fair*, March 2013 <https://www.vanityfair.com/hollywood/2013/03/stanley-donan-singin-in-the-rain> (accessed January 2019).
15. Jean-Paul Sartre, *Being and Nothingness*, trans. Hazel Barnes (New York: Philosophical Library, 1943/1956), pp. 55–70, 553–6. For an especially striking parallel, compare, pp. 55–6 with the Nichols and May skit *Teenagers in a Car* (1958).
16. Stephen E. Kercher, *Revel with a Cause: Liberal Satire in Postwar America* (Chicago: University of Chicago Press, 2006), pp. 126, 473.

17. David Riesman, Nathan Glazer and Reuel Denney, *The Lonely Crowd* (New Haven: Yale University Press, 1951/1961), pp. 1–30.
18. Cotkin, pp. 99–100.
19. John A. Hall, *Liberalism: Politics, Ideology and the Market* (Chapel Hill, NC: University of North Carolina Press, 1988), pp. 85–6.
20. Kyle Stevens, p. 25.
21. J. L. Austin, *How to Do Things with Words* (Oxford: Clarendon Press, 1955/1962), pp. 1–24.
22. Kashner.
23. Louis Menand, "Some Frames for Goffman," *Social Psychology Quarterly* 72:4 (December 2009): 296–9.
24. Erving Goffman, *The Presentation of Self in Everyday Life* (Edinburgh: University of Edinburgh, 1956), pp. 47–86.
25. Kyle Stevens, p. 27.
26. Kay Young, *Ordinary Pleasures: Couples, Conversation and Comedy* (Columbus: Ohio State University Press, 2001), p. 151.
27. Lahr.
28. Kashner.
29. Joyce Haber, "Very Early for May," *New York*, 22 July 1968: 51.
30. Thomas Thompson, "Whatever Happened to Elaine May?," *LIFE* magazine, 28 July 1967: 55.
31. Jonathan Rosenbaum, "Elaine and Erich: Two Peas in a Pod?," *Los Angeles Times Calendar*, 14 June 1987 <https://www.jonathanrosenbaum.net/1987/06/elaine-and-erich-two-peas-in-a-pod-tk> (accessed January 2019); Jeremy Bernstein, "How About A Little Game?" *The New Yorker*, 12 November 1966 <https://www.newyorker.com/magazine/1966/11/12/how-about-a-little-game> (accessed January 2019).
32. Examples are legion, but see David Blum, "The Road to *Ishtar*," *New York Magazine*, 16 March 1987: 35–43; Andrew Tobias, "For Elaine May, a New Film, But Not A New Leaf," *New York Magazine*, 6 December 1976: 59–69; James C. Udel, *The Film Crew of Hollywood: Profiles of Grips, Cinematographers, Designers, a Gaffer, a Stuntman and a Make-Up Artist* (Jefferson, NC: McFarland and Company, 2013), pp. 107–8.
33. "Elaine May in conversation with Mike Nichols." *Film Comment*, July/August 2006 <https://www.filmcomment.com/article/elaine-may-in-conversation-with-mike-nichols/> (accessed January 2019).
34. See Ray Carney (ed.), *Cassavetes on Cassavetes* (London: Faber and Faber, 2001), pp. 219, 267, 325, 357.
35. Stephen Saito, "Elaine May on Almost Getting Away With Murder in *A New Leaf*," *Moveablefest.com*, 1 January 2014 <http://moveablefest.com/elaine-may-new-leaf> (accessed January 2019).
36. Howard Thompson, "Elaine May Spends Her Summer Knee-Deep in Film," *New York Times*, 26 August 1969: 36.
37. "Elaine May in conversation with Mike Nichols."
38. Saito.
39. Tobias, pp. 60–1.
40. Chuck Stephens, "Chronicle of a Disappearance," *Film Comment* 42.2 (March–April 2006): 52.
41. Kashner. See Plato, *Symposium or Drinking Party*, ed. and trans. Eva Brann, Peter Kalkavage and Eric Salem (Indianapolis: Hackett, 2017), pp. 20–5.
42. Chuck Stephens, p. 52.

43. "Elaine May in conversation with Mike Nichols."
44. Richard Brody, "Screening Alert: Elaine May's Masterly *The Heartbreak Kid*," *The New Yorker*, 30 January 2015 <https://www.newyorker.com/culture/richard-brody/screening-alert-elaine-mays-masterful-heartbreak-kid> (accessed January 2019).
45. Julian Myers, "Four Dialogues 4: On Elaine May," *Open Space*, 28 August 2009 <https://openspace.sfmoma.org/2009/08/four-dialogues-4-on-elaine-may> (accessed January 2019).
46. Brody.
47. Jonathan Rosenbaum, *Placing Movies: The Practice of Film Criticism* (Berkeley: University of California Press, 1995), p. 246.
48. Sandra Shevey, "Playgirl Interview: Neil Simon," *Playgirl* 3.1 (June 1976): 138.
49. James Powers, "Dialogue on Film: Neil Simon," *American Film* 3.5 (1978): 33–48.
50. Brad Stevens, "Male Narrative/Female Narration: Elaine May's *Mikey and Nicky*," *CineAction* 31 April 1993: 79–83.
51. Samuel Beckett, *Waiting for Godot* (London: Faber and Faber, 1956), p. 72. The *Waiting for Godot* comparison also appears in Craig Keller's remarkable film essay *Elaine's* (2016), available at <https://vimeo.com/194607579> (accessed January 2019).
52. Tobias, pp. 61–9.
53. Charles Bramesco, "*Ishtar* at 30: Is It Really The Worst Movie Ever Made?," *The Guardian*, 15 May 2017.
54. "Elaine May in conversation with Mike Nichols."
55. Peter Biskind, *Star: How Warren Beatty Seduced America* (London: Simon and Schuster, 2010), pp. 346–65, 378–83.
56. Ibid., p. 350.
57. "Elaine May in conversation with Mike Nichols."

PART 3

Elaine May's Films as Director

CHAPTER 4

Kneeling on Glass—Elaine May's *A New Leaf* (1971) as Screwball Black Comedy

Samm Deighan

Elaine May's 1971 directorial debut, *A New Leaf*—which she also wrote and starred in—has been largely neglected by both critics and popular audiences. It deserves to be reassessed both as a watershed moment within May's career and as a film important to the development of contemporary American comedy cinema. This chapter will examine *A New Leaf* as a vital part of greater comedic traditions. Of these, I focus specifically on Pre-Code and 1930s screwball comedies, black comedies fixated on death and violence, and romantic films of the 1970s featuring unlikely couplings between unsympathetic protagonists. Working within these traditions, *A New Leaf* ultimately forges a connection between the themes of romance, finance, and mortality.

The film follows newly broke playboy Henry Graham's (Walter Matthau) plot to marry a wealthy woman, dispatch her, and inherit her fortune. He manages to attract a bumbling botanist (May herself), who agrees to marry him within a surprisingly short amount of time, but events don't quite go as he expected. I explore how this draws on a common theme within Depression-era Pre-Code comedies like *It Happened One Night* (Frank Capra, 1934), *My Man Godfrey* (Gregory La Cava, 1936), and the Preston Sturges-penned *Easy Living* (Mitchell Leisen, 1937), where a character on a determined, unsentimental search for fortune often crosses paths with another character trying to escape upper-class social pressures, resulting in an unconventional, unexpected romance. This is a theme that continued later in the decade with films like *Bringing Up Baby* (Howard Hawks, 1938) and throughout the work of Preston Sturges, both as a writer and as a director.

As one of the chief early directors of black comedies, Sturges' films, particularly *Unfaithfully Yours* (1948), evoke another important strain in *A New Leaf*: the connection to black comedies, particularly those concerned with murder, corpses, and crime, like Hitchcock's *The Trouble with Harry* (1955), with which *A New Leaf* has an important connection. *A New Leaf* represents an important development in this subgenre, as expressed in other similar films from the 1970s like *Harold and Maude* (Hal Ashby, 1971) and *Little Murders* (Alan Arkin, 1971). These are part of a broader web of relatively unsentimental romantic comedies of the 1960s and 1970s concerned with unlikely couplings such as Billy Wilder's *The Apartment* (1960) and May collaborator Mike Nichols' *The Graduate* (1967), and especially Audrey Hepburn-helmed comedies like *Breakfast at Tiffany's* (Blake Edwards, 1961) or *How to Steal a Million* (William Wyler, 1966). Essentially, all these films concern unlikely romances that develop as the result of a search for fortune.

The connection between *A New Leaf* and Pre-Code comedy may not initially be obvious; the Pre-Code Hollywood films are generally remembered for their transgressiveness, particularly in terms of representations of women, sexuality, and marriage. *A New Leaf* treads lightly, if at all, in its approach to sexuality, hinting at a marital sexual relationship between Henry and Henrietta, but refusing to depict this on screen. On the surface, their relationship is not particularly transgressive and does nothing overt to challenge gender stereotypes. Films like *Baby Face* (Alfred E. Green, 1933), *Blonde Venus* (Josef von Sternberg, 1932), and *Gold Diggers of 1933* (Busby Berkeley, Mervyn LeRoy, 1933) represent sex as a commodity and the films' main female protagonists as all too aware of its value and their control over it. In *Pre-Code Hollywood: Sex, Immorality, and Insurrection in American Cinema, 1930–1934*, Thomas Doherty summarizes the general theme of many of these films and the reason that they were considered so scandalous: "Outside of marriage, throngs of female libertines flirted and coupled for fun and profit."[1]

These unbridled depictions of women and sexuality brought about the Motion Picture Production Code in the early 1930s, which forbade or greatly restricted such themes. Depictions of women and sexuality on screen were again tightly leashed, with adultery and sexual passion particularly coming under fire. The Hays Code, as it was also known, above all sought to protect marriage. One of its main clauses spells this out in a literal sense: "The sanctity of the institution of marriage and the home shall be upheld . . . The treatment should not throw sympathy against marriage as an institution."[2] Despite this edict, marriage on screen was began to subtly shift in Hollywood films in the 1930s or 1940s, particularly in romantic comedies, thanks to writers and directors like Howard Hawks and Preston Sturges.

The cracks in the institution itself had been clearly revealed, showing marriage to be a legal and economic contract, essentially a business deal made between unequal partners—also a central feature of *A New Leaf*. The moral and religious reasons behind marriage were exposed by many of the Pre-Code films to be flimsy at best, a sham at worst. Doherty writes that in Pre-Code films, "marriage was a contract open to redefinition, amenable to renegotiation, and easily terminated by mutual consent."[3] Women were free to leave their marriages—even temporarily—to pursue lovers and new husbands. Divorce is portrayed in many of these films as a force for both liberation and hedonism. Much has been written about the so-called "comedies of remarriage," such as Hawks' *His Girl Friday* (1940), where a divorced couple reunite just before the woman remarries, and many of the other titles that fit into this loose designation also included plots where a couple is separated and then finally reunited just before the woman marries someone else, as in *It Happened One Night*.

These romantic comedies also often revolve around a central economic imbalance, in which one partner is wealthy and the other is poor; often the disadvantaged partner needs money for a specific reason. There are popular examples, including *It Happened One Night*, where a broke journalist falls for a headstrong heiress; *My Man Godfrey*, where a homeless man comes to work for a wealthy family after a chance encounter with two spoiled sisters; and *The Lady Eve* (Preston Sturges, 1941), about a glamorous con artist attempting to scam a millionaire.

The screwball comedies of the 1930s reflected the realities of The Depression, and many of the protagonists in these films are figuring out how to live from day to day, to feed themselves, and to stay alive in an increasingly chaotic and cruel world. This can be seen in *Easy Living*, about a young woman (Jean Arthur) who is mistaken for the mistress of a New York City industrialist (Edward Arnold) when a fur coat accidentally lands on her lap. She is punished for accepting his generosity as no one believes she acquired the fur coat by such innocent means. As a result, when she is invited to live in a luxury hotel (far beyond her own financial capabilities), she is not in a position to argue even though she does not understand why she is being so honored. She happens to cross paths with the industrialist's son (Ray Milland), who is attempting to make it on his own after a fight with his father, and the two fall in love. With her help, he is able to become independently successful and escape from under his father's thumb, their eventual marriage rescuing her from poverty.

A New Leaf belongs solidly to this tradition of romantic filmmaking that satirizes marriage as an economic institution, while showing the desirability and ultimately triumphant power of love, despite its seeming irrationality. It also borrows from a number of stock character types, including a clueless woman and an isolated, downtrodden man who must find maturity and economic success simultaneously. This dynamic is found not only in *Easy Living*, but *My Man Godfrey* and, most notably, in Hawks' screwball comedy classic, *Bringing Up Baby*, with which *A New Leaf* shares several elements. In a sense, *A New Leaf* functions as a combination of *Bringing Up Baby* and *The Lady Eve*, as it combines three plot elements found in varying combinations between the two films: the central conceit of one protagonist trying to get a considerable amount of money from the other, which is what draws the pair together; an absent-minded professor type; and a childish male character who is forced to mature by the end of the film.

In *Bringing Up Baby*, a timid paleontologist (Cary Grant) is trying to raise money to finish assembling a dinosaur skeleton ahead of his wedding. He crosses paths with Susan (Katharine Hepburn), the spoiled and scatterbrained niece of a potential donor, who proceeds to rapidly unravel his life as she falls in love with him, tries to delay his wedding, and comes into the possession of a pet leopard, the titular Baby. Grant's paleontologist, David Huxley, must politely tolerate Susan and keep her out of any number of scrapes in order to impress her aunt, because he is desperate for the donation of a potential million dollars from her.

The financial motivations in *The Lady Eve* are far less altruistic; Barbara Stanwyck's Jean Harrington is a con artist who targets Charles Pike (Henry Fonda), the heir to a fortune who is socially awkward and distracted by his obsession with herpetology, on a cruise liner. He falls for her, but her plans are waylaid by her own feelings for him. When he learns the truth about her life, he abandons her and she becomes determined to get revenge and take him for all he's worth. She reinvents herself as the Lady Eve, a wealthy woman whom he falls in love after a whirlwind romance; he's too gullible to believe that Eve is Jean in disguise. They marry and she reveals her real identity, but not even her various machinations can keep them apart.

Like Jean Harrington, Henry is interested in money only because of the lifestyle it will afford him and he begins in *A New Leaf* similarly obsessed with a specific lifestyle and no thought for anyone but himself. Like David of *Bringing Up Baby*, Jean and Henry all gradually fall for their respective targets because Charles, Susan, and Henrietta share similar traits: they are naïve, prone to accidents and social blunders, and are otherwise in need of a caretaker so they are not preyed upon by the world. While Susan is the strongest of the three characters, she finds herself in comic trouble in many scenes throughout *Bringing Up Baby*; Charles, meanwhile, narrowly avoids the attentions of other women only interested in his money, while Henrietta is being robbed by her lawyer and household staff.

This professorial type is an important element of both *A New Leaf* and *Bringing Up Baby*, with May's character in *A New Leaf* cast in the same mold, though with an updated twist to give her a female gender. Cary Grant's dotty professor is a central performance in the genre and helped establish the general trope within romantic comedy. In *Romantic vs. Screwball Comedy: Charting the Difference*, Wes D. Gehring writes, "The genre's favorite example of a profession nebulous to many Americans is the absent-minded professor, a type fully realized by the irreplaceable Cary Grant in Howard Hawks' *Bringing Up Baby*."[4] Gehring notes Hawks' preference for professorial characters, which undoubtedly popularized the type: they are also seen in *Ball of Fire* (Howard Hawks, 1941) and *Monkey Business* (Howard Hawks, 1952), with Grant reprising the role, while Henry Fonda's character in *The Lady Eve* is also "the ultimate milquetoast professor-like ophiologist."[5]

David, Charles, and Henrietta are all powerless against the attentions of their prospective suitors, partly because they don't have the life experience or social skills to resist. In particular, Charles and Henrietta are both dazzled by romantic attention of any kind from a member of the opposite sex. While Charles has been abroad in the Amazon and has only recently found himself back in polite society, Henrietta is so focused on botany and her professorial role that she seems unaware that she is not accepted by the upper-class social world. May turns the formula somewhat on its head in the sense that Henrietta channels Katharine Hepburn's profound sense of physical comedy in *Bringing Up Baby*. Gehring writes that "the one distinctive Hepburn trait in her *Bringing Up Baby* performance, beyond that signature forcefulness, is a gift for the physical in everything she does."[6] While Henrietta is less athletic, her quirks are revealed through an increasingly comedic and increasingly death-defying series of gags. The trope is also somewhat turned on its head because Henrietta's botanical obsession is transformed into a genuinely moving romantic gesture—naming a new species of fern after Henry and giving him a pendant with a preserved piece of the plant—which moves even his seemingly cold heart.

Gehring writes that in their absent-mindedness and seeming inexperience or emotional immaturity, these characters take on childlike qualities. In the case of Susan, Charles, and Henrietta, this manifests as a sort of infantilized role, where they need a more mature, adept character to literally provide them with care. But this is also true of David, Jean, and Henry, who are perhaps more self-aware, and aware of the world around themselves, but are immature in other ways and go through a journey of maturation throughout their respective films. Childlike male protagonists are a central feature of the screwball comedy—as Gehring notes with titles like *Holiday* (George Cukor, 1938), *My Favorite Wife* (Garson Kanin, 1940), and *Too Many Husbands* (Wesley Ruggles, 1940)—which often present male protagonists as needing to strike out on their own in the world and grow up before they can settle down as appropriate husband material. Molly Haskell writes that Hawks' films in general are concerned with this theme, particularly in how they are connected to American culture itself: "The intuitively American quality of Hawks' films expresses itself in themes of male–female competition, sexual inversion, and the struggle between adolescence and maturity for a grown man's soul."[7]

While David and Charles seem terrified of both women and marriage, the male protagonists of films like *Easy Living* and *My Man Godfrey* step out from under the protective wing of their wealthy fathers to temporarily live in poverty and learn how to be a man in the world. Henry is of a similar type; his fortune is depleted because he unwisely ran through it without planning ahead or being aware of the consequences. The lack of any money or financial stability forces him to mature, even though his plans initially come from a place of callous selfishness. What Haskell writes of Hawks' films applies to these screwball comedies concerned with immaturity in a more general sense. She writes that they are concerned with "the picture of man poised, comically or heroically, against an antagonistic universe, a nothingness as devoid of meaning as Beckett's, but determined nonetheless to act out his destiny, to assert mind against mindlessness."[8] In this world, "not only God but mothers are absent" and man has "evolved to a precarious ascendancy over nature and animals which he must fight to maintain."[9]

A New Leaf follows similar laws: not only mothers, but parents in general are absent and the only references to guardians include passing mentions of dead fathers, Henry's callous and malicious uncle, and Henrietta's lawyer, an exploitative, greedy figure who attempts to fulfill the role of husband, father, and legal caretaker, but is essentially ignored by Henrietta. As with screwball comedy protagonists, Henry and Henrietta are childlike and immature, which is revealed, in part, through their awkward interactions and obvious emotional inexperience. While Henry is openly selfish and obsessed with his life of comfort, Henrietta is similarly focused inward, so fixated on botany that she is unable to see how she is being taken advantage of by everyone around her. For example, she's so unprepared when Henry kisses her that she responds by stuttering, "Heavens, mercy . . . I mean gracious, heavens."

Childlike romantic protagonists are certainly present throughout the early screwball comedies, where the reluctant process of falling in love is accompanied by outbursts and temper tantrums, petty squabbles, impulsiveness, and overall emotional immaturity: the titular "screwball" behavior of the subgenre. The implication is that falling in love causes characters to take leave of their senses, often in dramatic and hilarious ways, at times causing surrounding characters to believe they are insane; for example, this is a central premise of *Bringing Up Baby*. Gehring suggests that love itself is responsible for much of this unhinged, childish behavior:

> The male also reveals his childishness in several other ways. Traditionally the screwball characteristic is associated with the female in the genre, but the male, too, may have a screwball tendency. While the heroine is . . . pleasantly potty to begin with . . . the male is just as likely to become a screwball as a result of female shenanigans.[10]

It has also been claimed by scholars such as Gehring that the central character type—the childish, isolated male protagonist—is a unifying feature with film noir and that screwball comedies act as an inversion of the standard noir plot tropes. Where the film noir ends in violence and tragedy, the screwball comedy ends in love and often marriage or implied marriage. In *Screwball Comedy: A Genre of Madcap Romance*, Gehring writes that films in both genres concern a "frequently irrational world with women hunting vulnerable men."[11] In *Screwball Comedy and Film Noir: Unexpected Connections*, Thomas C. Renzi further explores this connection: "The clever and conniving woman in the screwball was actually a comical sister of the self-serving seductress in noir. The screwball male, when portrayed as the object of the female's intentions, was oftentimes as hapless a figure as the doomed noir protagonist."[12]

Renzi notes that both screwball comedy and film noir are marked by a pronounced cynicism. While film noir protagonists are paranoid and persecuted, trapped in claustrophobic worlds of crime and violence, the characters of screwball comedies are products of the Depression. They are often skeptical of love, marriage, and conventional family life. As in *My Man Godfrey* or comedies of remarriage like *The Philadelphia Story* (George Cukor, 1940), sometimes they react to old heartbreak and emotional wounds. Unlike more conventional Hollywood romances, these films lack the rosy view that the idea of love or the act of marriage itself is enough to overcome obstacles between a couple. While these films often portray childish women as gripped in an irrational pursuit of a man, such as in *My Man Godfrey* or *Bringing Up Baby*, there are also colder, more calculated reasons for the pursuit, as in *The Lady Eve*. The male pursuit of female characters is often more complicated, such as in *It Happened One Night* (where the male lead will benefit from writing a story about a young woman), or the implications that Cary Grant's characters in *His Girl Friday* and *The Philadelphia Story* simply do not want their ex-wives remarrying.

In both film noir and screwball comedy, romance is not the journey of star-crossed lovers overcoming external obstacles, but manifests as an internal struggle between the protagonists themselves. Renzi describes both genres as depending "on two equal adversaries, a man and woman, locked in a love–hate relationship, the traditional battle of the sexes."[13] He draws a parallel between slapstick comedy and noir violence; certainly a film like *Bringing Up Baby* includes numerous scenes that end in near-death or destruction, such as a car accident, several falls, a night in jail, and two leopards on the loose. Parallels can be made between *It Happened One Night* and a film noir like *Detour*, where a man and a woman are effectively stranded on the road and are potentially subject to any number of horrors. Renzi notes that *The Thin Man* (W. S. Van Dyke, 1934) goes so far as to combine both genres on screen, thanks to the rapid-fire banter and friendly competition between happily married couple Nick (William Powell) and Nora Charles (Myrna Loy) as they solve a murder case.

These elements, which are the central focus of *A New Leaf*, are more closely connected to later films to come at the end of the screwball comedy wave, particularly Preston Sturges' grim romantic comedy, *Unfaithfully Yours* (1948). In the film, a composer, Sir Alfred (Rex Harrison), becomes suspicious that his beloved wife (Linda Darnell) is having an affair and is driven nearly mad with jealousy. He variously fantasizes about murdering her, nobly sacrificing his feelings and allowing her to divorce him, and dramatically committing suicide in revenge, but he ultimately decides to attempt to kill her. Like *A New Leaf*, which seems inspired by Sturges' film, *Unfaithfully Yours* hinges on the anxiety that this could become a romantic comedy, with a happy ending between the couple, or could become the tale of a man murdering his wife.

Renzi argues that *Unfaithfully Yours* is the final film of the classic screwball period, because it has come to rest almost equally between the two genres. "Symbolically, *Unfaithfully Yours*, with its potential to transition from comedy to tragedy, suggests that screwball has been pushed to its limits and cannot go any further without destroying itself."[14] Unlike May's film, Sturges' comedy was generally well received by critics, though it also did not make much of a splash at the box office and, in the years since its release, is often left out of discussions that group together Sturges' other comedic masterpieces. Jonathan Lethem writes that the film takes "a psychological subject with nightmare overtones: sexual jealousy, paranoiac daydreams, schemes for domestic murder" and explores "daydreams of sacrifice, derangement, depression, and revenge."[15]

Both *Unfaithfully Yours* and *A New Leaf* are essentially about a husband fantasizing about killing his wife and then planning her murder, an act that is prevented in large part by his own self-absorption and ultimately not carried out because he realizes how much he loves her. Sir Alfred is unable to complete the murder in the real world because he is much clumsier than in his fantasy; things simply go wrong, with much physical chaos and comedy ensuing. Similarly, Henry has opportunities where he could kill Henrietta, such as during a sequence where they are honeymooning and he is too absorbed in reading a book on poisons to notice that she is about to fall off a cliff and thus could be dispatched with only minimal effort.

Lethem writes that *Unfaithfully Yours* "satirizes the vanities and impostures of the artist."[16] While Sir Alfred is a great composer and much is made of his artistic temperament as being intimately bound up with his talent, May also presents Henry as a sort of artist, at least as a connoisseur, in the sense that he has turned being wealthy into an art form. His butler says to him, "You have managed in your own lifetime to keep alive traditions that were dead before you were born." There is the implication that he has a talent for being rich and for nothing else. Henry himself says, "I have no skills, no resources, no ambitions. All I am—or was—is rich. And that's all I ever wanted to be." Both

Sir Alfred and Henry seem to lack self-awareness or the kind of practical skills that allow other characters to function in the world; for example, Sir Alfred is the antithesis of the "starving artist" character type and much of his persona is bound up—like Henry—in a protective and isolating cocoon of wealth. To a degree, Sir Alfred treats his wife like a prized possession, a rare item that he must jealously guard. Henry, similarly, regards Henrietta not as a person, but as an object or an opportunity to bolster his wealth and protect his lifestyle. In a 1971 film, in particular, when countercultural movements had gained such prominence in American culture, it is difficult not to interpret this depiction of Henry as an attack on capitalistic greed. Part of his character growth in the film involves learning to progress beyond his obsession with wealth towards a more purposeful life.

This quality of self-absorption is similar to the aforementioned scatterbrained professor—another character type who exists within a protective cocoon of privilege—but is also found quite frequently in films about men who fantasize about murder, particularly about murdering their partners or spouses. It is likely this grisly quality that kept the film from being popular in its day; even with the happy, romantic conclusion, there is an ambiguity to the film and the sense that Sir Alfred *could* become a killer—nay, is well on his way to becoming one—that lingers. Lethem writes,

> *Unfaithfully Yours* is a film about marital homicide, and Sir Alfred is still sharpening his razor less than ten minutes before the film's happy ending. The exposé of "the perfect murder" recalls both Alfred Hitchcock, whose interest in this theme peaked with the "killing of Gromek" sequence in *Torn Curtain*, and Nabokov's novel *Despair*, which mirrors *Unfaithfully Yours*'s delight in showing the breach between a killer's self-flattering plans and their real-world result. *Unfaithfully Yours* might also be seen as a sort of happy version of Nicholas Ray's *In a Lonely Place*.[17]

Ray's 1950 film follows a writer, Dixon Steele (Humphrey Bogart), who is suspected of murder. His neighbor and new girlfriend (Gloria Grahame) impulsively acts as his alibi, but develops suspicions of her own when she gets to know his dark, troubled nature. *In a Lonely Place* lingers over whether or not Steele is the murderer and it is not revealed until the conclusion that he is innocent; of course, by then it is too late for his relationship to survive.

This focus on ambiguously violent men with murderous fantasies unites *Unfaithfully Yours, In a Lonely Place*, and *A New Leaf*, which are generally populated with unlikable (or at least unsympathetic) characters. All three male protagonists are given over to moments of violent fantasy even if they never actually become murderers. While these moments are generally more lighthearted in *A New Leaf*, they are off-putting in *Unfaithfully Yours* because of the overall comedic tone of the film. Renzi writes, "Two scenes are so grim and gruesome that the black humor balances precariously on the boundary between comedy and repulsive humor. In fact, Sturges' film may be called noir comedy because he melds the comedy with elements from film noir, including a femme fatale, chiaroscuro lighting, and a generally dark, cynical tone."[18]

Arguably, this tradition of black comedy, particularly romantic black comedy, rose up out of this merging of film noir and screwball comedy, and I would argue that without it, *A New Leaf* would not exist. While films like *Unfaithfully Yours* and *Arsenic and Old Lace* (Frank Capra, 1944)—starring Cary Grant as a man whose wedding day is nearly ruined when he discovers that his two aunts are poisoning lonely old men out of mercy and have hidden the bodies in the basement of the family home—began to explore these themes in the 1940s, they would more fully emerge in the following two decades, leading to an explosion of the loose subgenre in the 1970s.

An early example that bears a close relationship with *A New Leaf* is Alfred Hitchcock's *The Trouble with Harry* (1955), one of the director's favorites of his own films,[19] but one of the most critically and commercially neglected of his catalog. In autumn in a small Vermont town, local residents stumble across the corpse of a man named Harry (Philip Truex), which happens to be lying in the middle of the woods. All seemingly nonplussed by the body, various residents—including a retired captain (Edmund Gwenn), a painter (John Forsythe), a spinster (Mildred Natwick), and Harry's own wife (Shirley MacLaine)—are forced to team up because, in turn, they each believe they have accidentally killed Harry and must then hide his body.

Unlike Hitchcock's many other films revolving around a corpse, *The Trouble with Harry* is a comedy (even a romantic comedy), and the body is a device—the MacGuffin, a term popularized by Hitchcock himself, through it predated him[20]—to bring potential lovers together. The mystery of why Harry is dead, who killed him, and what they are going to do with his body is all but inconsequential to the plot as the two men fall in love with the two women. Likely disappointing his usual audience, Hitchcock ultimately reveals—after the foursome bury, dig up, re-bury, and hide the corpse several times—that Harry's death is due to natural causes and there is no murder mystery at all. François Truffaut called the film "a little metaphysical fable about a corpse" and wrote that it was "a film against humor, against funny stories, and against laughing audiences."[21]

While this is quite a departure from Hitchcock films like *The Lady Vanishes* (1938), about a missing woman believed to have been murdered, or *Rope* (1948), which is also concerned with the problem of a hidden corpse, *The Trouble with Harry* forgoes nefarious plots and both literal and figurative dark corners. Hitchcock himself said, "With *Harry,* I took melodrama out of the pitch-black night and brought it out into the sunshine. It's as if I had set up a murder alongside a rustling brook and spilled a drop of blood in the clear water."[22] Like *A New Leaf*, this is a film that juxtaposes sex and death; we are led to believe from the opening scenes that what will unfold is a thriller or crime film. Both also celebrate the natural world and present nature itself as a place where sex and death can hold equal sway.

May explained that the story that *A New Leaf* is based on—"The Green Heart" (1963) by Jack Ritchie—actually came from an Alfred Hitchcock omnibus collection of short fiction. She said, "I liked it because I realized the guy, the hero, was going to kill this woman. And he actually kills somebody else. And I thought he's going to kill her and he's not going to realize that he likes her."[23] She apparently intended the film to be a comedy in which someone gets away with murder, a territory also skirted by *The Trouble with Harry*. May said recently in an interview that *A New Leaf* was altered by studio interference and that she originally wanted Henry to get away with a murder—a scene that she actually shot but which was removed.[24]

While no one actually murders the titular Harry in Hitchcock's film, the gruesome element is that even if someone had, none of the characters seem to care. In *The Art of Alfred Hitchcock*, Hitchcock biographer Donald Spoto writes,

> No one really becomes very upset about Harry's demise, nor about the need (for a variety of reasons) to disinter him and then reinter him. The film implies that there are worse things in life than death, and that real maturity lies in accepting that, like everything else in nature "we all have to go sometime."[25]

Similarly in *A New Leaf*, only the butler Harold (George Rose) expresses mild concern over Henry's muttered plot to murder Henrietta, as if planning a murder is a routine activity with which no one really need concern themselves. Both films display a casual attitude about death and violence that seems to cover up very real anxieties. Spoto notes, "Laughing at death is thus like laughing at sex: it hides true feelings, and the laughter really betokens nervousness."[26]

At the time, *The Trouble with Harry* was noted for its somewhat brazen depictions of sexuality, including numerous scenes of flirting between characters, sometimes over Harry's body. This frank sexuality is not echoed in *A New Leaf*, which instead mimics the early screwball comedies; Henry and Henrietta are shown getting married, on their wedding night, and on their honeymoon, but there is no whisper of sex on screen. Perhaps surprisingly, it is not even used for comedic effect. In one of the first scenes of genuine pathos, Henrietta has tried to wear a feminine nightgown to bed, but has tangled the straps. In what could have been a comedic sequence, Henry is shown gently untangling her and putting the costume right.

Both films also show characters falling in love outside in nature, a place that complicates both sex and violence. Spoto argues that *The Trouble with Harry* is not as frank and casual about sex as it first seems and the lush Vermont greenery potentially conceals something as rotten as Harry's corpse: "Although Robert Burk's glorious cinematography gives it a vivid splendor, there is an almost palpable undercurrent of a dark and grotesque Puritanism in this picture. But whether the film affirms or satirically mocks that Puritanism is difficult to determine."[27] While it cannot be said that *A New Leaf* is especially puritanical, its complete absence of sex is disorienting. There is the implication that both Henry and Henrietta are too childlike to pursue sexual relationships until after their marriage.

Spoto writes that *The Trouble with Harry* "affirms the coexistence of evil and good as basic to the world; takes seriously the infinite capacities for criminal activity that lie within everyone; distrusts relationships and, in its schizoid attempt to deny the reality of the flesh, warns about the poisonous nature of sex."[28] In a similar way, *A New Leaf* seems to present sex—by its complete absence—as another distraction. Both films indicate a deeply cynical attitude towards intimacy of any kind, though both also ultimately have happy, if somewhat subdued, romantic endings. The characters in both films are generally flawed, often unlikable, and make fumbling attempts at breaking their own personal shells of isolation for hopeful social interactions with others; above all, they seem to seek to exert control over their insular and isolated environments. For example, it is remarked that Henrietta is "about the most isolated woman," which makes her perfect for Henry's scheme, but also underscores the film's theme about profound personal isolation, which it shares with many other unusual romantic comedies from the 1970s, particularly those that fit in with the cinematic movement known as New Hollywood Cinema.

Birthed in the mid to late 1960s, New Hollywood Cinema—to which May and collaborator Mike Nichols certainly belong—was strongly influenced by the French New Wave, which is reflected in the period's romantic films and comedies. Wes Gehring argues that New Hollywood Cinema, particularly its black comedies, borrowed three key ingredients from the French New Wave that differentiate them from Classic Hollywood, all of which are crucial to *A New Leaf*:

> First, instead of traditional admirable heroes, these films showcase anti-heroes—fascinatingly anti-establishment characters of a realistic, non-movie-star status. Second, rather than normal chronological narratives, the movies are often about slice-of-life existence which revels in disjointed storytelling, like the randomness of life—less a narrative than

a darkly comic cinematic mosaic . . . Third, in place of classic cinema's tidy upbeat conclusions, these counter-culture films end with a bittersweet honesty, from shattered dreams to death.[29]

Additionally, Gehring argues that the pre-cinematic nature of black comedy features "the omnipresence of death, the inherent absurdity of the world, and man as beast."[30] These are all central elements of *A New Leaf* and represent a departure from the influence of the early screwball comedies: the film's protagonist and, in a sense, its romantic hero is an opportunistic murderer who plans to seduce and marry a woman purely to steal her fortune. The film's plot is linear, but presents the "slice-of-life" approach discussed by Gehring, in the sense that May does not show what might be understood as the key beats of a romantic comedy. She depicts the "meet cute" at an afternoon gathering, where Henrietta is shamed for spilling her tea on the floor, and shows their hilarious wedding, but the wedding night is absent, as are expected moments where the characters are spontaneously tender towards each other and romantic feelings begin to unexpectedly develop (such as those shown in screwball comedies like *It Happened One Night* and *Bringing Up Baby*).

Gehring discusses one of the central features of New Hollywood Cinema as a reinvention, or reinterpretation of genre, resulting in "anti-genre" films. He cites Bob Fosse's later *All That Jazz* (1979) as an exemplary anti-musical and in a similar way, *A New Leaf* can be seen as an anti-romantic comedy. This builds on 1960s films like *The Apartment*, Nichols' *The Graduate*, and *Breakfast at Tiffany's*, all of which presented unconventional, complicated relationships that reflected a cynical attitude towards the sunny, perfect marriages seen in television shows like *Leave It to Beaver* (1957–1963) or *The Donna Reed Show* (1958–1966). Similarly, director Peter Bogdanovich scored a critical and financial hit with this loose formula in *What's Up, Doc?* (filmed before *A New Leaf* in 1970, but not released until 1972), another New Hollywood Cinema reinterpretation of the screwball comedy.

In that film, the chance meeting of four strangers with four identical pieces of luggage at a hotel results in the clumsy romance between a musicology professor (Ryan O'Neal) with "musical" rocks and an enthusiastic but disaster-prone young woman (Barbra Streisand). Like *Bringing Up Baby*, the female protagonist hatches a plot to get the professor a grant and to separate him from his uptight fiancée (Madeline Kahn), but there is also the slight inclusion of crime and espionage plots, as one of the suitcases contains secret government papers and another conceals jewels that are the target of thieves. Bogdanovich would explore these genre reinterpretations many times in his early career, through films like *Targets* (1968) or *Paper Moon* (1973). *What's Up, Doc?* was perhaps a bigger success than *A New Leaf* because it is much lighter in tone and includes more scenes of conventional slapstick comedy.

In general, New Hollywood Cinema dispensed with the straightforward, linear narratives Hollywood typically required. Endings, in particular, were often disjointed, confusing, or rejected obvious conclusions. While *A New Leaf* borrows some of these stylistic choices for its choppy narration—it barely touches on its protagonists' inner lives, for example—it appropriates equally from Classic Hollywood. For example, *A New Leaf*'s finale seems to come right from screwball comedy: the couple marry, Henry slowly warms to Henrietta, seemingly against his will, and though he continues to plan her murder, does nothing to execute either the plan or his wife. At the end of the film, when he stumbles across an ideal accidental death situation—alone, on a camping trip in the woods, in the river rapids—he cannot bring himself to go through with it and rescues her. In a strangely downbeat note, lacking the typical jubilance of a romantic comedy, he accepts the life she has proposed for him with quiet, yet seemingly pleased resignation. The film is devoid of any sweeping melodramatic moment, and it also lacks the suspenseful climax of a thriller.

In this sense, *A New Leaf* is a departure from the unconventional, disaffected youth films of the 1960s that served as a forerunner to New Hollywood, such as *Bonnie and Clyde* (Arthur Penn, 1967), and any reference to countercultural movements simply does not exist within the film. It is also in another universe from deeply pessimistic films like *End of the Road* (Aram Avakian, 1970), *Putney Swope* (Robert Downey Sr., 1969), or *The Last Picture Show* (Peter Bogdanovich, 1971), forgoing arthouse tropes in favor of a much more internalized cynicism. A lot of these films reflected the rapid social changes of the 1960s and 1970s—not just in the United States, but around the world—a time when gender roles were dramatically changing. The women's rights movement, in particular, progressed in leaps and bounds in the 1960s, both in terms of new-found legal permissions and career opportunities, and—for the first time—granting women access to financial and legal rights, new options for contraception and divorce, protection from domestic abuse, rape, and sexual harassment, and so on.[31]

In the 1970s, sexual liberation and women's rights essentially went mainstream. Reporting on the protest marches in New York City in 1970, *Time Magazine* states,

> The women's movement was most successful in pushing for gender equality in workplaces and universities. The passage of Title IX in 1972 forbade sex discrimination in any educational program that received federal financial assistance. The amendment had a dramatic affect on leveling the playing field in girl's athletics. Also, feminists made the workforce a more hospitable space for women with policies banning sexual harassment, something the Equal Opportunity Commission

recognized in 1980. Women's participation in college, graduate school and the professions has steadily increased over the past several decades, although a gender wage gap still exists.[32]

Anxieties around the transforming social order are reflected in many of the New Hollywood romantic films, which are concerned with issues of personal, political, and financial freedom, and the complications of love, courtship, sex, and marriage. A general mood of despair, mistrust, paranoia, and malaise is reflected in many of these films, and, like *A New Leaf*, many of them were set in New York at a time when the city became a symbol of rising poverty, violence, and urban chaos. These anti-romances were often bleak and cynical, focusing on ill-matched couples or couples who are miserable, destructive, or cruel to each other, highlighting some of the realities of partnership and marriage in a way not previously explored on screen.

Nichols, for example, was certainly a director who explored the complicated subject of romance and gender relations, in films like *Who's Afraid of Virginia Woolf?* (1966), *The Graduate* (1967), and *Carnal Knowledge* (1971). The latter follows two friends from college through to middle age and focuses on their contrasting experiences with dating, marriage, and divorce. Deeply cynical, *Carnal Knowledge* presents a more dramatic and less comedic, even mean-spirited view of similar themes at the heart of *A New Leaf*. These New Hollywood romance films, especially *Carnal Knowledge*, satirize romance and the Hollywood-sanctioned, on-screen depictions of love and marriage. They also offer up a visual representation in the changing morals of American society in the 1960s and 1970s; for example, *Carnal Knowledge* was among the first popular American films to frankly discuss sex and to actually include certain words in the dialogue, for which it was labelled "obscene material" in a related court case.[33]

Although May does not depict these themes in a similarly overt or confrontational way, I argue that a similar tone is buried within *A New Leaf*. In his book *Mike Nichols and the Cinema of Transformation*, J. W. Whitehead argues that this satire of romance and gender roles was at the heart of Nichols' and May's use of comedy, both as a duo and separately as directors. He writes,

> The first significant piece Nichols and May developed eventually came to be called "Teenagers." Two young people make out in a car, and the piece requires both physical and verbal dexterity. At one point they're so entangled that passing a shared cigarette becomes a comic ordeal.[34]

Whitehead notes a similar moment in *The Graduate* that involved smoking and kissing, but *A New Leaf* also includes a similar gag over drinking and spilling liquid on a carpet. This occurs when Henry and Henrietta meet, but also during the scene where he proposes marriage. He is forced to kneel in broken glass to propose, because the clumsy and distracted Henrietta has ruined yet another expensive carpet and broken yet another glass.

There was a wave of films with complicated and blackly comic explorations of romance in the early 1970s, including Nichols' films and *A New Leaf*, but many other titles with loosely similar relationships to death, violence, and absurdity. These include *Little Murders* (Alan Arkin, 1971), where a woman essentially forces a withdrawn, reluctant man to fall in love with her, but is abruptly killed by a random sniper attack during an outbreak of violence in New York City; Jerry Schatzberg's *The Panic in Needle Park* (1971), a grim tale about lovers whose lives are disrupted by heroin; and Peter Medak's *A Day in the Death of Joe Egg* (1972), where a married couple indulge in black humor and violent fantasies as a way to cope with their daughter's disability and their own crumbling sanity. Films like Arthur Hiller's *The Hospital* (1971) or Sidney Lumet's *Network* (1976) also juxtapose a budding if cynical romance with incredible violence: in the titular hospital, as a patient has gone on a murder spree, or on network television, where it jacks up the ratings. Both titles show the effect this violence has on a romantic relationship.

Like other films released in the same year—such as John Cassavetes' *Minnie and Moskowitz* (1971) and Hal Ashby's *Harold and Maude*—*A New Leaf* revolves around the idea of opposites attracting and the difficulties that might ensue from such a disparate match. And like the screwball comedies that present romance as a battle of the sexes, *A New Leaf* depicts these differences primarily as stemming from lonely, selfish individuals who must learn to cooperate and cohabit. But unlike a screwball comedy such as *Bringing Up Baby*, where Cary Grant's bumbling doctor happily accepts a new life with his future spouse, admitting that it's more exciting than the boring, sexless marriage he had been promised, *A New Leaf* belongs more firmly to the New Hollywood tradition where the ending is more ambiguous. It might not be as dramatic as films like *Little Murders* or *Harold and Maude*, where one member of the couple dies, but *A New Leaf* similarly has an unsettling resolution.

May explored this theme as a writer that same year—under the pseudonym Esther Dale—in Otto Preminger's *Such Good Friends* (1971), discussed at length elsewhere in this book. In that film, after a man (Laurence Luckinbill) slips into a coma after a minor medical accident, his wife (Dyan Cannon) learns of his infidelity. While he is unconscious, she uncovers more such affairs and has time to explore her feelings about their marriage, but he dies before she is able to confront him or resolve their issues. Though this was a project May took over from other writers such as Joan Didion, at the request of Preminger, it allowed her to explore themes of complicated romance and domestic strife outside the realm of comedy. Like *A New Leaf*, *Such Good Friends* follows the loose New Hollywood Cinema mold of rejecting the conventional happy ending. Tamar Jeffers McDonald writes,

Besides employing endings which evoked the openness of European art cinema, rather than the conventional Hollywood conclusion which saw all story strands nicely tied up, the radical romantic comedy was also prepared to end unhappily . . . While it is possible to say with certainty, therefore, that the romantic comedy before the 1970s was about love and romance, and would end happily with the couple's union, the radical romantic comedy, for a short period, was interested to see what became of the genre if more realistic elements were permitted space.[35]

Perhaps unexpectedly, *A New Leaf* straddles this ground between screwball comedy's happy ending and the more dissonant, even violent note struck by many of the New Hollywood romances. While it is suggested that Henry and Henrietta are on a more equal footing by the end of the film—he has at least abandoned his plan to murder her and seems to look forward to the responsibility of being her caretaker—there is nothing exciting or sexy about their relationship, which is presented as one of safety and comfort. As in *Unfaithfully Yours*, Henry also almost goes through with his plot to kill Henrietta and only turns back at the last possible moment, leaving somewhat of a downbeat tone to the film's last moments: Thanks to accidentally canoeing into river rapids, Henrietta nearly drowns, but does not attempt to save her own life and waits patiently for Henry to rescue her, which he does with a mixture of reluctance and resignation. As with Woody Allen's later film, *Hannah and Her Sisters* (1986), there is the suggestion that real love may not be bound up with passion and fireworks, but with comfort and stability.

A New Leaf can be seen as a political response to the rapid social and political changes of the 1970s, such as the violence of urban life, economic anxiety, dramatically changing gender dynamics, and the often harsh realities of marriage and romance. It deserves to be remembered at the forefront of the reemergence of screwball comedies within Hollywood, a series of films that regarded notions of romance critically. Intentionally, the conclusion of *A New Leaf* is less melodramatic than films like *Love Story* (Arthur Hiller, 1970) or *The Way We Were* (Sydney Pollack, 1973), but perhaps represents a more realistic portrayal of romance attuned to contemporary audiences. In this sense, *A New Leaf* stands in a unique position, at once looking backwards at screwball comedy tropes and forwards to a new kind of romantic drama that would allow filmmakers to explore more realistic, diverse types of romantic relationships— and May deserves to be celebrated as a filmmaker who anticipated comedic and romantic tropes that would come to dominate Hollywood in the 1980s and 1990s in the work of more renowned filmmakers such as Woody Allen or even writer/director Nora Ephron.

NOTES

1. Thomas Doherty, *Pre-Code Hollywood: Sex, Immorality, and Insurrection in American Cinema, 1930–1934* (New York: Columbia University Press, 1999), p. 114.
2. Ibid., p. 362.
3. Ibid., p. 113.
4. Wes D. Gehring, *Romantic vs. Screwball Comedy: Charting the Difference* (Lanham, MD: Scarecrow Press, 2008), p. 31.
5. Ibid., p. 31.
6. Ibid., p. 124.
7. Molly Haskell, "Masculine Feminine," *Film Comment* March/April 1974: 34.
8. Ibid., p. 34.
9. Ibid., p. 34.
10. Gehring, p. 37.
11. Wes D. Gehring, *Screwball Comedy: A Genre of Madcap Romance* (Westport, CT: Praeger, 1986), pp. 60–1.
12. Thomas C. Renzi, *Screwball Comedy and Film Noir: Unexpected Connections* (Jefferson, NC: McFarland, 2012), p. 2.
13. Ibid., p. 7.
14. Ibid., p. 12.
15. Jonathan Lethem, "*Unfaithfully Yours*: Zeno, Achilles, and Sir Alfred," *Criterion Collection*, 12 July 2005 <https://www.criterion.com/current/posts/772-unfaithfully-yours-zeno-achilles-and-sir-alfred> (accessed January 2019).
16. Ibid.
17. Ibid.
18. Renzi, p. 98.
19. Lesley Brill, *The Hitchcock Romance: Love and Irony in Hitchcock's Films* (Princeton: Princeton University Press, 1988), p. 273.
20. Todd McGowan, "Hitchcock's Ethics of Suspense: Psychoanalysis and the Devaluation of the Object," in Thomas Leitch and Leland Poague (eds), *A Companion to Alfred Hitchcock* (Oxford: Wiley-Blackwell, 2011), p. 514.
21. Wheeler Winston Dixon, *Early Film Criticism of François Truffaut* (Bloomington and Indianapolis: Indiana University Press, 1993), p. 96.
22. Donald Spoto, *The Art of Alfred Hitchcock: Fifty Years of His Motion Pictures* (New York: Anchor Books, 1992), p. 235.
23. "Elaine May in conversation with Mike Nichols," *Film Comment*, July/August 2006 <https://www.filmcomment.com/article/elaine-may-in-conversation-with-mike-nichols/> (accessed January 2019).
24. Ibid.
25. Spoto, p. 236. He quotes from Hitchcock's *Marnie* (1964).
26. Ibid., p. 237.
27. Ibid., p. 235.
28. Ibid., p. 238.
29. Wes D. Gehring, *Genre-Busting Dark Comedies of the 1970s: Twelve American Films*, (Jefferson, NC: McFarland, 2016), pp. 5–6.
30. Ibid., pp. 5–6.
31. See Flora Davis, *Moving the Mountain: The Women's Movement in America Since 1960* (New York: Simon and Schuster, 1991).
32. Sascha Cohen, "The Day Women Went on Strike," *Time Magazine*, 26 August 2015

<http://time.com/4008060/women-strike-equality-1970/> (accessed January 2019).
33. Warren Weaver Jr, "Court to Review Obscenity Case," *New York Times*, 11 December 1973 <https://www.nytimes.com/1973/12/11/archives/court-to-review-obscenity-case-carnal-knowledge-appeal-is.html> (accessed January 2019).
34. J. W. Whitehead, *Mike Nichols and the Cinema of Transformation* (Jefferson, NC: McFarland, 2014), p. 17.
35. Tamar Jeffers McDonald, *Romantic Comedy: Boy Meets Girl Meets Genre* (New York: Wallflower, 2007), p. 70.

CHAPTER 5

"Don't Put A Milky Way in Someone's Mouth When They Don't Want It": A Contemporary Feminist Rereading of Elaine May's *The Heartbreak Kid* (1972)

Clem Bastow

It's a question that keeps feminist film critics awake at night: is it possible to reclaim certain works as part of the feminist film canon, even if they were never intended as such? If Elaine May ever self-identified as a feminist, her public stance on the topic was one of comical obfuscation. "I don't think it's important whether you're a man, a woman or a chair," she said[1] in 1972, on the question of whether her gender had influenced her work. That same year, her second film, *The Heartbreak Kid*, was released.

Based on the Bruce Jay Friedman short story, "A Change Of Plan," and with a screenplay by Neil Simon, the film concerns the misadventures of Jewish sporting goods salesman Lenny Cantrow (Charles Grodin) as he attempts to dump his bride, Lila Kolodny (played by Jeannie Berlin, May's daughter), in order to get together with Kelly (Cybill Shepherd), the midwestern WASP princess of his upwardly mobile dreams, after they meet during Lenny's honeymoon with Lila. All that stands in Lenny's way is the fact of his marriage, and Kelly's anti-Semitic father, Mr Corcoran (Eddie Albert).

May might not have felt her gender was an important factor in her creative vision, but my immediate reaction upon viewing *The Heartbreak Kid* for the first time was that only a woman could have directed that film. Perhaps, as a feminist film critic, I am doomed to detect infinitesimal crumbs of feminist thought in even the most unlikely places, but watching *The Heartbreak Kid* stripped of its critical context, May's directorial position seemed clear: the film read as a critique of a very particular brand of 1970s manhood. You can imagine my surprise, then, when I discovered that contemporaneous feminist film critics did not, in fact, embrace *The Heartbreak Kid* as a searing indictment of Lenny, and instead considered May to be something of a traitor to the feminist cause. In her review for *The Village Voice*, feminist film critic Molly

Haskell took umbrage with the "egotistic male fantasies" of the film. Haskell wrote, of Simon's screenplay, that "May has softened the edges, making Lenny more enchanting than he has any right to be."[2] That anyone might come away from *The Heartbreak Kid* thinking Lenny an "enchanting" figure borders on the fantastical: Grodin's performance is a *tour de force* of appalling behavior. (Grodin himself said of Lenny, "I thought the character in *The Heartbreak Kid* was a despicable guy"[3]).

Haskell's take on the film set the tone for feminist critique to come. In her 1988 book on female filmmakers, *Women Directors: The Emergence of a New Cinema*, critic Barbara Koenig Quart went one step further, declaring in no uncertain terms that "Elaine May's work has no feminist content."[4] Koenig Quart remains vague on the specifics of the apparent "un-feminist" nature of May's work, except to say that the director's outlier status as a female director in a male-dominated Hollywood may have led to "the appalling vision of women in her work, as well as for her proclivity to work through male characters' point of view."[5] Knowing what we now do about the way May's directorial career unfolded, Haskell's and Koenig Quart's hostility towards her work stings a little. This is not to suggest that feminist film critics should be in the business of blindly propping up female directors, but the thought did occur to me that were *The Heartbreak Kid* to debut as a Sundance Film Festival feature or HBO limited series today, it's not hard to imagine May being heralded as a brave new feminist voice in the mold of Lena Dunham or Nicole Holofcener.[6]

Scouring for further feminist readings of *The Heartbreak Kid* turned up next to nothing: the film, it seems, slipped into the purgatory of second and third wave feminist film criticism, having the misfortune of being released a few years before the true advent of feminist film (the "first feminist mainstream filmmakers," in Koenig Quart's eyes, were Joan Micklin Silver and Claudia Weill[7]). This is assuming that feminist critics had seen the film at all: *The Heartbreak Kid* has remained difficult to access—so much so, that in 2015 *The New Yorker* critic Richard Brody penned a "screening alert"[8] to direct readers to the fact that the film was screening on the American cable network Turner Classic Movies.

I mention this not necessarily to suggest a sexist conspiracy on the part of the home entertainment industry—after all, many works of male directors are also out of print—but it does bear noting if only to possibly explain the absence of May's work from many feminist studies of film: it may be that the scholars and critics in question were simply unable to access her films.[9] It is my hope, then, that my contemporary feminist reading of *The Heartbreak Kid* might encourage fellow feminist film critics to reconsider May's work, not necessarily as expressly "feminist" in content, but certainly as significant within the canon of female filmmakers, and in its unflinching critique of second-wave-era gender roles, certainly worthy of feminist reappraisal.

In this essay, I reclaim *The Heartbreak Kid* from the second wave feminist critiques that dismissed it as sexist. I read the film through a contemporary feminist lens, specifically looking at May's framing of key scenes within the film as a representation of the "female gaze." Though that term is contentious, I use Laura Mulvey's notion of the male gaze, and an emerging interpretation of the female gaze by contemporary filmmaker Jill Soloway, and feminist psychoanalytical theory as a springboard for thinking about how the look works as a tool of power within *The Heartbreak Kid*. I also examine the contentious character of Lila, dismissed by many critics as a caricatured representation of Jewish womanhood, as key in May's critique of both the character of Lenny *and* the filmic canon of her male contemporaries. May looks beneath the caricature represented by Lenny's resentful and self-loathing gaze, and—working closely with her daughter, Berlin—finds the humanity within Lila.

JEWISH NEW WAVE, FEMINIST SECOND WAVE

The Heartbreak Kid's release came at the end of the Jewish New Wave (named for the concurrent Hollywood new wave), during which writers including Philip Roth, Mike Nichols, Elaine May, and Mel Brooks, and actors including Barbra Streisand, Dustin Hoffman and Elliott Gould, explored Jewish identity on screen by way of increasingly dark satire. J. Hoberman locates this moment between 1967 and 1973, beginning with *The Graduate* (Mike Nichols, 1967) and *Funny Girl* (William Wyler, 1968) and ending with *The Heartbreak Kid* and *The Way We Were* (Sydney Pollack, 1973). These films

> [f]eatured (mainly) young, (sometimes) neurotic, and (by and large) not altogether admirable Jewish male protagonists cut off from their roots but disdainful of a white-bread America. Self-hatred merged with self-absorption, narcissism seemed indistinguishable from personal liberation, and alienation was a function of identity.[10]

Of its place in the Jewish New Wave, Hoberman calls *The Heartbreak Kid* no less than the "masterpiece of the cycle,"[11] though if one film of this series of sorts has loomed large in critical assessments, it is *The Graduate*. That film, directed by May's former comic collaborator Nichols, covers much of the same ground—"The mismatched Jewish–WASP romance, the confused antihero, the generational bloodshed," as Saul Austerlitz put it[12]—but where Nichols' film was ultimately heartwarming, May's is excoriating. It's almost poetic, given the magnitude of Nichols' success and May's comparatively modest filmography, that their two works bookend this wave of films in such a manner. What's striking about May's film, positioned as it is in this short but significant movement, is how it functions as a critique of not just the narratives laid down by Nichols, Wyler and other Jewish New Wave directors (those "confused antihero[es]"), but even as a critique of those directors and writers themselves.

Ironically enough, this reading of *The Heartbreak Kid* was first posited by Koenig Quart. Her discussion of *The Heartbreak Kid* suggests that the film exists as much as a critique of a certain type of Jewish man's fantasy of the "shiksa goddess" as it does the entire (male) canon of the Jewish New Wave:

> ... It can also be seen as a film that only a feisty Jewish woman could make in answer to [Philip] Roth et al., a scathing portrait of those late 1950s/1960s ethnic young men on the make, who dominated the literary scene in those years.[13]

It is here that Koenig Quart's assertion that May's oeuvre lacks feminist content becomes shaky—what, then, is this satirizing of the work of the great young Jewish men of mid-century fiction and cinema, if not a feminist statement by a Jewish woman director? Perhaps, then, the simple fact of *The Heartbreak Kid*'s male protagonist is what has prevented its revisiting by contemporary feminist critics. Like Haskell's, Koenig Quart's critique points to an enduring issue in feminist film criticism: can a film with a patriarchal or sexist male protagonist be claimed as feminist?

RETHINKING THE FEMALE GAZE: FROM MULVEY TO SOLOWAY

While May has not identified as feminist, from a contemporary feminist perspective her work occupies a unique position in film history, in no small part precisely because of her grappling with contemporaneous notions of masculinity. Popular thought suggests that, as feminism is a women's movement, so feminist film must be well populated by female characters and, especially, female protagonists. This, of course, risks reducing feminism to its most superficial state, and has been a source of tension amongst feminist critics since the movement was in its infancy. As Mary Gentile wrote in her review of Koenig Quart's *Women Directors*, "To imply that a film is 'feminist' merely if women are not portrayed as victims, for example, is at best an oversimplification."[14] And yet, the idea that a feminist film must be "about" a prescriptive approach to female character persists. In the case of *The Heartbreak Kid*, it would be tempting to categorize the film as "sexist" rather than "feminist" simply by virtue of the protagonist's maleness, and his treatment—Haskell's "egotistic male fantasies," again—of the women around him.

May's decision to make "commercial" films, rather than "alternative" cinema, may have counted against her, at least in terms of feminist readings such as Koenig Quart's of her work, given that the annals of feminist film criticism are not overrun by "popular" film. The act of working within commercial cinema has not counted against the reputations of male directors such as Martin Scorsese or Quentin Tarantino. "We feel very comfortable discussing their individual styles, or at least their specific approaches to filmmaking," critic Stephanie Zacharek has said, despite the fact that many commercial female filmmakers who might be called auteurs have "a very distinctive voice."[15] There is certainly a distinct directorial voice present in May's work, though it may also be helpful here to consider the problem of the female gaze in *The Heartbreak Kid*. In Lenny's recoiling from Lila, and indeed his idealization of Kelly, one could accuse May of uncritically repeating the male gaze. That theory, which emerged from Laura Mulvey's polemical 1975 essay "Visual Pleasure And Narrative Cinema," employs the Freudian notion of scopophilia, deriving sexual pleasure from the act of looking, in positioning the woman in cinema as the object of heterosexual male desire. The look is central to Mulvey's theory of the gaze, and she associates three different looks with cinema: "that of the camera as it records the pro-filmic event, that of the audience as it watches the final product, and that of the characters at each other within the screen illusion."[16]

The enduring nightmare of the male gaze is its inescapable quality; that even when women are protagonists, audience members or directors, they can still only see themselves *through* the male gaze. No doubt aware of her essay's larger-than-life presence within feminist film criticism, Mulvey has cautioned against the application of the gaze as one-size-fits-all theory, noting in an interview with Roberta Sassatelli that her essay had concerned a very particular period in Hollywood cinema where censorship had led to highly structured narratives "in which sexuality was absorbed into image," and that even at the time of writing "Visual Pleasure", "there were always some cinemas that were less repressed about sexuality, in which relations between the genders had always been more complex."[17]

Perhaps because of the limitations of applying the male gaze to contemporary film—where female and gender-diverse protagonists abound, as do their equivalents in the director's chair—the question of the female gaze has continued to intrigue and confound critics (in the same interview, Mulvey herself said, regarding the state of contemporary cinema, "there surely are many gazes around"). Attempts to define the female gaze, beyond the presence of a female director, have often focused on whether or not a film's protagonist is female, but the notion remains ephemeral and locked in binary opposition to the male gaze.

The notion of the female gaze has become popular in discussion of the so-called contemporary "golden age of television", where female showrunners (in effect, televisual auteurs) like Shonda Rhimes (*Grey's Anatomy*, *Scandal*) and Amy Sherman-Palladino (*Gilmore Girls*, *The Marvelous Mrs. Maisel*) have taken up the mantle traditionally held by men such as David Simon (*The Wire*) and Matthew Weiner (*Mad Men*). And, intriguingly, a particularly compelling recent reading of the female gaze comes to us not from the academy, but from a practitioner: *Transparent* creator Jill Soloway. While Soloway is a filmmaker, not a theorist, their attempt to investigate the notion of the female gaze offers compelling possibilities for a feminist re-reading of *The Heartbreak Kid*. In their 2016 Toronto International Film Festival address, Soloway attempted to define the female gaze as a way of "feeling-seeing": "I take the camera and I say, hey, audience, I'm not just showing you this thing, I want you to really feel with me."[18] In Soloway's "triangle"—a nod to Mulvey's "three looks" of cinema—the female gaze covers feeling-seeing, the gazed-gaze (representing how it feels to be the object of the male gaze), and the subjectivity, via authorial voice, to name the male as the object. Soloway's model of the female gaze also suggests a "heroine's journey," a new spin on the monomyth of *The Hero's Journey* as posited by Joseph Campbell in 1949. Soloway uses Martin Scorsese's *The King of Comedy* (1982) as their example: "we fall backwards with Rupert Pupkin, spiraling in an ever illuminated self-punishing story of having enraged or engaged the male gaze."[19] In Soloway's view, the heroine's journey is not a structure that can only be applied (as some feminist film criticism would suggest) to a female protagonist.

In Lenny, *The Heartbreak Kid* finds a protagonist whose mores seem utterly at odds with the emerging feminist movement of the early 1970s: he views the women in his life only as infuriating (Lila) or idealized (Kelly) obstacles to his own personal fulfilment, is emotionally unfaithful and psychologically abusive, and seems threatened by more enlightened men. However, it is precisely *within* this unflinching presentation of Lenny's foibles that May's film reveals itself as a critique of this man-child. May allows Lenny's actions to speak for themselves during excruciatingly long takes, and often locating him, within the frame, within the eyesight and earshot of disapproving female onlookers; they are stand-ins for May's own gaze upon Lenny. May leaves nothing to chance in her vision of *The Heartbreak Kid*, making crucial use of Owen Roizman's cinematography[20] to further drive home her scathing critique.

REREADING *THE HEARTBREAK KID*

We can assume, from her reluctance to identify as a feminist (let alone a feminist filmmaker), that May's intention was not born of a desire to put gender politics front and center in her authorial voice, but my textual critique of its male protagonist argues that *The Heartbreak Kid* is a compelling site for feminist film criticism. In this re-reading, I examine key moments in *The Heartbreak Kid*, employing both Mulvey's notion of the male gaze and Soloway's of the female gaze as a way to read May's unique and unflinching use of mid-shots and long takes as critique of Lenny's behavior. It is impossible to examine Lenny's gaze without acknowledging that, through it, we are encouraged to view Lila as nothing short of abject, so I will also employ at times Julia Kristeva's famous notion of abjection[21] in my reading of both Lila, and Lenny's recoiling from her. In the characterization of Lila, May cannily presents a young woman whose unselfconscious sensuality—she is "living her truth," as contemporary online feminists might put it—is read as abject by Lenny, further cementing May's feminist critique of a man whose self-loathing and desperation for assimilation leads him to view his bride as nothing short of a horror. Through May's female gaze, we see Lila as human, but through Lenny's male gaze, Lila represents the caricatured Jewess of his nightmares.

In the film's introductory montage, and even during the wedding sequence, Lila seems pleasant enough: a good-time girl who clearly only has eyes for Lenny. It's during the wedding sequence that May first hints at the "gazed gaze" that will characterize many of the film's key moments. Here, she introduces her visual chorus of disapproving women. As the couple's Jewish ceremony unfolds, the camera finds faces in the crowd of loved ones; a few initially beaming expressions are gradually replaced with sorrowful ones. Through their concerned expressions, we are invited to search our own misgivings about the newlyweds' future, given the hasty nature of the courtship and resulting nuptials. In picking out these female onlookers, May drives home her critique of Lenny: through them, we gaze at him. This visual chorus is a motif she will return to, in a moment of even more scathing critique, at the end of Lenny and Lila's marriage

It is only once the couple leave for their honeymoon that we are first invited to view Lila through Lenny's gaze. Lila's freely expressed sexuality terrifies Lenny; when she yanks open her blouse to expose her bosom, Lenny becomes a mess of anxiety, concerned that passing truck drivers will see her, as though their opinion of his wife has preempted his own. They make their first of a number of stop-overs in Virginia, where they finally consummate their marriage in a motel. Lying in bed in a post-coital daze, Lenny can't even bear for Lila to touch his chest. "Are you gonna be grouchy for the next fifty years?" she asks as she stomps off to the toilet. As the sound of Lila urinating issues from the bathroom, an expression of existential dread floods Lenny's face. This is the first (but not last) time May positions Lila as, through Lenny's eyes, an embodiment of the abject, her loud toilet break an aural evocation of "the horror within."[22] The Kristevan "bad object"[23] looms once more when Lila returns to bed and unwraps a chocolate bar for a midnight snack. When she tries to feed her husband, Lenny protests, "Don't put a Milky Way in someone's mouth when they don't want it," refusing the Milky Way as though it were the breast. In these intimate scenes, May dresses Berlin in matronly nylon bed coats and nightgowns. Through this, coupled with Lila's baby-talk—going "pee-pee," sulking about Lenny's grouchiness—we begin to see Lenny hear her bedroom chatter not as dirty talk or flirting, but as the dreaded maternal voice.[24]

When the couple finally make it to Miami Beach and check into their hotel, May doubles down on the gaze's possibilities. In Kelly's first appearance, she is positioned solely through Lenny's male gaze: the afternoon sun a blinding halo behind her tanned skin and flaxen hair, yellow beach towel tossed over her shoulder, she's the "shiksa goddess" as literal golden girl. The erotic impact of Kelly's introduction is striking, and her presence—sexy swimsuit and all—typifies the *"to-be-looked-at-ness"* of Mulvey's gaze. But, if we consider Soloway's "gazed-gaze," then Shepherd's knowing performance (and May's direction of her) indicates that Kelly deploys her *"to-be-looked-at-ness"* as a weapon. Despite Shepherd's winning performance, it's Berlin's Lila who is the film's beating heart,[25] and whose scenes with Lenny invite a closer feminist reading of the film. May interrogates the gaze in the three key scenes that unfold in Miami: Lenny's lying to Lila, his cocktail hour meeting with the Corcorans and, most devastatingly, in his break-up dinner with Lila.

In the first, Lenny returns to their room and spins Lila a wild fabrication about needing to meet with an old army buddy before dinner. "He's a big redneck jerk when it comes to having a conversation," he says, explaining that he's made their dinner reservation for 9 p.m.—the first of many times he tries to dazzle Lila with the promise of a lobster dinner with "yummy pecan pie." Lila is devastated: "You won't forget me?" she says (see Figure 5.1). Once more, May—working symbiotically with Berlin—stays with Lila's heartbreak. Here, again, is Soloway's "feeling-seeing," where "the emotions are being prioritized over the action."

As Lenny tries to put Lila off with his increasingly elaborate lies, May positions Lila in front of a mirror. Through this sequence, Lenny fusses with his outfit in the mirror. This is immensely powerful, because *we* see devastation dawn on Lila's face, but *Lenny* gazes into the mirror, seeing only the back of his wife. This shot, like so many in *The Heartbreak Kid*, is working on two levels: in the *mirror*, we see Lenny's male gaze, but in the *shot*, we gaze at the gaze. We, as viewers, recognize both Lila's sense of, per Soloway, "having been seen," but also our own. We see Lila not as the abject, Solarcain-daubed figure Lenny looks at in previous scenes, but as a hopeful young woman. Crucially, however, in May's framing of the scene, we never see Lila's gaze upon Lenny; there's no reverse shot where we see Lenny through Lila's eyes to position him as object. Instead, we see only Lenny's gaze, reflected in the mirror.

The second of these key scenes amplifies May's gaze to almost excruciating

Figure 5.1 We see what Lenny refuses to see (from *The Heartbreak Kid*, 1972).

levels. In an unflinchingly long one-take mid-shot, May frames the Corcorans alongside Lenny and Kelly during their pre-dinner cocktails, setting the stage for Lenny to debase himself in real-time. Lenny even relates his love for Kelly as being the result of Mulvey's third "look" of cinema.[26] Explaining how quickly he fell for her, Lenny says "One good look did it, if you want to know the truth"; his "love" for Kelly springs solely from his gaze upon her. As the increasingly delusional Lenny reveals his truth, including his prospector-like plans to "lay claim to your lovely daughter," as though making polite dinner conversation, Mrs Corcoran's face melts from broad smile to horrified blank stare (see Figure 5.2). In the unwavering gaze of May's mid-shot, we see, per Soloway, the authorial subjectivity to name the male as object.

The shot is held so long (the length of the entire five-minute scene) that it becomes almost unbearable; feeling-seeing once more. Lila is not physically present in the scene, but her *presence* can be felt—gazing at the gaze—in Lenny's discussion of her as though she is a mere speed-bump on the road to certain happiness with Kelly: "There is a slight complication, uh ... I happen to be a newlywed." (Lenny is also willing to submit to Mr Corcoran's heavily implied anti-Semitism, assuring the patriarch that Lila—his "big mistake"—is "not really my type.") Lenny's self-debasement only gets worse from there. Even in this unflinching and extended moment of critique, May, ever the comedian, cannot resist the opportunity for humor. Mr Corcoran responds with horror to Lenny's suggestion that, once he gets a divorce, he might get together with Kelly: "Not if they tied me to a horse and pulled me forty miles by my tongue." When Lenny thanks the patriarch for his frankness, Mr

Figure 5.2 The claustrophobic May mid-shot (from *The Heartbreak Kid*, 1972).

Corcoran drives it home: "Not if they hung me from a tree and put a lit bomb in my mouth." When Lenny assures Mr Corcoran of his respect for Kelly and the family, Mr Corcoran explodes, "Get him out of here before I take him into the men's room and break all the respect in his body." In this moment, as May and the viewer gazes at Corcoran's gaze, it's Lenny who has become "abjectified".

The third and most devastating of these scenes occurs immediately after this, when Lenny finally takes Lila out for the lobster dinner he has been promising her since their arrival in Miami Beach. May foreshadows Lenny's debasement at his own hands by opening the scene with a brief shot of a lobster presented on a silver platter; when the hapless crustacean twitches, still alive, the unseen waiter's hand knocks it on the head until it lies, unmoving, on the platter.[27] The couple's romantic dinner goes from bad to worse as Lenny tries to muster up the courage to tell Lila their marriage is over. In a visual echo of the wedding scene, the other diners who react with suspicion and horror to Lenny's behavior are almost all women (see Figures 5.3 and 5.4).

May locates these women at the edge of the frame, and on occasion between Lenny and Lila, regarding Lenny with raised eyebrows and concerned glances as he debases himself first with his tantrum about the promised pecan pie dessert, and then with lies and exaggerations as Lila falls apart. Lenny never recognizes their gaze—none of them are to be looked upon, by him, as sexual objects—but once more, May's gaze and our own zeroes in on these women's gazing at the gaze. It's one of the film's most explicit textual critiques of Lenny, easy to miss if one zeroes in on Lenny and Lila, but hiding in plain sight nonetheless.

Figures 5.3 and 5.4 Female onlookers gazing at the gaze (from *The Heartbreak Kid*, 1972).

The lobster dinner sequence bookends Lila's position (in Lenny's eyes) as abject. This is echoed in Lenny's assertion, regarding the pecan pie, that he's been "talking about that pie as far back as Virginia"; Virginia is also the first time we see Lila as abject through Lenny's gaze. When Lenny laughs and tells Lila, "I want out of the marriage," she is dumbstruck. Immediately, tears tumble down her cheeks as she tells her husband she's going to be sick. Unable to cope with her response, Lenny forces her to drink water, chastising her for making a fuss (oblivious to the fact that every woman in the restaurant has been critiquing him with her gaze all night), even as she begs him to help her to the ladies' room so she can throw up.

Once more, May radicalizes the objectified female subject as Lila's hurt and disappointment threaten to explode in a geyser of vomit; once more, in Lenny's eyes, she becomes abject. However, in being freed (although against her will) from Lenny, Lila emerges, in a manner later articulated by Kristeva: "During that course in which 'I' become, I give birth to myself amid the violence of sobs, of vomit."[28] As Lila sobs, gasping for air, Lenny once more, as he did in Virginia, criticizes the sounds she makes, her cries disrupting his Symbolic Order.

It is Lila's final appearance in the film, and with her exit the warm heart of the film is snuffed out; the film literally goes cold when she is removed from the narrative, plunging Lenny into snow-capped Minnesota. It's not over for Lenny, of course, and it is in Minnesota that Lenny delivers Simon's masterstroke of male idiocy—the famous "There is no deceit in the cauliflower" speech over dinner—as he reveals his complete lack of understanding of midwestern American life. Through it all, Lenny is fixed in the laser-like stare of Mr Corcoran, and once more Soloway's notion of the Heroine's Journey being represented within a male protagonist's, "spiraling in an ever illuminated self-punishing story of having enraged or engaged the male gaze," rings true.

May reserves one final claustrophobic mid-shot for the film's final image (see Figure 5.5), and in positioning Lenny as alone at his own wedding to Kelly, May once more allows her framing to deliver her critique of her protagonist. It's a haunting final image, but it's also, on May's part, damning: Lenny has abandoned everything about himself—his Jewish identity and family, his sense of belonging—in pursuit of his fantasies of assimilation, and found himself ultimately alone. This is no accident; as Vincent Canby wrote in his review for *New York Times* at the time of the film's release, "behind the laughs there is, for a change, a real understanding of character—which is something that I suspect, can be attributed to Miss May."[29] May reserves one final barb for the closing credits, over which "The Theme From The Heartbreak Kid" is revived. This time, in contrast to the Simon & Garfunkel-esque folky arrangement that locates Lenny in his New York Jewish world in the film's opening, the song plays in a far glossier, overproduced arrangement

Figure 5.5 One last gaze at the gazer (from *The Heartbreak Kid*, 1972).

that suggests, in its Carpenters-esque tone (The Carpenters, after all, were the ultimate Californian Methodist musical group) Lenny's assimilation into the midwestern WASP nightmare.

Through the film's second half, the specter of Lenny's mistreatment of Lila looms large; as Lenny abandons Kelly at their own reception in order to talk business with guests, we're led to assume that he will, one day, drift away from Kelly (though perhaps for different reasons). Writing for *Cine-File* on the eve of a 2017 screening of *The Heartbreak Kid*, Kathleen Sachs sees May's gender as, not separate from her Jewishness, but key to her scathing critique of the character: "Lenny doesn't know he's a schmuck, but she does, and so do we—thus it's we who have the last laugh."[30] May and Berlin's presentation of Lila finds the human being inside the caricature, through whose eyes we gaze back at Lenny's gaze—we have Sachs's "last laugh." In this way, *The Heartbreak Kid* provides a compelling site within which to explore both existing and emerging notions of the gaze within feminist film theory and criticism, and it should be considered essential viewing.

NOTES

1. Anna Fields, *The Girl in the Show: Three Generations of Comedy, Culture and Feminism* (New York: Arcade Publishing, 2017).
2. Molly Haskell, "Stir Until Marriage Dissolves," *The Village Voice*, 28 December 1972.
3. Nathan Rabin, "Interview: Charles Grodin," *The AV Club*, 20 May 2009 <https://www.avclub.com/charles-grodin-1798216629> (accessed January 2019).

4. Barbara Koenig Quart, *Women Directors: The Emergence of a New Cinema* (New York: Praeger, 1988), p. 39.
5. Ibid., p. 39.
6. I thought of May casting her unflinching eye on Lenny when I watched Holofcener's tragicomic *The Land of Steady Habits* (2018), the writer-director's first film to focus on a male protagonist; Anders, that film's depressed divorcee, is as floundering as Lenny was determined.
7. Koenig Quart, p. 51.
8. "Screening Alert: Elaine May's Masterly 'The Heartbreak Kid'," Richard Brody, *The New Yorker*, 30 January 2015 <https://www.newyorker.com/culture/richard-brody/screening-alert-elaine-mays-masterful-heartbreak-kid> (accessed January 2019).
9. Indeed, for the purposes of this essay I had to rely on a YouTube upload of the film; a second-hand, now out-of-print DVD copy of the film was listed on Amazon for the price, at time of writing, of $99.99.
10. J. Hoberman, "Flaunting It: The Rise and Fall of Hollywood's 'Nice' Jewish (Bad) Boys," in J. Hoberman and Jeffrey Shandler (eds), *Entertaining America: Jews, Movies and Broadcasting* (Princeton: Princeton University Press, 2003), p. 221.
11. Ibid., p. 242.
12. Saul Austerlitz, *Another Fine Mess: A History of American Film Comedy* (Chicago: Chicago Review Press, 2010), p. 437.
13. Koenig Quart, p. 43.
14. Mary Gentile, "Review: *Women Directors: The Emergence of a New Cinema* by Barbara Koenig Quart," *Film Quarterly* 44 (1990): 63.
15. Shelley Farmer, "Why Aren't More Female and POC Directors Considered Auteurs?" *Paper*, 4 November 2015 <http://www.papermag.com/ava-du-vernay-sofia-coppola-elaine-may-auteurs-1438731738.html> (accessed January 2019).
16. Laura Mulvey, "Visual Pleasure and Narrative Cinema," *Screen*, 16.3 (October 1975): 18.
17. Roberta Sassatelli, "Interview With Laura Mulvey: Gender, Gaze and Technology in Film Culture," *Theory, Culture & Society* 28 (2011): 130.
18. Jill Soloway, "The Female Gaze—TIFF: Master Class," Topple Productions, 11 September 2016 <https://www.toppleproductions.com/the-female-gaze> (accessed January 2019).
19. Ibid.
20. Roizman worked on countless Hollywood new wave films, including *The Exorcist* (William Friedkin, 1973), *The Stepford Wives* (Bryan Forbes, 1975), *Network* (Sidney Lumet, 1976) and *Tootsie* (Sydney Pollack, 1982), on which May was an uncredited writer.
21. Julia Kristeva, *Powers of Horror: An Essay on Abjection* (New York: Columbia University Press, 1982), p. 1.
22. Ibid., p. 53.
23. Ibid., p. 45.
24. As Kaja Silverman writes, the maternal voice "functions as the acoustic mirror in which the male subject hears all the repudiated elements of his infantile babble"; *The Acoustic Mirror: The Female Voice In Psychoanalysis And Cinema* (Bloomington: Indiana University Press, 1988), p. 81.
25. It is a feeling shared by members of both the Academy of Motion Picture Arts & Sciences and Hollywood Foreign Press, who bestowed Best Supporting Actress nominations upon Berlin at the 1973 Academy Awards and Golden Globes, respectively.
26. "That of the characters at each other."
27. Amusingly, Soloway's TIFF address concludes with a poem that draws a comparison

between the female gaze and "the green stuff you find in the brain of your lobster . . . it has a million generations of lobster in it, no wonder it is scary."
28. Kristeva, p. 3.
29. Vincent Canby, "'Heartbreak Kid': Elaine May's 2nd Effort as Director Arrives," *New York Times*, 18 December 1972.
30. Kathleen Sachs, "Crucial Viewing," *CINE-FILE* (no date) <http://www.cinefile.info/?offset=1513364114709&reversePaginate=true> (accessed January 2019).

CHAPTER 6

Mikey and Nicky (1976)—Elaine May and the Cassavetes Connection

Jeremy Carr

"Like a moon in the solar system of John Cassavetes, there is Elaine May's *Mikey and Nicky*."

—David Thomson[1]

Elaine May's *Mikey and Nicky*, released in 1976, bears an obvious indebtedness to John Cassavetes, not just because of his commanding presence as one of the film's two primary stars, but in a kindred approach to cinematic form, acting style, genre adherence and modification, and narrative construction. This is not to take anything away from May, however, for what makes *Mikey and Nicky* the phenomenally original work that it is has to do with her own idiosyncratic vision, and how she absorbs and manipulates the Cassavetes persona and the Cassavetes formula to suit her own ambitions. It is evident May built the film around a particular brand of filmic drama, one conducive to an unpolished aesthetic Cassavetes helped popularize. It is candid cinema, hinging on unrestrained, painfully intimate physicality and an audacious desire to push all facets of viewer engagement beyond the norm. Each influencing and complementing the other, May and Cassavetes revel in a shared penchant for authentic spontaneity, improvisational interactions, and turn-on-a-dime digressions.

That May and Cassavetes would eventually unite for a feature film should not be surprising, as each grew out of similar performative environments. Cassavetes' enrollment in New York's American Academy of Dramatic Arts led to opportunities in regional theater acting with the Army Reserves' performing group, and finally, to appearances on television and his first starring film role, in 1957's *Edge of the City*. Around that time, using whatever clout he was able to accumulate, he and theater director Burt Lane formed The

Cassavetes-Lane Workshop, where actors arbitrarily created scenes based on rough character outlines and scenarios. The plan was to take these cursory inventions and develop the result into a feature film, a methodology that motivated Cassavetes' 1959 directorial debut, *Shadows*, an unrefined passion project heavily indebted to the illuminating process of improvisation. Manic and wildly unpredictable, this form of filmmaking produced works of profound visual, emotional, and tonal vitality. It was a process that continued throughout Cassavetes' career, relatively consistent in the films he wrote and directed, though seldom achieved in his roles for other filmmakers. *Mikey and Nicky* is the great exception.

Of course, there are also aspects of *Mikey and Nicky* that originate from May's own sundry background, from the Philadelphia setting, where she was born, to her appreciation of free-wheeling collaboration. May studied acting in Los Angeles before moving to Chicago in 1955, where she became a member of The Compass Players, a theatrical group that, much like Cassavetes' clique, was devoted to artful improvisation, with a decidedly more comedic, satirical bent. May's most prominent early alliance was with Mike Nichols, who attended the University of Chicago with May and with her formed the improv comedy duo, Nichols and May. In 1960, the recording of their Broadway debut, a sold-out event, won a Grammy Award for Best Comedy Performance, but in late 1961 the two went their separate ways. Just over ten years later May wrote, directed, and starred in her first film, *A New Leaf* (1971). A dark take on the romantic comedy, *The Heartbreak Kid*, followed up in 1972.

Mikey and Nicky began as a potential one-act play written between May's late-teenage years and her time with The Compass Players. Peter Falk first heard of the project when he was acting with her in in the 1967 film *Luv*, adapted from Murray Schisgal's acclaimed Broadway comedy. As Falk tells it, "In the course of one night, Elaine told me about this story, it was based on real people in a real neighborhood, people that were close to her, whom she had known when she was child. She remembered it very vividly and it caused in her a need to write it. I thought it was a helluva story."[2] May was concurrently swept up in the whirlwind of John Cassavetes' social and creative circle, showing up for readings of his latest screenplays and talking about *Mikey and Nicky* as her newest venture. An intrigued Cassavetes told Falk that if May were to direct and Falk were also to appear, he knew it would be a good film.[3] What nobody could know at the time was that *Mikey and Nicky* would also be May's penultimate feature.

Once May secured funding for *Mikey and Nicky*, accomplished only after she had made *A New Leaf* and *The Heartbreak Kid*, she and her team were off and running, and she and Cassavetes were firmly united in a riotous coalition. As Marshall Fine puts it, "She matched his tenacity with her own neurotic perfectionism," and the two shared a "maverick spirit and sense of cinematic adventure."[4] It was a mutual pursuit molded by collective ideals and a reciprocated artistic temperament, manifest throughout the production, starting with the script. While the extent to which Cassavetes influenced the screenplay remains debatable (in any event, only May received credit), many involved with *Mikey and Nicky* presume a fair amount of cooperation. "Though it was definitely May's film," writes Fine, producer Michael Hausman said Cassavetes was a strong influence: "For them, it was like a personal, private movie," he said. "She admired Cassavetes as a filmmaker and they had a lot of discussion of how to shoot it."[5] Frank Yablans, former president at Paramount, similarly stated, "I'm sure John had input to the script. John and Elaine were very close,"[6] and, as Fine also contends, on *Mikey and Nicky*, May was "always in consultation with Peter and John. It was a lot of collective effort, a lot of time spent discussing stuff."[7] That said, this collaborative atmosphere did little to reign in the production's unfettered status. For May, this was a long-gestating project, having undergone various prior iterations, and the problem, as May associate Hausman puts it, was that she had wanted to make the film for so long that it became hard to commit to one idea: "She'd seen it so many ways in her head," he said. "Certain people shouldn't be put in that kind of box."[8]

The permissiveness of *Mikey and Nicky's* formation carries over to the realization of its character types, emphatically personified by Cassavetes' character Nicky Godalin. Disheveled and distraught, whiskers peppering his exhausted, angular face, Nicky's physical condition and expressions of bewilderment are only enhanced by the haphazard way in which May initiates the narrative and begins to move the film along. What she holds back in terms of exposition and development, she communicates in behavior, in this case Nicky's evident anxiety. Like the vivid settings that house Cassavetes' own filmic spheres, scenic details also prove indispensable to the inhabited world of *Mikey and Nicky*. The film is built from an assembly of everyday details, rather than grand storylines, forming an intricate tapestry of textures, as authentic as they are revealing: an ashtray loaded with crumpled cigarettes, wrinkled, untucked clothing, streaked car windows, cracker crumbs and empty beer cans. In other words, people live here, and here, gun in hand, Nicky is a paranoid mess. Amidst a perilous preexisting drama, the camera's erratic focus reflects his own touch-and-go coherence.

May will not immediately shed light on the situation; only gradually will she introduce ostensibly random bits of background and current concern. What is revealed, in abstract at first, is that a contract has likely been placed on Nicky's life, decreed by mobster David Reznick (Sanford Mesiner) and enacted by low-rent hitman Kinney (Ned Beatty). It seems Nicky stole money from his underworld bosses and, as such things go, his life is now in danger. None of this is divulged straightaway, and truth be told, it is the least interesting part of what occurs in the film. In any case, to assist in his plight, to perhaps provide some answers, or, minimally, to keep him company, Nicky rings fellow gangster Mikey (Falk), his best friend of more than thirty years. Their obvious closeness, based if nothing else on the fact that Nicky instinctively beckons Mikey before anyone else, suggests their mutual value and promotes a critical familiarity. Surpassing the fundamental plot of *Mikey and Nicky*, then, is the expansion of the personal and professional history of these two men, a framework littered with defects and detours. In this way, *Mikey and Nicky* is perpetually incomplete. Like much of Cassavetes' work, which tends to exist in the here and now with no cognizance of the past or future, there is something that resembles forward momentum in *Mikey and Nicky*, propelled by spatial movement and temporal advancement, but it is as if the gaps in this course have simply been glossed over in favor of a more heedless, arguably more bona fide immediacy.

It is clear, though, that there is the instant potential of a double-cross, and yet even this development mirrors a classic Cassavetes pattern, wherein a given narrative component generates reserved trepidation, because of what is left indefinite or never processed in full. Disquiet is therefore born from not knowing what a certain character is planning, and what he or she may do next, from one minute to another. Anything seems possible. This unbound suspense lingers throughout *Mikey and Nicky*, largely because of its piecemeal portrait, a sketch that leaves the viewer unassured and doubting of its intentions. There is from this a connected edginess and resulting discomfort, as one witnesses a film in which nothing proceeds as it would in a conventional drama. As is common in Cassavetes' films, characters do not behave as they do in "normal" movies. Rather, and this is quite different from even May's other three features, the two noted above and the ill-fated *Ishtar* (1987), these people are not "movie people"; they are more realistic, existing in an only slightly removed, fabricated existence that is unnerving because of just how faithfully impulsive it all is.

Nevertheless, May sustains a story within the madness of *Mikey and Nicky*'s surface form, effectively confirming Nicky's suspicions about Mikey and his role in the impending hit, bringing to light their past antagonisms and disclosing impartial glimpses of the two men and their homelife; Nicky's wife, Jan (Joyce Van Patten), has left him and taken their children to her mother's house, while Mikey's wife, Annie (Rose Arrick), sits up all night with their young son. But even these instances of substantial character accompaniment are referred to in roundabout ways or briefly seen as superfluous asides, almost as a way of filling in the blanks and cultivating a modicum of backstory while adding plot points that may or may not prove relevant but form a blanket narrative field: they are details to enliven the film, not necessarily to substantiate it.

Mikey denies Nicky's repeated suspicions with attempts to assure him and calm him down, but Nicky's apprehension grows increasingly apparent, initially and effectively ratified when the two are preparing to depart Nicky's motel and Nicky insists Mikey and he swap coats, lest there be an assassin lying in wait. The request indicates his warranted skepticism, but it also hints at the unsound integrity of their relationship, where a passive-aggressive trust is tinged with implicit misgiving. The thorny sensation continues when they arrive at a local tavern, where Mikey slips away to phone Kinney and tension mounts as he routinely checks the clock, awaiting an affirmative rejoinder. In scenes like these, banking on Falk's affable screen persona, his inclusion proved ideal casting for May, not only because of his established relationship with Cassavetes, adding meta-weight to their depicted friendship, but because of his genial status on TV's *Columbo* (1971–2003). It is part of May's blatant inclination for deception and upending expectations. Surely, one thinks while watching this beloved, bedraggled nice guy, he could not be sneaking around and plotting to have his supposed best friend killed, a friend played by John Cassavetes no less. Such an on-/off-screen association likewise distinguishes Cassavetes' work, where the small stock company could generate a fictional overlap with reality.

Although he is evidently on edge for his own duplicitous reasons, Mikey is a relatively reassuring presence, the yin to the yang of Cassavetes' Nicky in terms of composure and communication. Falk plays the comparatively rational caregiver, one not far removed from his Nick Longhetti in Cassavetes' 1974 film, *A Woman Under the Influence*, where he similarly attends to his partner (Gena Rowlands' unstable Mabel), who is also in a state of physical and emotional hysteria. Conversely, Mikey acts toward Nicky like a doting parent or protective older sibling, a type of familial relationship with parallels in prior and subsequent Cassavetes work: see the discordant family of *Shadows*, for example, or later, the madcap brother and sister of 1984's *Love Streams*. Nicky's desperation as he arranges for their meeting ("Mikey, I'm in trouble") is countered by Mikey's arrival, his sing-songy pleading, his assurances based on their past relationship ("What way am I gonna see you I haven't seen you before?") and his paternal embrace, hands clasped around a sobbing Nicky's head. As if attending to a child, Mikey is essentially required to force-feed his partner in crime, introducing Nicky's ulcer medicine with, "Open the door. Let the train come in." He also worries about him catching a cold on top of the stomach condition: "That's all I need." This is standard terrain for both Cassavetes *and* May, with each having explored problematic relations before and since, where the protagonist is seldom a solo player but is part of a family unit or partnership, romantic or otherwise. As far as *Mikey and Nicky*, this theme appears to have additionally significant autobiographical connotations for May. As Jonathan Rosenbaum writes, Stanley Kauffmann (who called *Mikey and Nicky* "the best film that I know by an American woman") notes that the picture's title echoes the name Mike Nichols (just the names of two

Figure 6.1 From *Mikey and Nicky* (Elaine May, 1976).

people call to mind a performing theatrical team), and "even a detail in a speech by Mikey towards the end of the film—about his kid brother losing all his hair—may have been prompted by Nichols having lost his hair as a boy."[9]

Falk's placement in *Mikey and Nicky* has its own incentive, from his association with May and Cassavetes to the import of his iconic identity, but this type of performance art is most aptly suited to Cassavetes himself. He appears naturally at home with such material and, by comparison, does not give the impression of playing a character, at least not a unique character, so much as he seems to fit into a recognized personality seen elsewhere in his own directorial crop, embodied by himself or others. There is an elusiveness to the behavior of both men, with so much suggested by shrewd gestures and glances and, especially when it comes to Cassavetes, his sweaty grimaces, his wild, wide-eyed paranoia, his pained fretfulness, and his mischievous grin, hinting at what may dwell beneath the simmering insanity. Cassavetes' expressions divulge a recklessness and a teeming energy just waiting to burst forth. But with so much inferred by facial contortions and irregular movements, by what is implied and unsaid, one is left to interpret these mannerisms without a firm compass. "It would be hard to overstate the unusualness of Cassavetes' decision to let the actors bear the expressive burden in his work," writes Ray Carney in reference to Cassavetes' own authorial stance. "It is extremely rare for a director to use the acting—the faces, bodies, and movements of individuals—and not the impetus of the narrative, the abstract meaning of characters' speech, or the visual and acoustic style, to carry the meaning."[10] Rare, but perfectly emulated by May, who likewise induces, indeed demands, active spectator commitment. As Carney insists, "Conceptions are easier to deal with than perceptions. Statements of intention are easier to understand than presentations of behavior."[11] Tracing this strain of influence to *Mikey and Nicky*, this is Cassavetes doing Cassavetes, but only so far as May dictates. By contrast, one need look no further than the actor's Oscar-nominated turn in *The Dirty Dozen* (Robert Aldrich, 1967) or his appearance in *Rosemary's Baby* (Roman Polanski, 1968)—two fine performances, but neither quintessential achievements—to see that he and May are riding a similar wavelength. Their respective crests are what gives *Mikey and Nicky* its tangible vibrancy.

Making such connections even more demanding is the often abhorrent conduct of not just Mikey and Nicky, but other comparable Cassavetes protagonists who are similarly keen to pick fights and seem to desire external struggle. One obvious antecedent is Seymour Cassel's oddball charmer Seymour Moskowitz, from Cassavetes' *Minnie and Moskowitz* (1971). He too has an awkward social disposition, struggling to fit in with orthodox society and communicating too much and yet not enough, usually to the mutual befuddlement of himself and whoever it is he interacts with. Some of this has to do with an innately gregarious personality, outgoing and vociferous, but more perplexing is the tendency to engage in unnecessary conflict, as when Nicky picks a fight with unknowing African-American men at a bar. Why do it? What is there to gain?

Mikey and, especially, Nicky have a sheer lack of societal awareness, and a refusal to adhere to customs of decorum. It is a stance that informs *Mikey and Nicky* as a whole. With its occasionally off-putting tone—for many, it is too erratic for its own good—the film and its characters are utterly unconcerned with anything beyond their immediate situation, forgoing the perception of complete understanding and rescinding to the here and the now and the insular. For men like Mikey and Nicky, for men like Seymour Moskowitz, for those who live within a self-absorbed shell with little regard for the outside world and the people who inhabit it, someone like erstwhile prostitute Nellie (Carol Grace), one of Nicky's presumed stable of lovers, is an individual curiosity. When she declares her responsiveness to what is happening in Indochina, Mikey and Nicky are bemused by her attention. On one hand, Mikey says it is unusual for pretty girls to also be smart, but on the other, this disbelief stems from the customary view that, in most cases (in nearly all of Cassavetes' work, save for *Shadows* with its racial significance), these characters have little interest in current affairs, and the films themselves exist apart from such a broad context. Only May's *Ishtar*—a film discussed at length in the next chapter—has any trace of geopolitical acuity, and that is pushing it to say the least.

When individuals like Mikey and Nicky, or those in Cassavetes' films, do participate in the outside world, the peripheral interactions are rarely crucial but are an illustrative part of their mania and their strained social interface. At times, there is a peculiar fascination in this communal incompatibility, as when Nicky insults a stranger on a bus, blowing her a raspberry in an act of childish, impetuous humor—it is still humor all the same. And when he and Mikey repeatedly revert to teenage shenanigans, careless belligerence, and juvenile banter, it is equal part Cassavetes' conversation, part May's comedic schtick. But the bus ride scene in *Mikey and Nicky*, with its verbal back and forth and brutal crescendo, epitomizes the best and worst of this interactive manner. The hapless female victim of Nicky's abuse asserts her reluctance to start up with his "element," a phrasing that reduces Nicky to a giddy, perverted schoolboy, but that train of thought is derailed when Mikey casually observes, "You got big hands." So far, so innocent, and securely amusing. Yet as May continually overturns moments of consolation, after what seems like good-natured ribbing, Nicky lashes out at the bus driver with an unruly assault.

The men in Cassavetes' *Faces* (1968) and *Husbands* (1970) are the same way. They have a devilish charm, unbridled and unable to be contained, happily existing in their own world, clomping down stairs, screaming, and kicking at doors. They live in a world of unaffected instability, an unending in-joke where only they know the punchline. But this can go too far, even between Mikey and Nicky. Any wavering resentment between the two tottering friends comes to a head and reaches a point of no return when Nicky tosses Mikey's cherished watch, a gift from his departed father, and it shatters. As Mikey laments the item he has prized for twenty years, Nicky quips, "That's long enough." And as they pick up the pieces, Nicky adds insult to injury: "You don't have the time, do you?" It is darkly funny for the viewer, and Nicky, but Mikey is not laughing. "You think this is a joke?" he responds. He has had enough and seizes the moment to voice a latent agitation with their friendship generally, with the sort of brutal honesty so patent in Cassavetes' own brand of cinematic catharsis, especially in *Faces* and *Husbands*, as noted above, but even in a less representative example like *Too Late Blues* (1961), in which Bobby Darin's jazz musician has a transformative falling-out with his buddies. "I don't think you love anyone but you," Mikey says. "Don't you have any notion of anything that goes on outside of your own head? Don't you have any idea how people feel?" Nicky takes his jokes too far. He is the worst of Cassavetes' own penchant for shiftless, insensitive protagonists; he takes advantage of his already soured rapport with Mikey, which, who knows, may have been a catalyst for his betrayal to begin with. "I don't want you to be my friend just when there's nobody else around," Mikey remarks. "Unless you're sick or in trouble, you don't even know I'm alive."

Although Mikey is the reasonably tamer of the two, he is nonetheless prone to his own emotional eruptions, leaping over a counter and assailing a cashier who will not sell him cream without coffee. His agitated exuberance is perhaps generated by his genuine concern for Nicky, but it is also likely the result of what he knows he has to do or has already done. After this creamer incident, he slips and falls while rushing back to the motel, a bit of artless, accidental business far more common in the Cassavetes canon than it is in May's. Akin to Cassavetes' output, *Mikey and Nicky* commonly accentuates physicality, with bodies in ceaseless motion and combustion, with the titular companions falling all over their setting and each other. This can at times be naturalistic, as in the simple act of tripping, but the extent of their commotion also seems inflated, as if there were no physical filter for their acting out, playfully rolling around, or violently fighting, and doing so in excruciating proximity to one another and the public at large. They can never settle at a stable condition, which in turn affects the constitution of the picture itself, which seems capable of heading any which way no matter the expectations of a given situation.

Again, this is an aspect of *Mikey and Nicky* that makes it difficult for one who may feel left out or realigned within the narrative, but it reinforces the stress on two old friends who have an overpowering informality. Though their friendship is lasting, it is also untenable. While they are best friends frequently joking with each other, goading each other on, these are not the likable cohorts seen in May's buddy comedy *Ishtar*, lovable rogues played by equally likable actors Warren Beatty and Dustin Hoffman. The opposition between Cassavetes and Falk is acerbically affectionate, like that between Cassavetes, Falk, and Ben Gazzara in *Husbands*, where individual quirks work against a firm cohesion of sympathetic personalities. It is also as if they, and by extension May, could not care less about relatable protagonists so long as they convey genuine traits, heightened by unfiltered emotions and uncertainties. To that end, rather than a conventional plot, the friendship of this contentious tale is where the heart of it lies, while the story remains a largely immaterial consideration.

Subtly growing from this syndrome (though subtle seems strange to say given the voraciousness and indulgence of the film) is a portrait of effusive male bonding. In this, *Mikey and Nicky* has its most obvious equivalent with Cassavetes' *Husbands*. As also seen in that film, the relationships between men can yield an anomalous antagonism, so fiery one wonders how they ever became friends to begin with, and what exactly is the basis for their enduring solidarity. The rapport between Mikey and Nicky has been ongoing, yes, but was it ever that strong? How can people like this stand to be around one another? These are questions worth posing in more than one Cassavetes film, most of which bristle with constant quarrels and verbal and physical outbursts, and they are certainly questions germane to *Mikey and Nicky*.

Still, as alarmingly genuine as it may be (to be sure, these characters can at times be downright despicable), one is willing to entertain a degree of discomfort and revulsion, so long as the true colors shine through. Of men like Mikey and Nicky, Hausman commented, "I don't think you wanted to be them, but you know them."[12] Just as this was common with May, who filled her prior two films with rather dislikable male protagonists, Cassavetes also recognized the complexity of his creations, who may be abrasive but are undeniably sincere. "You can *trust* my characters," he argued. "Whatever they are—and they're not always nice—at least they're upfront."[13] And somehow, they can even end up endearing. Nicky expresses an inkling of regret when he acknowledges Mikey's unwillingness to help any further—"I did too much to him"—and for his part, Mikey's shame comes though when he cries out to be removed from Kinney's car as it appears to hurtle toward a fleeing Nicky; later, there is the slight suggestion Nicky was possibly delaying the murder all along. So, while *Mikey and Nicky* has a murderous finale, as far as its fundamental themes go, the conclusion is open-ended. As I've written elsewhere, "There is a wobbly acclimation process that wraps up *A Woman Under the Influence*, both for the viewer and the characters. But as with the unsettled conclusions of *Faces* and *Husbands*"—and this applies to *Mikey and Nicky*—"the question of whether anything has been accomplished remains."[14]

Though it is like Cassavetes' *Husbands*, May's interest in male camaraderie and paradoxically bonding enmity is unique to her prior productivity, with nothing to previously indicate such insight. Filmmaker Jesse Noah Klein writes, "The relationship between Mikey and Nicky is the fullest, barest, most honest depiction I've seen of the knotted entanglements—the resentments so scarring they can only be born of love—that exist in a fraternal bond."[15] And just as it is in Cassavetes' cinema, so too is the masculine mold of *Mikey and Nicky* shaped around a precarious amalgam of cruelty, honesty, and volatility, all of which threaten the limitations of time-honored cordiality. "May uses the pair's dichotomy to deliver her most blistering critique of male sociality," writes Jake Cole, "no mean feat," he adds, "for the maker of *The Heartbreak Kid*."[16] Mikey and Nicky pride themselves on their autonomy, but they prove to be roundly dependent, not only on men of their same criminal set, but also their family, to whom both ultimately go running. *Mikey and Nicky* "mocks their bravado and projected cool," states Cole, "but it uses the two men to make a larger comment on how men interpret the notion of responsibility and self-reliance."[17] This holds true with *Husbands*, where for all their carousing and determined independence, two of the three male leads revert back to their familiar domestic arenas.

At the same time, for films so preoccupied with the all-purpose predominance of male behavior, entries like *Mikey and Nicky* and *Husbands* are nevertheless revealing studies of male–female contention. As Richard Brody observes:

> The lack of sympathy, even the cruelty, of men toward women in Cassavetes's films is one side of a battle in which men are fighting with

and against women—even the women they love—for their lives and their identities, against their better natures and better judgment. For May, the stakes are different.[18]

"May's judgment on manhood is harsh," he continues, "it entails renunciation, submission, humiliation, and the willingness to betray and to break the relationships forged in the heat of male bonding. Or, to be a man, one must stop being one of the guys."[19] It is certainly the case that with just four features to her name, betrayal is one of the dominant motifs of May's directorial corpus. "All four of her films to date include the same obsessive theme," Rosenbaum notes, "the secret betrayal of one member of a couple by the other ... But only in *Mikey and Nicky* is this theme pushed to its limits, beyond comedy."[20] To be sure, there is a marked tonal difference between *Mikey and Nicky* and *A New Leaf*, *The Heartbreak Kid*, and *Ishtar*. As Vincent Canby observes, the earlier two "were comedies of sometimes inspired and often touching lunacy, mostly about the uncertain progress of romantic love between men and women." While those films take shape as fairly commonplace comedies, with duplicity played for laughs and seldom suggesting dire repercussions, *Mikey and Nicky* "is something else entirely."[21]

"Films about the fierce bond of platonic male friendship litter cinema," writes Cole, "but *Mikey and Nicky* suggests that such a thing is illusory, and that a quintessentially masculine drive for self-preservation will always override loyalty for one's buddy."[22] But this cannot be. Despite all that is revealed, an optimistic audience holds out hope that Mikey and Nicky will not just make amends but will reach some sort of understanding and place of safety. It is a testament to the trusting nature of their friendship, and it especially testifies to Nicky's perseverance, his not wanting to believe in what he sees and suspects, his desperation for a few more good times before it all comes crashing down. A similar fatalism infuses *Husbands*, where the prospect of looming death prompts the living to make the most of whatever time they have left. It is to May's credit, and to the credit of Falk and Cassavetes in tandem, that the potential for peace is so obstinately persuasive.

Their consequent conduct begs the question of whether or not their view of what transpires can be trusted or validated. As character guides, these two men are highly unreliable. Nicky's delusional demeanor is conceivably deceiving while Mikey's denials are obviously upended by his actions. And still, so convincing are these performances—Cassavetes' and Falk's, Nicky's and Mikey's—that the eccentricity seems par for the course. Cassavetes liked to keep audiences similarly off balance and insecure with his material, with scenes that "begin and end in what would be the middle of the scene in a more conventional film," as Fine writes.[23] Ray Carney elaborates on this:

Explicit motivations and predictable plotlines were in many ways inconsequential and deliberately discomforting: "That's why my pictures are so long! Hours of beginnings, no endings."[24]

Earlier in this book, Carney noted:

Cassavetes played mind games with his actors to elicit desired results and he took a similarly antagonistic approach to audiences ... He did not care what people thought of his films. What mattered most was the instinctive response, good or bad. "It doesn't matter whether audiences like it; it matters whether they *feel* something," he explained.[25]

What makes the betrayal of *Mikey and Nicky* so powerful is the longevity of the friendship presented. The lineage of Mikey and Nicky, though indiscriminately developed, is potent enough to add a corresponding worth to what is at stake. The two address this directly, as Nicky in a way pleads for his shelter by encouraging the remembrance of things past, in the hopes it may provide a buffer to assuage the tension or at least buy him some time. "I think that's the reason we're such good friends," he says at one point. "Because we remember each other from when we were kids. Things that happened when we were kids that no one else knows about but us in our heads. That's how we know they really happened." But Mikey is not buying it. "What are you talking about? I really know what happened when I was a kid." Nicky is not immune to the compelling proposition of memory, though. He is genuinely in awe that Nicky can remember the piano keys taught to him by his sister, and he wants to make sure his wife likes to hear about his childhood. When they visit the grave of Nicky's mother (Mikey attended the burial), the two contemplate issues of life, death, love, and friendship, with the same sort of casual profundity that Cassavetes incorporates into his work. This understated emphasis on the past is unusual for a film generally consumed by the central present, but *Mikey and Nicky* finds a satisfying balance. In fact, it adds considerable weight to the final suburban showdown of the film, where, as critic Don L. Stradley notes, Mikey "knows that Nicky's murder will knock a hole in his past. (In Denmark, the movie was released as *Chased by the Past*, which is an apt title.)"[26]

As all of this is happening, May drops in scenes of the pursuit, obligatory reminders that Kinney is still on the trail and that within this thematic frame there is still a basic premise taking place. Even so, Kinney's search is representative of her broader structural orientation. Almost as a self-conscious reflection of thwarted progression, his quest is halted in a model example of real life impeding the constructed device of the film; he gets lost and has to ask for directions, he has to drive around because of No Parking signs, and he shows up too late and just misses Mikey and Nicky. For all of its apparent randomness, though, these types of scenes were, for May, all part of her stimulating strategy, even if what happened as a result could deviate considerably. A script was written and generally followed but May encouraged breaks from the written word and allowed deviations and additions from both actors.

Writing about the making of *Ishtar* in the 16 March 1987 issue of *New York Magazine*, David Blum attributes May's penchant for radical indulgence and extensive improvisation as a possible cause for her lack of productivity. "To understand why Elaine May had not worked behind a camera in over a decade," he states, "it is necessary to flash back to *Mikey and Nicky*." He goes on to relay the oft-cited time when May was shooting well into the early morning hours and, even though she had already gone through several cameramen and the film was "way over budget with hundreds of hours of film in the can," she continued to allow the camera to roll as Cassavetes and Falk "talked to each other in and out of character about whatever happened to be on their minds." At one point, Blum continues, "Falk had walked down the block to talk to a friend, and Cassavetes wandered off the set entirely. Still, the camera kept running ... After several minutes of shooting film of a scene with no actors in it, the new camera operator called 'Cut!' and turned off the camera." To this, May jumped from her seat and chastised the cameraman, arguing only she, as the director, was permitted to say "cut." The camera operator agreed but added that the two stars had left. "Yes," came May's reply, "but they might come back." As Blum suggests, and as May herself acknowledged when the Museum of Modern Art honored *Mikey and Nicky* in 1986, such leniency left the powers-that-be rather wary of her methodology. "It was difficult for me to get directing jobs because I seemed sort of crazy," she said.[27]

Nevertheless, this freedom produced a film abounding in circuitous dialogue, a word salad of insinuations and references, and a deference to spur-of-the-moment decision-making. Mikey and Nicky could go see a girl, or maybe to a movie; maybe they would just get a drink. This indecisiveness, as if there was a basic plan but May, Cassavetes, and Falk were free to go any direction from there, yields a series of vacillating arrangements, as if the film was at the whim of these aimless characters. Liberated from traditional plot structures, celebrating a non-narrative and episodic format, the release comes through in the film: "What are you talking about?" Mikey asks Nicky, as if he himself is confused by the path of their conversation. And when Nicky arrives at his mother's tombstone, he hesitates: "Now that I'm here, I don't know what to do."

That this casual construction still manages to work so well has to do with *Mikey and Nicky*'s relatively rudimentary scenario and the fact that, as Cassavetes would often do, May operates within a durable form, where the intricacies of the set-up are allied with the superficial qualities of a given genre. As a result, the customary plot development is not entirely necessary, so long as the formulaic basics are established, providing a sort of buffer against which the more polemical and unusual features can be bounced. With its stress on criminals and hit men, the gangster genre is a convenient place for *Mikey and Nicky*, helpful for the promotion of the film and substantiating it on a foundation of familiar tropes. Such genre reworking was assuredly familiar for Cassavetes, who took a similar approach with his version of romantic comedy (*Minnie and Moskowitz*), backstage drama (*Opening Night*, 1977), and the gangster film (*Gloria*, 1980 and *The Killing of a Chinese Bookie*, 1976), where there is a similar sense of basic generic groundwork, but what succeeds from there is where each film's originality lies.

By resisting broad conformity, Cassavetes' films and a film like *Mikey and Nicky* stand apart from the Hollywood mainstream. "Cassavetes' films cannot be considered as either simply belonging to Hollywood narrative traditions or simply serving as part of some anti-Hollywood project," writes George Kouvaros. "Cassavetes' films and career mark out a resolutely 'impure' or hybrid form of film practice, later carried on in the work of directors such as Elaine May, [Martin] Scorsese, Paul Schrader, and others, that operates on the fringes of Hollywood filmmaking, using its traditions and narrative forms but at the same time undermining the cohesiveness and drive to resolution of those narrative forms."[28] *Mikey and Nicky* may have its mob bosses in plush leather chairs, its card games and shootouts, but like *The Killing of a Chinese Bookie*, "the binding scenarios of film noir—betrayal, murder, and conspiracy—are reworked according to a different tempo and dramatic rhythm. Also in both films the displacement of determining action allows the filmmakers to focus directly on the dynamics of male performance."[29]

Figure 6.2 From *Mikey and Nicky* (Elaine May, 1976).

"Like the work of May, Scorsese, and Schrader," Kouvaros continues, "Cassavetes' films force us to reexamine our assumptions concerning the Hollywood cinema, its operation, and its possibilities."[30] *Mikey and Nicky*'s gritty urban texture, while hardly unique in the 1970s, was nevertheless a familiar milieu within which Cassavetes and his stalwart on- and off-screen associate Falk could flourish. Insofar as its recognizably coarse landscape, its indicative social set, its revelatory asides, and the infantile roughhousing between men burdened by antipathy and unwavering loyalty, May's film also recalls, as J. Hoberman has pointed out, "the period's other great non-Cassavetes Cassavetes film, *Mean Streets*."[31] And yet even this 1973 Scorsese feature has its roots tracing back to Cassavetes, who chided Scorsese for making the exploitation film *Boxcar Bertha* in 1972 and encouraged the budding auteur to do something personal, something that meant something, something where Scorsese could infuse his individual voice and utilize his own personal experiences. It was advice that seemingly found its way through the ether and made its way to Elaine May, who similarly based the milieu and characterizations of *Mikey and Nicky* on an indefinite, though apparently illicit, incident involving her older brother back in Philadelphia.[32]

For whittling down what amounted to more than a million feet of film (almost three times as much as was shot for *Gone with the Wind*, 1939),[33] acknowledgment goes to editors John Carter and Sheldon Kahn, the former having worked with May on *The Heartbreak Kid*. So much seems to be happening, so many places are visited and side characters introduced, that *Mikey and Nicky* would seem to be a much longer film that it is, which with a surprisingly condensed narrative, comprising just a few hours, runs only 119 minutes. Furthermore, much of what distinguishes *Mikey and Nicky*, and emphasizes its Cassavetes-esque parallels, is also attributed to the film's five cinematographers, among them Lucien Ballard and Victor J. Kemper, who left the production after a few days' worth of arguing with May. "Her filmmaking style," writes Jessica Kiang, "which was to have three cameras left rolling for long periods of time as the actors worked and reworked the scenes, gives it an almost unbearably naturalistic feel that owes a great debt to, and arguably surpasses, some of Cassavetes' own directorial work."[34] (Indeed, Cassavetes himself stepped behind the camera for at least one sequence, filming from the backseat Ned Beatty's vehicular crusade.) The stopover to see Nellie is one of the more uncomfortable moments in the film, evoking *Faces*, where two or more people are encased in a combustible arena with added sexual tension. As Nicky advances on the unenthusiastic young woman, it is almost as if Mikey steps into the position of the audience, as an uncomfortable detached observer witnessing the unpleasant action, helpless in the dark but to bear witness to this repellant behavior. Eventually, though, his view become interactive, and he shifts from eyewitness to a part of its abusive surge.

Figure 6.3 From *Mikey and Nicky* (Elaine May, 1976).

May and Cassavetes have an aptitude for the detached, fly-on-the-wall depiction of intensely private moments (should we even be privy to such a scene?), where the intense juxtaposition of characters and camera placement mingle with obstinate movements in which the frame is practically bursting at the seams and preparing to overflow with action and emotion, creating a formal capriciousness. It is what Cole terms an "invasive, almost vivisectional approach." He writes that the camera's proximity is "a means for reading emotions in real time and poring over surfaces for weaknesses. Cataloging the duo like an entomologist peering at critters under a telescope."[35] Shot in natural light with hand-held buoyancy, May's inconsistent compositions are unlike her other films, which communicate a prescribed harmony of linear editing and a fixed *mise-en-scène*. Here, more like a Cassavetes film, the camera's position is occasionally extraneous, often obscured (as in *Faces*), and moving in and out of close-up with portions of the action repeatedly obstructed by the backs of people's heads or inanimate objects. The framing can be disordered, but the camera can also be unobtrusive and intimate, canvasing the characters in their oppressive settings, barely able to contain with the drama. Writes Canby, "It's a melodrama about male friendship told in such insistently claustrophobic detail that to watch it is to risk an artificially induced anxiety attack. It's nearly two hours of being locked in a telephone booth with a couple of method actors who won't stop talking, though they have nothing of interest to say, and who won't stop jiggling around, though they plainly aren't going anywhere."[36]

Whatever the on-set contention that resulted from her directorial decisions, that behind-the-scenes drama was just the start of what would soon afflict

Figure 6.4 From *Mikey and Nicky* (Elaine May, 1976).

Mikey and Nicky and, more forcefully, May as a feature filmmaker. Shot in sequence, with sixty days in Philadelphia and an additional fifty in Los Angeles, production stopped after just a few weeks for Falk to start a new season of *Columbo*. That lasted for about a month. The film's original budget of $1.8 million ballooned to more than $4.3 million and the editing was "a laborious process made more difficult by May's inductiveness." "By the end of the process," writes Fine, "even Cassavetes had lost patience with May's dithering over the editing. Jay Cocks said, 'the film was too nuts even for John, and that's saying something.'"[37] Distributed by Paramount Pictures, *Mikey and Nicky* originally had a summer 1976 release, but delays set it back to 21 December, which in turn allowed the studio to possess the film and enact its own final cut privilege. Sporadic acquisitions and intermittent exhibition continued throughout the following decade. What looked bleak for May was only intensified by her fourth and final feature film as director, *Ishtar*, considered one of the biggest debacles in American film history. May would not direct another film until 2016, when she helmed a television documentary about Mike Nichols.

In words that could describe nearly every film written and directed by John Cassavetes, Sam Price writes that *Mikey and Nicky*, "hangs in an odd limbo between comedy and drama; between financial disaster and artistic accomplishment. It's a maudlin, fitfully comical piece that always feels as if it's on the verge of darting off a precipice—something that was surely mimicked off-screen as well as on." But, he continues, "What Peter Biskind pejoratively wrote off as May's downfall—her 'looniness'—I see as her primary attribute as director."[38] Josh Larsen is not convinced. The question remains whether

Mikey and Nicky "might have been something greater in the hands of another director."

Clearly May is invested in the material—she wrote it—and deserves credit for creating a fruitfully improvisational atmosphere. Yet she doesn't leave a very distinct signature here, such as the social satire she brought to *A New Leaf* and *The Heartbreak Kid*. And in terms of craft, *Mikey and Nicky* actually represents a step backwards. Aside from focusing issues and even an instance of an errant boom mike, the movie evidences no coherent strategy for filming the volatile interactions between these two men. (The framing of a shot in a prostitute's apartment, with Nicky and the woman in the foreground darkness and Mikey in the background, standing in the illuminated kitchen, is a rare exception.)[39]

Reflected in these divergent observations, the view of *Mikey and Nicky* is complex, partly due to its own formal constitution, and partly due to its clear resemblance to the films of John Cassavetes. "The film was buried by reviews and ignored by the public," writes David Thomson. "Yet, like many of the Cassavetes projects, it has a seething intelligence at work that is reluctant to accept any formal discipline. It's not just that these two guys are unlikable (they are). It's more that their situation is not very interesting . . . All one can say is this picture serves to enlarge the strange story of her undoubted but unresolved talent."[40] Alternatively, "*Mikey and Nicky* isn't just an unusually accomplished riff on the sweaty intensity of its iconoclastic stars' oeuvre; it ranks alongside Cassavetes' best films," writes Nathan Rabin. "It's remarkable that an artist with such a strong personality and sensibility . . . was able to channel another artist's personality so compellingly and convincingly."[41] The Cassavetes influence is undeniable, but *Mikey and Nicky* is not a John Cassavetes film. This is an Elaine May film, made by someone with a reverence for the groundbreaking work that came before her, but also by someone who successfully carves out her own niche in American cinema. "Among other things," writes Hoberman, "*Mikey and Nicky* is the greatest Cassavetes film Cassavetes never made."[42] It is that, but it is so much more.

NOTES

1. David Thomson, *Have You Seen . . . ? A Personal Introduction to 1,000 Films* (New York: Alfred A. Knopf, 2008), p. 552.
2. Marshall Fine, *Accidental Genius: How John Cassavetes Invented the American Independent Film* (New York: Hyperion, 2005), pp. 314–5.
3. Ibid., p. 315.

4. Ibid., p. 315.
5. Ibid., p. 316.
6. Ibid., p. 316.
7. Ibid., p. 316.
8. Ibid., p. 316.
9. Jonathan Rosenbaum (2003), "Mikey and Nicky," DVD essay, *JonathanRosenbaum.net* <https://www.jonathanrosenbaum.net/2003/10/mikey-and-nicky-liner-notes> (accessed January 2019).
10. Ray Carney, *The Films of John Cassavetes: Pragmaticism, Modernism, and the Movies* (Cambridge: Cambridge University Press, 1994), p. 14.
11. Ibid., p. 17.
12. Interview with producer Michael Hausman on the Homevision Entertainment DVD of Elaine May's *Mikey and Nicky* (DVD: 2004).
13. Ray Carney, *Cassavetes on Cassavetes* (London: Faber and Faber, 2001), p. 170.
14. Jeremy Carr, "Great Directors: John Cassavetes," *Senses of Cinema*, 79 (2016) <http://sensesofcinema.com/2016/great-directors/john-cassavetes/#fn-27065-26> (accessed January 2019).
15. Jesse Noah Klein, "Why I Keep Returning to Mikey and Nicky," *Talkhouse* 2017 <http://www.talkhouse.com/keep-returning-mikey-nicky> (accessed January 2019).
16. Jake Cole, "Spotlight on Fandor: Mikey and Nicky," *Movie Mezzanine* 2015 <http://moviemezzanine.com/spotlight-on-fandor-mikey-and-nicky> (accessed January 2019).
17. Ibid.
18. Richard Brody, "DVD of the Week: Mikey and Nicky," *The New Yorker* (no date) <https://www.newyorker.com/culture/richard-brody/dvd-of-the-week-mikey-and-nicky> (accessed January 2019).
19. Ibid.
20. Rosenbaum (2003).
21. Vincent Canby, "'Mikey and Nicky': Film on Amity," *New York Times*, 22 December 1976 <https://www.nytimes.com/1976/12/22/archives/mikey-and-nicky-film-on-amity.html> (accessed January 2019).
22. Cole.
23. Fine, p. 260.
24. Carney, *Cassavetes on Cassavetes*, p. 493.
25. Ibid., p. 257.
26. Don L. Stradley, "This Dazzling Time, Mikey and Nicky," Don L. Stradley Blog, March 2016 <http://donstradley.blogspot.com/2016/03/mikey-and-nicky-1976.html> (accessed January 2019).
27. David Blum, "The Road to *Ishtar*," *New York Magazine*, 20.11 (16 March 1987): 34–43.
28. George Kouvaros, *Where Does it Happen? John Cassavetes and Cinema at the Breaking Point* (Minneapolis: University of Minnesota Press, 2004), pp. 91–2.
29. Ibid., p. 92.
30. Ibid., p. 92.
31. J. Hoberman, "May Days," *The Village Voice*, 14 February 2006 <https://www.villagevoice.com/2006/02/14/may-days/> (accessed January 2019).
32. Rosenbaum (2003).
33. Blum.
34. Jessica Kiang, "Retrospective: The Directorial Career of Elaine May," *IndieWire*, August 2013 <http://www.indiewire.com/2013/08/retrospective-the-directorial-career-of-elaine-may-95011/> (accessed January 2019).

35. Cole.
36. Canby (1976).
37. Fine, p. 317.
38. Sam Price, "Films that you probably haven't seen but definitely should #8—Mikey and Nicky," *Permanent Plastic Helmet,* 24 July 2011 <https://permanentplastichelmet.com/2011/07/24/films-that-you-probably-haven%E2%80%99t-seen-but-definitely-should-8-mikey-and-nicky-1976-dir-elaine-may/> (accessed January 2019).
39. Josh Larsen, "Mikey and Nicky," *Larsen on Film* (no date) <http://www.larsenonfilm.com/mikey-and-nicky> (accessed January 2019).
40. Thomson, p. 552.
41. Nathan Rabin, "Unpacking the short but prickly filmography of Elaine May," *The AV Club*, 2013 <https://film.avclub.com/unpacking-the-short-but-prickly-filmography-of-elaine-m-1798235875> (accessed January 2019).
42. Hoberman.

CHAPTER 7

Cartographies of Catastrophe— Elaine May's *Ishtar* (1987)

Dean Brandum

For Columbia Pictures the deal was irresistible: Warren Beatty, one of the world's most successful film stars had pitched them a script that was both broad farce about a pair of bumbling fools and a hat-tip to classical Hollywood comedy. Penned by a celebrated woman writer, Beatty had convinced his friend—an equally major star—to play alongside him and it was to be directed by a member of the famed Nichols and May comedy duo. Columbia hastily agreed but not long after shooting began the production became troubled and when the film was finally released it was savaged by critics and shunned by audiences.

That film was *The Fortune*. Released in 1975 and starring Warren Beatty and Jack Nicholson, this homage to 1930s screwball comedies was written by Carole Eastman and directed by Mike Nichols. Although rarely revived or discussed today, for a while its title was easy fodder for industry wags to quip about the amount Columbia lost in financing the flop. It did not take long for most of the participants to move on and Beatty was soon celebrating the success of *Shampoo* (Hal Ashby, 1975), while Nicholson won an Academy Award for *One Flew Over the Cuckoo's Nest* (Milos Forman, 1975), and Nichols, after focusing on Broadway, received critical acclaim for his return feature, *Silkwood* (1983). Unfortunately, Eastman, best known for her work on *Five Easy Pieces* (Bob Rafelson, 1970) would not have another screenplay produced until 1992.

The failure of *The Fortune* should have been a lesson to all involved that the combination of top talent will not necessarily result in a quality commodity if the project is not suited to the individual and collective strengths of those involved. Yet, enamored by the successful run that Beatty would immediately enjoy after that debacle, Columbia was prepared to forget (or perhaps conveniently overlook) the lesson of *The Fortune* when, a decade later, he would pitch to them a project that sounded remarkably similar in terms of concept and the talent involved. This film was to be known as *Ishtar* and, unlike *The Fortune*, it would be long remembered.

From 1980 to 1995 cartoonist Gary Larson created a highly successful and widely syndicated single-panel comic strip called "The Far Side." In one titled "Hell's Video Store" he depicted a set of video store shelves adjacent to the roaring flames of its location. For the unfortunate denizens of hell the only film stocked in the store was copious copies of *Ishtar* (May, 1987).[1] In 1992 when this comic was included in an anthology of his work, Larson offered this commentary:

> When I drew [the cartoon], I had not actually seen *Ishtar* . . . Years later, I saw it on an airplane, and was stunned at what was happening to me: I was actually being entertained. Sure, maybe it's not the greatest film ever made, but my cartoon was way off the mark. There are so many cartoons for which I should probably write an apology, but this is the only one which compels me to do so.[2]

Ishtar has the unenviable appendage *Film Maudit* attached permanently to its reputation. There are few filmmakers who have endured labors of love that have been scorned by critics and rejected by audiences, but to be credited *Film Maudit* is an acknowledgement of vainglorious failure in a league of its own. Although Jean Cocteau initially applied this label in 1949 to a festival of curated films that had been disparaged and overlooked, the term, translated as "cursed film", has found a place in cinema mythology.[3] In Hollywood, there exist a number of films to which *Film Maudit* may be applied: as far back as *Greed* (von Stroheim, 1924) to more recent examples such as *Cleopatra* (Mankiewicz, 1963), *Heaven's Gate* (Cimino, 1980) and *Waterworld* (Reynolds, 1995). In each instance these films were plagued by production problems, experienced budgetary and schedule overruns, suffered bad press during production and opened to hostile critical receptions and below-average box-office. No matter the inherent quality of each film, any such assessment was preceded by an overawing negative reputation. Such is the fate of *Film Maudit*—perpetually damned without either evidence or true testimony. Gary Larson recanted, but many years after the damage had been done.

Ishtar remains a blind-spot in May's brief filmography as a director. Her previous works, although occasionally colored with distractions of (generally forgotten) studio interference and rancor, are still able to be easily discussed as contained texts. The backstories, critical reaction, audience reception, and historical legacies of *A New Leaf*, *The Heartbreak Kid* and *Mikey and Nicky* are, depending on a writer's focus, of secondary importance, the additional spice to add some contextual flavor to the anchoring critical theory. Yet, whilst the production of *The Heartbreak Kid* seemingly went smoothly enough, this was not the case on either *A New Leaf* or, to a far more worrying extent, on *Mikey and Nicky* (in which release dates were not met, and Paramount's legal team were kept busy). These were warning signs that should have been seen within the industry but were either misread or ignored completely. Instead, Hollywood arrived at *Ishtar*.

Nothing would please your author more than to write of *Ishtar* "only" as an Elaine May film, yet such is the film's infamous status as one of the most mocked and expensive box-office failures in the history of the American film industry, the broader ramifications of *Ishtar* are impossible to ignore. One such consequence of the film's impact is that this book is devoted to a director of only four feature films. Therefore it is impossible to separate the text from the object of *Ishtar*. However, although the film's production has been recounted with a form of gleeful relish by a number of industry historians, few have also discussed the film itself. This chapter aims to rectify that situation, positing that *Ishtar* is one of the most scathingly subversive major Hollywood releases of the 1980s; a film that was equally critical of the then (and now) orthodoxy of unfettered American geopolitical influence and of an ideology that rejects individuality and sincerity in favour of success and conformity. Yet, in the three decades since its release the text of the film has become enmeshed with the legend of its production and reception. For those with even the most basic knowledge of *Ishtar* it is impossible to disentangle the reputation from the viewing experience. Rather than attempting that near-impossible task, it is just as fulfilling to embrace *Ishtar* as a near-meta text, one which is self-fulfilling in its own prophecy of grandiose ridicule, rejection, and failure.

On paper, *Ishtar* must have sounded like a promising commercial proposition. Although May's previous experience behind the camera had proven difficult for both the director and studios that employed her, in the decade since she had redeemed her reputation by earning an Academy Award nomination for co-writing (with Warren Beatty) the comedy *Heaven Can Wait* (1978) and by providing valuable, uncredited rewrites on the historical drama *Reds* and the gender-subverting comedy *Tootsie* (Sidney Pollack, 1982). Importantly, all of these films had been hits with the public, and within the industry it was known that much of their success was due to May's input. Beatty for one, had championed May's work and was willing to use his clout to assist her return to the director's chair. May had the idea of updating the "Road To" comedies that had starred Bob Hope and Bing Crosby. These comedies featured the duo (usually as some form of conmen) bumbling through various far-flung parts of the world (but never leaving the Paramount backlot) and falling for a local girl (Dorothy Lamour). Beginning in 1940 with *The Road to Singapore* (Victor Schertzinger, 1940) a further five adventures followed. Highly popular with audiences, the series incorporated genre pastiche and musical interludes.

Crucially, they also parodied the personae (on screen and off) of the leading men.

May proposed a story of a pair of out-of-touch songwriters who find their way into the Middle East and due to inadvertently coming into possession of a recently unearthed mythical map that foretells the arrival of two saviors (for whom they are mistaken) become embroiled in helping overthrow a cruel despot. With a working title of "Blind Camel" (an animal introduced into the plot for further comedic interaction), Beatty agreed to star as one of the songwriters (Lyle Rogers) and, at May's suggestion, convinced Dustin Hoffman to come on board as his partner, Chuck Clarke. Eventually Isabelle Adjani would be cast as the mysterious revolutionary they both fall for, with Charles Grodin and Jack Weston—who had both appeared in earlier May films—as, respectively, a CIA chief and the songwriters' agent. May would receive $1.5 million to write and produce, Beatty and Hoffman would be paid $5.5 million to star, with the former receiving an additional $500,000 to produce the film.[4]

In terms of the narrative the map is nothing more than a MacGuffin, for although it is emphasised that knowledge of its existence could inflame the region, it simply serves as device to propel the plot. However, it is the fabled story of the making of *Ishtar* in which it seems an inverse map has been carefully followed, one in which warning signs were carefully placed and stubbornly ignored. Each, we could imagine, read "Warning: Ishtar lies ahead." In early 1985 Beatty took the project to Guy McElwaine, his friend and former press agent, now head of production at Columbia Pictures. Beatty promised that, even with location shooting in the Middle East, the film could be ready for release by Christmas 1986 on a budget of no more than $25 million.[5] Although dubious of this prospect McElwaine signed off on the deal, with better instincts deferring to the hope that fostering a good relationship with Beatty and Hoffman would be beneficial for future business prospects. Columbia had recently been taken over by the Coca-Cola Company, which, as a neophyte in the industry, was keen to ensure a good rapport with Hollywood heavyweights.

That May was a meticulous director with an exacting (and often exasperating) attention to detail was well known in Hollywood. Suitably, for a potentially difficult location-based shoot, her working methods required a strong producer on hand to ensure the filming remained on schedule and budget. However, in entrusting Beatty to fill that role they had employed a second director legendary for shooting copious takes of scenes and running over budget. Like May, Beatty favored finding the film in the editing suite and only then deciding upon which of the many takes was suitable to the tone and rhythm he desired. Beatty had insisted upon the role so as to shield May from studio interference (and possible removal). This would appear a highly magnanimous gesture by the star, however his recent producing successes were those that he had also directed and for which his reputation was most at stake. Were either *Reds* or *Heaven Can Wait* to have failed, he was squarely to blame, on *Ishtar* the attention would be elsewhere. Additionally, although only employed to act in the film, Dustin Hoffman had a known track record of requiring placation upon set. Three major talents synonymous with individuality, stubbornness, and profligacy, one of whom was entrusted with containing the others (and himself as an actor), was a combination a less star-struck employer should have seen as a red flag for worry. It was another landmark ignored on the road to Ishtar.

That the film was patterned on the "Road" movies was apparent within *Ishtar*'s general storyline, however, the key to the success of that series had been the rapport between the stars and their ability to make fun of their own personae and, in the process, allow the audience the pleasure of sharing a joke designed specifically for them. Additionally, Crosby was a one of the most successful singers of his time and Hope could adequately carry a tune. Both could also convincingly manage the dance sequences some numbers required. They were, in effect, playing variations of themselves and, as entertainers, actually entertaining. May, in updating the concept, decided to have her actors play against type, with Hoffman's Chuck the more naturally confident of the pair and Beatty's Lyle socially awkward and seemingly virginal (in one scene, as they attempt to chat up two women at a New York bar, Chuck's small talk and bravado seem to be having the desired effect, as Lyle, wearing a ridiculous fur hat, can barely mumble a word to his bored companion). Although Hoffman had enjoyed success with a variety of character roles, Beatty's recent successes, *Heaven Can Wait* and *Shampoo* (1975), had emphasised his attractiveness and sexuality both as a screen persona and in his private life, which had included relationships with many famous and desirable women. To subvert this may have been amusing as a skit on a television sketch show with Beatty as a guest, but to build the entirety of a major film around the conceit was a risk. To compound this, throughout *Ishtar* it would appear that the directive to the costume designer was to clothe the protagonists in the least attractive garbs possible. Similarly, in casting the versatile Isabelle Adjani as the revolutionary Shirra Assel, May was brave in keeping the actor's head swathed in head scarves for most of its duration, robbing audiences (and publicity departments) of her beauty.

Another distancing from the "Road" series was that neither Hoffman nor Beatty was known for their musical prowess. Previously Beatty had played lounge singers/comedians in *Mickey One* (Arthur Penn, 1965) and *The Only Game in Town* (George Stevens, 1970) and that neither made any impression upon the public should have warned studio executives to keep him away from a piano. But whereas Hope and Crosby could professionally entertain, May's idea was for Rogers and Clarke to be purposely bad, with the entertainment value to be found in the ridiculousness of the songs they have written (composed by May and Paul Williams) and their delivery. May's estimation of the public's willingness to discern "bad in a funny way" from just plain "bad" was another, uncalculated, risk. But surely such subversion should have been underwritten by the mammoth box-office clout of the two actors, for whom success had come so naturally?

Celebrating the fiftieth anniversary of *Bonnie and Clyde* (Arthur Penn, 1967), the stars of the film, Warren Beatty and Faye Dunaway were invited to present the Best Picture winner of the 2017 Academy Awards. Beatty, upon opening the winner's envelope, mentally noted a discrepancy and, unsure what to do, passed it to an impatient Dunaway, who announced the winner as *La La Land* (Damien Chazelle, 2016). Chaos ensued as production staff rushed the stage to confirm that the wrong envelope had been given to the presenters and *Moonlight* (Barry Jenkins, 2016) was the actual winner. This controversy created international headlines (possibly the most coverage the awards had received in years) and brought the two, often reclusive, stars back to an unwelcome spotlight. In the following days a number of news outlets began reacting to a social media query, "Who are Warren Beatty and Faye Dunaway?" To some aghast older film buffs this was a case of the millennial generation having scant regard for history. However, a personal indulgence will distort that belief.

In 1987, as a high school student, I asked a classmate on a date to see *Ishtar*. When told it starred Warren Beatty, she replied, "Who's Warren Beatty?" To the average teenage filmgoer in 1987 Warren Beatty was an unknown quantity, a fifty-year-old actor who had not been on screen since 1981 and, even then, in a long and verbose drama about disillusioned American communists from the beginning of the century. Few stars can risk removing themselves for extended periods from the popular consciousness, for fear of being forgotten by a fickle public. During the Second World War both James Stewart and Clark Gable volunteered for military duty and upon return both suffered initial box-office disappointments and difficulty in reconnecting with their audience. More recently, Arnold Schwarzenegger's return to the big screen after a foray into politics was met with middling audience interest. Pop culture churns over at such a hectic rate that the six years Beatty took off from appearing on screen saw an influx of new and younger performers capture the public's attention.

To place this in perspective, since Beatty had last appeared on a cinema screen, Eddie Murphy had progressed from being one of the most popular performers on television's *Saturday Night Live* to having made five feature films, four of which were huge box-office hits. Beatty and Hoffman were not alone in being uncertain box-office quantities at this time, with a number of their contemporaries also enduring patchy form. In the 1960s and 1970s they were performers popular with the baby boomer generation, but as that audience had aged and settled into a domesticity that was more inclined to be entertained by renting a VHS tape than visiting a cinema, it was the audience that followed in their wake—those loosely referred to as "Generation X"—with whom the boomer film stars needed to connect, but they had uneven results. Jack Nicholson, Clint Eastwood, Jane Fonda, Burt Reynolds, and Robert Redford had all endured box-office disappointments in the 1980s and Al Pacino, having received caustic notices and poor returns for the big budget *Revolution* (Hugh Hudson, 1985) had effectively retired to the stage. An examination of the Top 10 box office hits of 1986 reveals that none included a star popular with the boomer generation, with the twenty-four-year-old Tom Cruise starring in the year's highest grossing film, *Top Gun* (Tony Scott) and the surprise hits of Paul Hogan in *Crocodile Dundee* (Peter Faiman) and Rodney Dangerfield's *Back to School* (Alan Metter) performed far more strongly than those with Nicholson or Fonda, which barely scraped into the Top 40.[6] Beatty and Hoffman did retain a box-office cachet, yet it had been untested for several years. Although Hoffman's previous film, *Tootsie*, had been a major favorite and, with its star in drag for much of its screen time, had provided him the opportunity to display his talents for broad comedy, Beatty's track record (*The Fortune*) was not so certain.

Filming on *Ishtar* progressed at a lagging pace as the budget steadily grew. Stories from dissatisfied crew on the set were leaked to the press, most of which centered on May as a "difficult" director. There is an anecdotal history of filmmakers castigated for wasting time and resources to try and control or change weather, geography, and seasonal change. Rather than attempt to work within the constraints of what is available, these directors display the characteristics of megalomania in order to achieve perfection at the expense of budget considerations, scheduling, and the exasperated proletariat of a crew. Such a reputation was unshakably latched to Michael Cimino during the making of *Heaven's Gate* (1980) when, deciding that a large open field located for a battle sequence was not appropriately green for his liking, insisted that it be cleared and levelled and that an extremely expensive irrigation system be installed to encourage grass to grow.[7] The stories of excess on that production were duly related by the media, helping to create a climate in which the film was doomed to failure and, in the process, bankrupting its studio (United Artists) and stalling Cimino's career (he would next helm a major studio production in 1985). From the set of *Ishtar* came the news that, having initially requested her location scouts find a suitable area of sand dunes for a desert sequence, upon inspection May changed her mind and two weeks were wasted in which bulldozers flattened the terrain to a level that pleased her.[8] Production difficulties that were once industry gossip were now becoming public knowledge and it seemed that no one at Columbia was able to exert any form of damage control.

The lack of executive action was only exacerbated when Coca-Cola, disturbed by the lukewarm performance of a number of Columbia releases, dismissed Guy McElwaine as head of production. His replacement was David Puttnam, the British film producer who had enjoyed great success at home with a number of acclaimed features, some of which had broken through the confines of the arthouse ghetto in the United States. Puttnam was a great believer in "quality" product and despised Hollywood excess. He also had an unpleasant history with Hoffman, with whom he clashed during the making of *Agatha* (Michael Apted, 1979), which Puttnam produced and the actor starred in. Of greater concern was Beatty's intense dislike of Puttnam, due to the latter's disparaging remarks about the former's labor-of-love, *Reds*, in the lead-up to the 1981 Academy Awards, in which the Puttnam-produced *Chariots of Fire* (Hugh Hudson, 1981) beat Beatty's film to the Best Picture Award. Beatty (and Hoffman) refused to deal at all with Puttnam and the new head of production only agreed to take the position if he could divorce himself from *Ishtar*, which he saw as a hangover from the previous regime.[9]

So it evolved that *Ishtar* continued without full executive oversight and, as if to provoke dissent, the production continued to fall behind schedule and over-budget. That Puttnam took a hands-off approach to the highest budgeted film on the studio's slate is a decision that is curious in hindsight, but what is truly baffling is that Puttnam admitted to never taking the time to view the film during his tenure as head of production at Columbia (it is probable that he is still yet to see it). At one point in the film the CIA place a tracking device in Chuck's jacket and they follow his progress on a computer screen. However, the jacket is lost in a sandstorm and is swirling across the desert sands, causing a senseless display on the screen. This sequence is analogous to this stage of the film's production. It is not that the warning signs were no longer heeded: no one was even consulting the map.

Ishtar missed its proposed release date of the Christmas of 1986, leaving Columbia without a product to feature in that most lucrative of release dates. The Christmas holiday release schedule had traditionally been the key focus of the studio slate until the late 1970s, when it was usurped by the potential delivered by the slots within the summer schedule. However, for family-oriented, unchallenging material (i.e. PG-rated comedies) it remained a boon-time. For that period the highest-grossing release was *Star Trek IV: The Voyage Home* (Leonard Nimoy, 1986) followed by the Eddie Murphy comedy *The Golden Child* (Michael Ritchie, 1986). In relation to other Christmas periods, 1986 was a flat performer, with the other major comedy releases—*Three Amigos* (John Landis, 1986) and *Little Shop of Horrors* (Frank Oz, 1986)—performing below expectations. Speculative hindsight is always fraught, but had *Ishtar* been released, as first proposed, at that time it is possible that by avoiding the bad publicity that dogged its final months of post-production, it may have been presented as a viable comedic alternative to the adventures of the Enterprise and to the comic stylings of Murphy (in what was not a critically well-received film). However, having missed that release date *Ishtar* was destined to perform in the cutthroat summer period, for when all studios readied their most promising and broadly appealing product. By 1987 the most successful of these titles were likely to be "high-concept" films.

"High-concept" filmmaking was the integration of production and marketing: in the commercial sense the film could be promoted through soundtrack music sales, posters, fashion, and other commodities associated with the film. Simultaneously, the film would promote these products, in which the studio had a financial stake. Although tie-ins had long been part of Hollywood's marketing strategies, the progressive takeover of the Hollywood majors by multi-national conglomerates had seen the once independent studios reduced to film-making divisions within an often-diverse portfolio of business interests. With its potential to engage a willing audience, the film-making division was readily able to promote existing or newly created commodities and services within other divisions housed under the conglomerate's umbrella or in partnership with outside businesses when potential promotional opportunities arose. In advancing the merging of interests known as "synergy" the most successful studio was Paramount, most specifically their producers Don Simpson and Jerry Bruckheimer. Keys to the success of their films lay within the branding and marketing of their product in which *Flashdance* (Adrian Lyne, 1983), *Beverly Hills Cop* (Martin Brest, 1984), and *Top Gun* all had titles that explained the narrative and iconic advertising imagery that sold the appeal of the product and simultaneously displayed a fashion-consciousness, respectively the off-the-shoulder sweatshirt, baseball jacket, and Rayban sunglasses. Each of these films also had chart-topping soundtrack albums, comprised of newly composed songs and others sourced from the publishers' catalogs that could be inserted into the film (diegetically or otherwise).

The marketing imperative of high-concept was also the consideration of the narrative itself. Producer Peter Guber has stated that the narrative for such films "is very straightforward, easily communicated, and easily understood."[10] In the case of the Simpson–Bruckheimer films, the narratives do not differ greatly from how one may visualize the film after seeing the poster. In terms of casting, high-concept draws upon the audience expectations of the character a particular star will play and adheres as closely as possible to their most appealing traits. Incorporated within this are the look and sound of the high-concept film, the form being greatly influenced by the popularity of MTV and high-end advertising campaigns (a number of successful high-concept directors, including Adrian Lyne and Tony Scott, had previously worked in the advertising business). Quick cutting, a glossy aesthetic, a focus on the body and matching the visuals to music (often in the form of montage) were key traits to the high-concept film.

This was new terrain for May, Beatty, and Hoffman. For although low-concept films, in which nuance and ambiguity were favored, continued to find audiences if they were of a desirable quality and suitably marketed, *Ishtar*'s trailer, with its focus on broad comedy, international intrigue and action, appeared to be trying to sell the film as a high-concept product. This could only confuse audience expectations once the film was released. For *Ishtar* is the strangest of hybrids—the 1970s ideology of low-concept, contained within the contemporary trend of high-concept and aggressively fighting it. It appears that, with every opportunity provided, May's instincts turned towards confounding the most popular aesthetic tropes then on display in American cinema. As has been mentioned, the actors were cast against type and their garb purposely unappealing. The songs, sung off-key and purposely "bad", were not likely to provide a hit soundtrack album, and the title itself, whilst as succinct as *Flashdance*, conveyed little of the film's tone or content. In her previous films as a director May had displayed an eye for striking framing and juxtaposition of shots between edits that could have the tendency to appear ostentatious. In *Ishtar*, her use of film grammar calls attention to itself due to its sheer minimalism. While high-concept cinema could rarely keep a camera still nor seem to hold a shot for more than a matter of seconds, May stubbornly kept shots lingering long after others would cut. The standard master-two shot-reverse shot progression is often reduced to only the master within a stationary frame. It recalls the proscenium arch effect of early cinema, yet this approach is deliberate, with May's use of *mise-en-scène* filling the background of each long-held frame with bits of theatrical business that provide pleasure to the viewer's wandering eye in a style that recalls the semi-silent technique of Jacques Tati. A number of these scenes are those that involve the camel, where the beast's spontaneous movements contrast with the carefully rehearsed performances of the actors, but others involve intimate moments containing crucial dialogue, where the expected over-the-shoulder reverse shots are dispensed with in favor of holding to a two-shot. The traditional two-shot allows for the reactions within the conversation to be expressed in a temporal and spatial "reality," rather than in the distancing an over-the-shoulder reverse-shot provides. Thus, rather than focus on the speaker within the conversation the viewer is allowed to drift towards the listener, who acts accordingly, in the knowledge that their reacting (rather than just the back of their head) will be on screen. It is a highly effective technique that increases the comic possibilities and results, but in a climate of music video-influenced quick cutting it is also disconcerting in its lack of movement.

Oddly, May also refused to alter her style during a sequence when Rogers and Clarke are attacked by helicopter gunships in the desert. Her framing is so economical that it appears she is directing for the stage, with much of the filming taking place from a low angle behind the protagonists, with the enemies approaching from the air in the background. May refused to utilize the potentials of space and distance that this scene offered (it is said that Beatty quarreled with May over how this should be shot, with May steadfast in her resolve). There seems little reason for this stylistic choice, which dilutes the sense of danger within the conflict, other than May's inexperience with action filming; or perhaps it was shot (and then edited) in a manner that would conform to the rest of the film's strict anti-high-concept policy.

In the lead-up to the release of *Ishtar* there were two stormfronts brewing, one blowing in from the left and the other from the right. Most pressing to Beatty was the return of Gary Hart to the presidential race.[11] Hart, the Democrat senator from Colorado, had first met Beatty in 1972 when they were both campaigning for the election of George McGovern. That effort was unsuccessful, with Nixon winning a second (albeit aborted) term in office, yet the two remained friends. In 1982 Beatty had helped organize fundraisers and used his appeal and contacts to elevate the young senator's profile, and utilized his media savvy to coach Hart on the most effective way to answer questions from news organizations. Hart lost the Democrat nomination to Walter Mondale, but from a low base at the beginning of the race he turned it into a tight contest. It was not until 13 April 1987 that Hart decided to throw his hat into the ring for nomination and Beatty, heavily ensconced in the editing booth of May's film, was again called on to assist with his clout and expertise.[12]

It should be noted that although friends, Beatty, as a dyed-in-the-wool Roosevelt New Deal-era Democrat wished for the more centrist Hart to take a more leftist stance with his policies. Hart refused to acquiesce to Beatty's implorations, believing that such a stance against the strongly conservative (and still highly popular) Republican government would be unsuccessful. Although taken by surprise at the late nomination and the less stringent policy line than he would have preferred, Beatty jumped on board, but the optimism was shortlived. Before long photographs emerged of the attractive and young Donna Rice sitting on (the married) Hart's knee aboard a yacht and the ensuing tabloid furor prompted Hart to leave the race on 8 May, a week before *Isthtar*'s opening. Convinced the storm would blow over with some admissions and regrets, Beatty convinced his friend to reconsider and he did, in December of that year, but due to the media scorn his re-entry was shortlived and he shortly withdrew for good.

Beatty's thinking that the same standards would be held to a Democrat nominee as would be to himself was, to a degree, indicative of the actor's naïvety. However, as Bai has noted, although the media had a history of discretion towards the infidelity of high-profile politicians, the confluence of "family values" rhetoric that had gained traction in the nation's move to conservatism, women's liberation decrying the notion of powerful men treating wives and girlfriends as objects, and the rise of cable news media devouring the salacious and sensational left Hart fair game to be taken down.[13] For Beatty this was not only a crushing blow for his own political aspirations, but evidence that the persona and lifestyle he had popularized a decade earlier was out of touch with the current American mood. The rejection of Hart was the rejection of Beatty, and on the eve of his comeback film the timing could not have been worse.

The second stormfront had been brewing since late the previous year, when news leaked of American government officials bypassing an embargo and selling arms to Iran in exchange for hostages being held in Lebanon. In a convoluted, covert operation, the deal involved Israel sending the arms to Iran, the U.S. taking the payment, resupplying Israel and using the funds to free the hostages. At some point in the proceedings the payments were diverted to fund anti-Sandinista Contra forces in Nicaragua. The complexities of the operation and its legalities are too broad to discuss within the confines of this chapter, however, among the key players to feature in the evolving story was Colonel Oliver North, who authorized the diversion of funds with assistance from the CIA. Over the course of early 1987 the story grew as more details emerged and the focus turned to question how much President Reagan knew of the deal. In November of 1986 the President had authorized the Tower Commission to investigate the evolving scandal, and their findings, delivered in late February 1987, found the President to have been incompetent in not knowing of (let alone controlling) the actions of those under his command. In July of that year North would appear before televised hearings in which he admitted his role in the affair, lying to Congress, altering some official records and shredding others. In 1988 North was found guilty of a number of charges relating to the scandal, but these were dismissed in 1991.

It is an old show business adage that "any publicity is good publicity"—so the seemingly ridiculous subplot of *Ishtar*, in which our bumbling heroes become key figures in a CIA operation to remove left-wing opposition to a ruthless Middle-Eastern dictatorship (along with allusions to pan-national and even inter-statist arms deals), which was not *that* far removed from the contemporary scandal, should have worked in the film's favor. Instead, the narrative was never so simple. To many, North, although operating outside his legal parameters, was an American hero—in attempting to overthrow the communist regime his intentions were those of a patriot and in America's best interest. It was a story that would only intensify after *Ishtar*'s release (when the televised hearings began). Towards the end of *Ishtar* Rogers and Clarke blackmail the CIA into supporting a communist regime's overthrow of a fascist dictator (along with producing and promoting the duo's record album). During their recorded concert they ask for the house lights to be trained on Shirra Assel—the revolutionary now leading the country—and announce that "Our next song is for our little lady of the left." Here, May not only ridicules the CIA and the military complex but also promotes the elevation of a female communist leader into a position of power in a key (albeit imaginary) nation state of the world's flashpoint region. Prior to the concert, the CIA hack Jim Harrison is seen taking a phone call from the singers' agent, who lists their demands, to which a check-mated Harrison must agree. Countering his flustered state, his office is sparsely decorated, intentionally so, allowing May to let the viewer concentrate on the two items behind him. Over his right shoulder is the flag of the stars and stripes and over his left a framed portrait of a smiling Ronald Reagan (who, it is suggested, is furiously screaming at Harrison on the red phone). It has long been a tradition that, in fictional narratives, Hollywood seldom depicts or namechecks "real" presidents, even more rarely when they are still in office, and big-budget blockbusters hardly ever, perhaps never, actually mock them. Except for *Ishtar*—a major summer family release in which the dictatorial Amir, when promised American protection by the CIA, reminds the audience that such promises did little for the fates of either Egyptian President Anwar Sadat (assassinated in 1981) or the Shah of Iran (who was deposed, and died in exile). This is a film in which the American Dream has crushed two middle-aged men, the pressure to succeed driving one to the brink of suicide and both to losing their partners, who can no longer countenance their failed ambitions. As Lyle tells Chuck: "It takes a lot of nerve to have nothing at your age, don't you understand that? Most guys'd be ashamed, but you've got the guts to say 'to hell with it.' You say that you'd rather have nothing than settle for less, understand?"

Ishtar is a tract on American unexceptionalism. Lyle and Chuck, oblivious to anything outside their own ambitions (at one point, Chuck has to be reminded that Gaddafi is a person, not a country), bumble their way into controlling the fate of the Middle East and the CIA (and, by association, the American military and government). For American dreamers like Chuck and Lyle success will never be found at home. Instead their only chance of acceptance is to be found in the mythical land of Elaine May's imagination.

The sentiments expressed and the ridicule dished out to institutions and the then U.S. head of state would have been well suited to a counter-culture piece made circa 1970. Yet it should be remembered that, even in those more cynical and free-wheeling years, few such films were overly popular at the box office. For every cynical *The Graduate* (Mike Nichols, 1967) or *M*A*S*H* (Robert Altman, 1970) that was a hit with the public there were numerous others that made little or no impact. For although the collective cultural memory situates the late 1960s as years of progressive idealism and activism, it ignores the fact that vehement reactionary opposition was simultaneously taking place, manfully trying to maintain a conservative status quo (this was the electorate that voted in Richard Nixon in 1968 and preferred him to Beatty's McGovern in 1972). In both 1970 and 1987 conservatives comprised at least half of Hollywood's audience. The countercultural hits of New Hollywood were modestly enough budgeted to succeed even without attracting a large contingent of the conservative crowd (it was a bonus if a number were lured to see what the fuss was about). In a business built on risk aversion, no fiscally sensible studio would green-light a big-budget blockbuster with political sensibilities that would be likely to deter half their potential audience.

With its release date approaching *Ishtar*'s fate appeared sealed. The film's accumulated bad press had created a public sense that a failure was to be unleashed and the same insecurity infected the executive suites of Columbia once May handed in her final cut. *Ishtar* had the appearance of a film that had been purposely designed to lack appeal either within the film itself or in sealed extracted elements that were marketable. That Puttnam refused to publicly praise the film was less damning then his refusal to condemn it—his silence was a distance from which he could watch the humiliation with blameless detachment. Beatty took complete control of the film's marketing strategy and in a move that went against the perceived wisdom of concise minimalism, chose the design of a double one-sheet poster, incorporating a painted image of the two actors, rope in hand, attempting to pull a reluctant camel across the dunes of two posters. Apart from the logistical headache faced by theaters requiring two adjacent display frames, the design did replicate May's adherence to master shots at the expense of depicting the marketable commodity of the faces of two of the most successful actors of the previous twenty years. Traditional orthodoxy deems that when a studio has little faith in its product turning a profit it is best to cut the advertising budget and reduce the losses. However, at Beatty's insistence the advertising was increased to the point where the audience was saturated with the knowledge that its arrival was imminent.

The reviews for *Ishtar* were almost uniformly savage. Stuart Klawans has stated that during industry previews in Los Angeles anyone who laughed during the film was glared at with disdain by surrounding audience members.[14] There was blood in the water and critics relished the myriad flesh wounds the film enabled them to inflict, from the politics, the performances of the leads, and that May's humor was just not "funny," to aspects outside the realm of the presented product—the budget, the production difficulties, the delays and the inner turmoil it caused within Columbia.

Ishtar opened in 1,139 theaters on 15 May 1987. However, due to the fact that there is only limited data available for the total of North America's theatrical market, the analysis will be derived from that published in *Variety*'s weekly Top 50 grossing films chart, which evaluated the returns from around twenty to twenty-two key territories—mostly within capitals and other major cities. These accounted for approximately 12 to 15 per cent of all screens across the country, but as the venues delivering the results were usually first-run houses in populous areas the data sample is in the ballpark of reflecting 30 per cent of a film's overall box-office gross. The week prior to *Ishtar*'s opening, distributors had decided to be cautious, for although May's film was encumbered by bad press, the names involved should still account for huge audience interest, swamping the prospects of other titles on screen. Thus in the week of 8 May, a post-Vietnam drama, a teen comedy, a low-budget action flick and a highly regarded arthouse feature were the only new films presented. Other than the limited release of Tim Hunter's *River's Edge*, all performed poorly.

Holding onto the top two positions on the chart were the comedies *The Secret of My Success* (directed by Herbert Ross) and Blake Edwards' *Blind Date*, respectively in their fifth and seventh weeks, and although both had been reasonably popular features, these late spring releases were running out of legs as the summer blockbusters prepared to move in. Thus, *Ishtar* was provided with clear air. With its only new wide-release competition being Tibor Takács' low-budget horror *The Gate*, May's film had no excuse not to perform strongly. After the opening week's figures were collated the results from the survey sample read as follows:

As expected, *Ishtar* had claimed the number one position, but by a margin of only $40,000 ahead of *The Gate*. Rarely could such a victory have been such an embarrassment for a major studio. To provide further damning context to the opening week's performance, *Ishtar* managed the lowest opening week's gross of any film to claim the number one position during 1987, and of the 338 new releases as recorded on the *Variety* charts, it ranked fifty-first in opening numbers, placing it between Clive Barker's *Hellraiser* and John Carpenter's *Prince of Darkness*, a pair of R-rated horror films devoid of sellable stars with restricted audiences and niche genre interest. Furthermore, of the forty-nine films opening on 200 or more screens, *Ishtar*'s average of $7,668 placed it in thirty-second position. As poor as this is, the use of this metric actually disguises the film's wretched performance. For of all fifty-two films ranked number by *Variety* in 1987, *Ishtar* had the second lowest gross and per-screen average occurring in a week that had the second lowest overall gross ($10,203,001) over the course of the year. In fairness it must be stated that as the sample size of venues was never static over the sample period, overall gross is an unreliable indicator. However, taking the per-screen average of venues used in each survey provides a clearer indicator and thus, the average of $3,771 earned by each of the 2,706 venues in *Ishtar*'s opening week also places it second last. It should be noted that the worst week recorded was that immediately prior to *Ishtar*, when nothing of notable audience interest opened and *The Secret of My Success*, in its fifth week, held the number one position. Finally, the metric of measuring the film's performance within the Top 10 shows that, by only accruing 21 per cent of the Top 10's total gross although the market was the second softest of the year, the distribution of audience interest was not strongly geared towards the new film. This metric tends to find such results in markets that are very strong (in which several popular films are released

Table 7.1 Box office takings in *Ishtar*'s opening week

Title	Dist	Gross	RK	CTS	TS	Ave	W	Cume	% TT
Ishtar	Col	$1,541,381	1	16	201	$7,668	1	$1,541,381	21
The Gate	NCV	$1,510,050	2	16	215	$7,023	1	$1,510,050	21
Secret . . . Success	Uni	$1,033,957	3	18	213	$4,854	6	$10,749,295	14
Creepshow 2	Nw	$623,047	4	9	188	$3,314	3	$3,168,263	9
Gardens of Stone	Tst	$553,656	5	18	158	$3,504	2	$1,292,293	8
Lethal Weapon	Wb	$513,658	6	16	148	$3,470	11	$18,579,114	7
Hot Pursuit	Par	$432,051	7	16	158	$2,734	2	$1,009,513	6
Platoon	Ori	$365,312	8	19	142	$2,752	22	$37,955,130	5
Project X	Fox	$359,894	9	13	141	$2,552	5	$4,106,300	5
Raising Arizona	Fox	$294,396	10	16	98	$3,004	10	$6,325,731	4
Hour of the Assassin	CCD	$100,000	19	1	26	$3,846	1	$100,000	
The Barbarians	Can	$86,000	21	1	16	$5,375	1	$86,000	
Personal Services	Ves	$75,000	23	3	4	$18,750	1	$75,000	

simultaneously and share the viewership) or very weak, in which films long into holdover are still cornering the market and new releases are of limited interest. Even if *Ishtar*'s numbers were below expectations, it should have gained a larger distribution of the audience. However, in direct comparison to *The Secret of My Success* (an efficient, though hardly blockbuster performer), two out of five viewers still favored seeing the Michael J. Fox comedy in its sixth week in preference to the new release. One may occasionally read of filmmakers complaining that their film failed due to being released in direct competition to a popular blockbuster and being unable to find an audience. In terms of being provided clear air with little to no competition of note, *Ishtar* could not have asked for more ideal conditions in which to open and could not have delivered a less impressive result.

Ishtar's opening week was notable for its appalling performance across a number of indicators. Although it was clear that the film would suffer a financial loss, it was hoped that a strong word of mouth would negate the vicious critical reviews that plagued its opening. Unfortunately, its second week was the one in which Tony Scott's *Beverly Hills Cop II* was released—the film which achieved the best results against most of those same indicators.

As the above table shows, *Ishtar*'s second week's gross fell by only 7 per cent, however, this was achieved by the addition of another forty-one screens. On a per-theater basis, its already mediocre gross fell by 22 per cent. Such a second-week decrease actually matches the historical average, indicating that word-of-mouth was ambivalent but from such a low opening base the result was of little help. It is clear to see that all films that week were eclipsed by the performance of *Beverly Hills Cop II*. Not only did the Eddie Murphy comedy achieve the highest gross and wide release average of the year, it also accounted for 53 per cent of all tickets sold in the 2,830 surveyed theaters. If the $12,124,310 grossed by the film is subtracted from the total survey set gross of $22,720,447 it leaves an overall market gross of $10,596,137, which is very close to the market result in *Ishtar*'s opening week. Determined by the 1987 average ticket price of $3.91, an estimated 3.1 million more people attended the cinema that week simply to see the *Beverly Hills Cop* sequel. This was the potential audience available the previous week, the audience that *Ishtar* was unable to rouse to leave their homes.

In the third week *Ishtar* maintained its theater count but lost 43 per cent of its audience. Then began the gradual withdrawal from screens so by its sixth week it had fallen from the Top 10 and by its eighth had fallen out of the Top 50 entirely.

In terms of rentals (the distributor's remainder of the gross once the exhibitors had deducted their share), *Ishtar* managed to return $7.4 million to Columbia from a gross of $12.7 million. *Variety* ranked it sixty-fourth on its rentals list for 1987. That year the average production budget for a Hollywood

Table 7.2 Box office takings in *Ishtar*'s second week

Title	Dist	Gross	RK	C	TS	Ave	W	Cume	% TT
Beverly Hills Cop 2	Par	$12,124,310	1	19	366	$33,126	1	$12,124,310	62
Ishtar	Col	$1,440,217	2	20	242	$5,951	2	$2,981,598	7
Ernest Goes to Camp	Uni	$1,286,523	3	16	226	$5,652	1	$1,286,523	7
The Gate	Nev	$1,285,380	4	18	243	$5,289	2	$2,777,812	7
Secret . . . Success	Uni	$1,084,900	5	19	225	$4,821	7	$11,886,719	6
Chipmunk Adventure	Wb	$812,400	6	15	173	$4,655	1	$812,400	4
Lethal Weapon	Wb	$412,651	7	14	111	$3,717	12	$19,019,013	2
Gardens of Stone	Tst	$406,594	8	19	152	$2,674	3	$1,724,814	2
Platoon	Ori	$293,800	9	17	111	$2,646	23	$38,277,685	2
Project X	Fox	$269,976	10	13	108	$2,499	6	$4,401,379	1
Enemy Territory	Emp	$135,000	16	1	68	$1,985	1	$135,000	
Amazing Grace Chuck	Tst	$89,087	23	6	16	$5,612	1	$89,087	
Tampopo	Ny	$27,000	40	1	1	$27,000	1	$27,000	

Table 7.3 Takings in the first seven weeks of *Ishtar*'s U.S. cinema release

Wk	Gross	Cume	Gr % ch	Rank	Cities	TS	Ave	Av % ch
1	$1,541,381	$1,541,381	—	1	16	201	$7,669	—
2	$1,440,217	$2,981,598	−7	2	20	242	$5,951	−22
3	$815,759	$3,797,357	−43	4	21	240	$3,399	−43
4	$465,016	$4,262,373	−43	6	19	208	$2,236	−34
5	$248,253	$4,510,626	−47	9	16	113	$2,197	−2
6	$106,516	$4,616,142	−57	13	14	67	$1,590	−28
7	$14,173	$4,630,315	−87	32	6	12	$1,181	−26

film was $17 million. It is estimated that $51 million was spent on completing *Ishtar*, with a further $20 million outlay for prints and advertising, leaving Columbia in the red to the tune of over $60 million. Devoid of other licensing opportunities (a soundtrack album was recorded but pulled from release) there was little chance of any more of its budget being recouped, with the company shielding itself from further losses by quietly dumping it into foreign markets with limited advertising campaigns. In a number of international territories, the carefully designed, Beatty-approved artwork was ditched in favor of a garish cartoon camel wearing sunglasses singing into a microphone, the stars' images reduced to publicity headshots below the title. The film that began as "Blind Camel" ended its theatrical life being sold on that one aspect.

For Columbia *Ishtar* was a disaster, its problems not mitigated by any smash hit that could help erase some red ink from the company's ledger. In the course of 1987 only Fred Schepisi's *Roxanne* and Luis Valdez's *La Bamba* were profitable to their moderate budgets. Other releases, including John Boorman's *Hope and Glory*, David Jones's *84 Charing Cross Road* and Bill Forsyth's *Housekeeping* were inexpensive, well-regarded fare shepherded by Puttnam that did not break out of the arthouse ghetto. Jeff Bleckner's *White Water Summer*, Harold Becker's *The Big Town* and Ridley Scott's *Someone to Watch Over Me* were all planned commercial products that made little impression upon audiences. For Christmas it was hoped that the tide would turn with Paul Weiland's $27 million comedy *Leonard Part 6*. Television's most popular star, Bill Cosby, was the lead in the spy spoof which he also produced and for which he provided the story. That film received a worse reception from critics than *Ishtar* and audiences stayed steadfastly away. By September that year Puttnam had resigned from his position at the studio. In some consolation for the former head, a film he had picked up for the company, Bernardo Bertolucci's historical drama *The Last Emperor*, won the Best Picture award and returned (considering its subject matter) some handsome returns. Two years later, Coca-Cola, frustrated at the unpredictability of the movie business, sold Columbia to the Sony Corporation.

Ishtar bears some comparison with Martin Scorsese's *The King of Comedy* (1982) in which the socially awkward Rupert Pupkin dreams of becoming a famous stand-up comedian, yet rather than working his way up through the regular channels, he is determined that his debut performance will be on the popular "Jerry Langford Show" (a stand-in for Johnny Carson's Tonight Show, with Jerry Lewis as Langford). When his attempts to gain a booking for the show fail he decides to kidnap Langford with the ransom being Pupkin to deliver a set on that night's program. After his appearance Pupkin is arrested by the police; however, such is the media and public interest in the story that he becomes a sensation. Scorsese's film is a caustically critical examination of the role of celebrity in American culture—those who crave it, the media's role in promoting it, and the public's embrace of it, no matter the reasons for the particular fame in question. In *The King of Comedy* the inept Pupkin gains what he desires, albeit through nefarious means and as such this becomes an indictment upon those who enabled him—the media and the public.

Ishtar also ends with its protagonists enjoying the performance they have been allowed but due to cunning, rather than talent. As they sing the frame freezes and graphics are painted across the screen—"Rogers and Clarke In Concert Live!" This is the cover to the album they have been promised will be produced and promoted by the CIA as part of the deal for the map. The camera then pulls back to reveal the album on display in the window of a record store—the same one Rogers and Clarke gazed into as earlier dreamers. Risk-averse Hollywood cinema would use this scene as a moment of triumph—perhaps including a storefront notification that this was now the number one album in the country. However, in this film so drenched in cynicism, the album sleeves are attached with signage stating "On Sale" and "Special Low Price." Already in the bargain bin as soon as it is released, Rogers and Clarke have been rejected by the American public. Once losers, always losers. Intriguingly, as the camera tracks backwards revealing more of the shopfront we can see other titles on display surrounding their album and, with their titles, one may think this was no arbitrary piece of set dressing. "True Blue" (Madonna) emphasizes friendship over adversity, "Life, Love & Pain" describes the effort that went into the production and—most prominently visible due to its stark sleeve—Peter Gabriel concurs with the audience response, "So?" The map of *Ishtar*'s journey has reached its prophesized destiny: Rogers and Clarke are May, Beatty and Hofman, the live album is *Ishtar* and its rejection is the film's rejection.

As this sequence leads into the credits, the song "Dangerous Business" segues from the concert performance to a relic of 1980s musical over-production. This is also the song that they are seen developing over the opening credits. The lyrics (in part) are worth reproducing here.

"Telling the truth can be dangerous business.
Honest and popular don't go hand in hand.
If you admit that you can play the accordion,
No one'll hire you in a rock 'n' roll band.

But we can siiinnnngggggg . . . our hearts out (all night)
And if we're lucky, then no neighbors complain.
Nobody knows where the beginning part starts out (sing all right)
But being human we can live with the pain."

Watching *Ishtar* Elaine May just might have been the finest figurative accordion player of all who somehow got hired in the rock and roll band of high-concept

Hollywood. In doing so she created one of the greatest "fuck-you" films the industry has received. Once the dust of the *Ishtar* debacle had settled most of its main players recovered. Hoffman teamed with high-concept star Tom Cruise the following year for Barry Levinson's *Rain Man*, which was a box-office hit and garnered him his second Academy Award for Best Actor. Beatty turned to what would become the most high-concept of all genres—the comic book adaptation—starring in and directing *Dick Tracy* (1990), teaming up with pop star Madonna as his femme fatale leading lady. Although costly, it turned a small profit due to a heavy marketing campaign.

In the years following, *Ishtar* became shorthand for costly, vanity flops. Although it has found some admirers in the age of the internet it has yet to find the kind of resurrection that *Heaven's Gate* has enjoyed in recent times, with critical revision turned in its favor. At the time this book was in production *Ishtar* made the news due to Dustin Hoffman's being accused of a number of historical incidents of sexual harassment and abuse on film sets, including claims that he inappropriately touched a woman in a sound booth whilst looping his singing on the song sequences during post-production. It seems as if nothing positive will ever be associated with the film.

If we can return briefly to the fate of the Bill Cosby bomb *Leonard Part 6*, the film's director was Paul Weiland, a veteran of British television commercials making his film debut. The reception that film received could have ended any future career in Hollywood. Yet, in 1994 he was handed the reins on *City Slickers II: The Search for Curly's Gold*, a sequel to Billy Crystal's 1991 smash hit comedy western. Although she has served as a screenwriter (both credited and not) on films of distinction, has acted in films and been busy on stage, *Ishtar*'s director Elaine May has never directed a feature film since and probably never will, no matter her previous track record. Dangerous business. For some, anyway.

NOTES

1. Gary Larson, *The Complete Far Side: 1987–1994* (Kansas City: Andrews McMeel Publishing, 2003), p. 351.
2. Ibid., p. 351.
3. Colin Burnett, *The Invention of Robert Bresson: The Auteur and His Market* (Bloomington: University of Indiana, 2016), p. 64.
4. David T. Friendly, "Ishtar Delay No Issue—Beatty" *Los Angeles Times*, 4 September 1986 <http://articles.latimes.com/1986-09-04/entertainment/ca-13860_1_warren-beatty> (accessed January 2019 via keyword search).
5. James Robert Parish, *Fiasco: A History of Hollywood's Iconic Flops* (Hoboken: John Wiley & Sons, 2006), pp. 173–4.
6. "Big Rental Films of '86" *Variety*, 14 January 1986: 25.
7. Steven Bach, *Final Cut* (New York: Onyx, 1987), pp. 301–2.

8. David Blum, "The Road to *Ishtar*," *New York Magazine*, 16 March 1987: 36.
9. Andrew Yule, *Fast Fade: David Puttnam, Columbia Pictures and the Battle for Hollywood* (New York: Delcorte, 1989), p.190.
10. Justin Wyatt, *High Concept: Movies and Marketing in Hollywood* (Austin: University of Texas Press, 1994), p. 8.
11. At the time of writing, *The Front Runner* (2018) was readying to be released in theaters. Directed by Jason Reitman, it stars Hugh Jackman as Gary Hart and focuses on this moment in American history. Although a number of real-life figures are portrayed in the film, it appears that the character of Warren Beatty is missing entirely. His enigma remains intact.
12. Steven J. Ross, *Hollywood Left and Right: How Movie Stars Shaped American Politics* (New York: Oxford University Press, 2011), pp. 324–48.
13. Matt Bai, "How Gary Hart's Downfall Forever Changed American Politics," *New York Times*, 18 September 2014 <https://www.nytimes.com/2014/09/21/magazine/how-gary-harts-downfall-forever-changed-american-politics.html> (accessed January 2019).
14. Stuart Klawans, *Film Follies: The Cinema Out of Order* (London: Cassell, 1999), p. 161.

PART 4

Collaborations/Revelations

CHAPTER 8

In/Significant Gestures— Elaine May, Screen Performance, and Embodied Collaboration

Alexandra Heller-Nicholas

> She's the finest actress I've ever worked with . . . and I've never expressed an opinion about a leading lady before. I've had opinions, but I've never expressed them. I think Elaine is touched with genius, like Judy Holliday. She approaches a scene like a director and a writer, not like an actor, and she can go so deep so fast on a scene, and her mind works at such great speed, that it's difficult for her to communicate with other actors.
> —Actor Jack Lemmon on working with Elaine May in *Luv* (Clive Donner, 1967)[1]

Six years after Elaine May and Mike Nichols called an end to their hugely successful comedy partnership at the behest of the former,[2] Thomas Thompson wrote a lengthy feature on Elaine May in *LIFE* magazine that would, as Sam Kashner noted, be May's last really in-depth written interview until his own appeared in *Vanity Fair* in 2013.[3] While reflecting on Nichols' newfound status as "a spectacularly successful Broadway and Hollywood director," his enquiry is focused on another question, that of his feature article's title: "Whatever Happened to Elaine May?" In 1967 Elaine May returned to the screen, appearing as an actor on screen in a range of capacities in three films: Nichols' own New Hollywood classic *The Graduate*, Carl Reiner's *Enter Laughing*, and Clive Donner's *Luv*, in which she co-starred with Lemmon and Peter Falk. At the time Thompson's feature was published in July that year, these films had not yet been screened: *Luv* had just wrapped shooting, *Enter Laughing* was yet to be released in cinemas, and *The Graduate* (in which she only appears briefly in an anonymous-looking but beautifully filmed cameo) would not reach cinemas until December. Regardless, May as a screen actor already had a dedicated fan in Lemmon at least. "She put a 10% coating on top of her role, another level of 'comedy by attitude'," he continued. "She has one of the greatest pusses of all time, and some of our finest footage is where she's not saying a word but just reacting."[4]

Across her impressive career, the manifestation of Elaine May's remarkable skillset reveals itself primarily through a three-pronged attack of writer, filmmaker, and performer. That these overlap so significantly in her 1971 debut feature film as director-writer-actor *A New Leaf* typify how difficult it is at times to individually extract each thread for analysis, yet this chapter seeks to do precisely that. With an eye towards May's smallest and most nuanced movements and gestures, I argue that the foundations for what have made her so unique a comedy performer are apparent in her physical techniques from her early comedy career with Nichols, through to her most recent screen performance in Woody Allen's 2016 Amazon series, *Crisis in Six Scenes*. May's gestures—particularly the movement of her hands, often right down to the very ends of her fingertips—throughout her career as a performer frequently suggest either actual self-control and assuredness, or (even more interestingly perhaps) bely at their most extreme when assessed and in terms of dialogue and context a desperately feigned *performance* of control and assuredness. In these latter cases, comedy often arises when those expressions of confidence are obviously very far from the truth. As an actor, May's body reveals a reality that her character's words often do not or cannot.

"Acting came first in the chronology of Elaine May," Thompson notes, recounting the oft-cited tale of her being effectively born into the theater through her father.[5] From this perspective it is unsurprising then that later critics would place emphasis on May's understanding of the nuance of performance. In his review of *Ishtar* at the time of its release, David Ansen, for example, pinpoints May's greatest talent as lying within her deep understanding of "the inside moves, the comedy of social embarrassment, the offhand behavioral ties of her actors that will suddenly bring a scene to fresh satirical life."[6] In 2016—also discussing her directorial talents on *Ishtar*—Richard Brody noted that "Her comic framings, her sense of distance and proximity as well as timing, are matched by her sense of gesture and inflection."[7] Yet as a performer in her own right, May was not just gifted but highly trained: while Nichols studied Method Acting with Lee Strasberg, May herself was under the tutelage of the revered Maria Ouspenskaya, a renowned teacher and character actor in her own right.[8] According to Edward Dwight Easty, Ouspenskaya was a Russian ex-pat who formed a splinter group from her original teacher Stanislavsky, and her teaching methods heavily emphasized what were called "animal exercises," which Easty describes as "a limitless number of acting exercises in animal characterization" that have in part the purpose "to assist the actor in a more complete understanding of his fellow man in order to portray him more truthfully."[9] Ouspenskaya would also teach

Lee Strasberg, who would famously open his own acting school in the United States,[10] and Ouspenskaya's focus on the physicality of "animal exercises" and how they assist an actor to engage with others is fundamental to how May uses her body (even its slightest nuance) as the cornerstone of her performance technique.

As a performer, May herself is first and foremost a wholly *physical* presence in that she communicates as much bodily as she does verbally, and often the two complement or, as noted, even contradict each other. Even when not acting, when watching Elaine May on screen it is difficult not to notice that her hands are almost always moving. In a Q&A with Nichols after a screening of *Ishtar* in 2006, she wears a white blouse with a pirate-style detail at the front, laced up with a gold chain. She is playing with the chain throughout their conversation, so unconscious a movement that it is barely noticeable until the chain breaks. From a 2018 perspective, the moment is a significant one, for she has just begun to talk about the now scandal-plagued Weinstein brothers, Harvey and Robert: we never find out what she was going to say as her chain snaps and she verbally draws our attention to it, pulling out the cord and placing it to her side. Weinsteins aside, this is a curious moment because until then her twiddling registered with only a passing awareness on our part, dismissed perhaps as nerves, jitters; a habitual fidgeting. While clearly comfortable talking to Nichols himself, physically she is also clearly somewhat anxious about being in the spotlight. This tension is both revealed and broken at the very moment the chain itself snaps. While certainly an unconscious, unplanned moment—there is nothing to suggest otherwise—the sudden change in her body when all eyes are on her and with the unexpected cessation of this one repetitive gesture cease is a fruitful way of beginning to think through May's relationship to gesture and performance.

Much has been written on gesture and performance more generally, particularly in its relationship to comedy. In his book *Acting Comedy* (2016), Christopher Olsen underscores that gestures are not specific to hands and can be expressed through any body part that starts a gestural process of communication. For Olsen,

> The purpose is for performers to widen and deepen their arsenal of gestures by exploring them more comprehensively. Instead of just coming up with a predictable gesture expressing only one thought, the process of going from abstract to concrete exploration can produce not only a more original gesture but one that can be expressed from a variety of perspectives.[11]

Emphasizing the importance of repetition and comic gestures,[12] with particular emphasis on the many one-on-one comic encounters that mark

May's performance career (May/Nichols, May/Lemmon, May/Falk, May/Matthau, May/Allen, etc.), Olsen also privileges the role of exaggeration in allowing gestures to "contribute to developing the relationship between two comic characters and heighten the confrontation within a scene."[13]

Beyond the realm of comedy acting, Adam Kendon defines gesture as "a label for actions that have the features of manifest deliberate expressiveness." For Kendon, "They are those actions or those aspects of another's actions that, having these features, tend to be directly perceived as being under the guidance of the observed person's voluntary control and being done for the purposes of expression rather than in the service of some practical aim."[14] Crucially, according to his understanding of the term, gesture is fluid and adaptable and can change according to its context: "What may be 'gesture' in one circumstance may be 'incidental movement' in another," he notes. "What will be counted as intentionally expressive and treated as such may vary from one situation to another."[15] Kendon's definition is as follows:

> What is the status of gesture? On the one hand it has been valued as a component of self-presentation and public performance, even cultivated as an art. On the other hand, it has been looked upon as something to be avoided, its use betraying a lack of proper self-control or an inadequate command of spoken language.[16]

From this perspective, May is a curious figure: in her gesture-heavy performances, she in fact straddles both of these considerations. The art May has cultivated as a performer is recognizable *precisely* as being linked—in some of her most famous roles at least (Henrietta in *A New Leaf*, May in Woody Allen's *Small Time Crooks*)—to characters that both "lack proper self-control" and have an "inadequate command of spoken language." As an actor, one of May's strongest and most formidable skills is the ability with which she utilizes consciously constructed gesture to communicate a sense of the unconscious workings in what therefore result in dense and often complex characterizations.

As a comic actor there is, arguably, also the important role of gender to consider here. Linda Mizejewski's 2014 book *Pretty/Funny: Women Comedians and Body Politics* argues that "in the historic binary of 'pretty' versus 'funny,' women comics, no matter what they look like, have been located in opposition to 'pretty,' enabling them to engage in a transgressive comedy grounded in the female body—its looks, its race and sexuality, and its relationships to ideal versions of femininity." She continues "in this strand of comedy, 'pretty' is the topic and target, the ideal that is exposed as funny."[17] May is a fascinating figure to consider in relationship to Mizejewski's observation that

[w]omen who write and perform their own comedy have been far fewer as mainstream figures in modern popular culture, and most often they've gotten far because they were willing to be funny-looking: Fanny Brice, Phyllis Diller, Carol Burnett, Lily Tomlin. Or, like Mae West, they were willing to camp up or otherwise make fun of traditional femininity.[18]

May again straddles both categories: while not "funny-looking" herself as such in the same way that Mizejewski clearly means Brice, Diller, Burnett, and Tomlin might be understood, in the case of *A New Leaf*'s Henrietta and *Small Time Crooks*'s May, as an actor Elaine May herself deliberately renders her body—through wardrobe, costume, and most of all, gesture and body language—"funny-looking." But at the same time, she does this with a spirit of mock exaggeration, mimicking a particular *kind* of femininity: instead of West's hypersexualized blonde bombshell, May's stereotype of choice is the awkward cliché of a nervous Jewish woman.

There is, however, arguably much more going on here than May's simply "making fun" of these characters. As filmmaker Chantal Akerman said of Delphine Seyrig's repetitive, gesture-heavy performance in the title role of her 1975 film *Jeanne Dielman, 23 quai du Commerce, 1080 Bruxelles*, "the daily gestures of a woman . . . are the lowest in the hierarchy of film images." She continues, "If you choose to show a woman's gestures so precisely, it's because you love them. In some way you recognize those gestures that have always been denied or ignored."[19] Repetition is therefore crucial here, echoed in Judith Butler's suggestion that gender "is an identity tenuously constituted in time—an identity instituted through a stylized repetition of acts." For Butler, "gender is instituted through the stylization of the body and, hence, must be understood as the mundane way in which bodily gestures, movements, and enactments of various kinds constitute the illusion of an abiding gendered self."[20]

While the notion of gendered performativity is a useful critical lens through which to begin to consider May's predominantly (although not exclusively) signature hyper-anxious femininity in many of the characters she has played on screen, it would be erroneous to reduce her craft solely to the terrain of gender politics. As I argue in this chapter, as a screen actor[21] May has utilized across her film career an enduring and dynamic performance toolkit within which sit a number of key gestures, reutilized and redeployed in different ways for different—and sometimes even contradictory—results. This chapter considers her key screen performances including *Luv, Enter Laughing, A New Leaf, California Suite* (Herbert Ross, 1978), *Small Time Crooks* (Woody Allen, 2000) and *Crisis in Six Scenes* (Woody Allen, 2016) in a linear chronology that maps out how these precise performative movements not only play a significant part in her own character development, but also exist almost always in direct relationship to another actor, rendering her performance technique as not merely embodied but wholly collaborative. As Lemmon said of working with May on *Luv* in the context of mainstream Hollywood: "it was a marvelous experience to act *with* somebody and not *at* somebody. It's damn rare out here."[22]

A PERFORMANCE HISTORY OF ELAINE MAY'S HANDS, 1967–2016

Of the three films Elaine May appeared in during 1967, her briefest appearance is in a film that is with little doubt the most famous –and yet the most covert— of all the movies in which she appeared on screen. In an uncredited cameo, May appears in Nichols' *The Graduate* as an unnamed roommate of Katherine Ross's character. In reality, May was closer in age at the time to Anne Bancroft, who played Ross's character's mother, the iconic Mrs Robinson, than Ross herself, but these specificities are irrelevant when considering closely how May's short scene is presented. When Ross's Elaine decides to break up with Benjamin Braddock (Dustin Hoffman), she asks her roommate at Berkeley to give him a note. The scene with May takes approximately only twelve seconds of screen time, in which May's face is completely obscured as she walks in silhouette down a long, dark corridor. Yet despite the absence of her facial features, May is vaguely recognizable from her familiar hair style and body shape. Wearing a dark navy pinstripe skirt suit, she walks directly towards the camera in a sequence marked by an extraordinary formal style as the camera fades to black as it homes in directly on her genital area. While certainly neither a complex characterization nor one particularly reliant upon May's skills as a performer, it is even so significant in that this cameo in Nichols' blockbuster New Hollywood masterpiece symbolizes her simultaneous presence and invisibility throughout their future collaborations as screenwriter and director.

That same year, May's first role as a jobbing screen actor was as Angela Marlowe in Reiner's *Enter Laughing*. Following protagonist David Kolowitz (played by Reni Santoni), the young cinema-obsessed man finds himself in late 1930s New York City with aspirations of becoming an actor. Deciding to join an off-Broadway theater group, he endures a complicated relationship with the company's director, Harrison B. Marlowe (José Ferrer), and at the same time is pursued aggressively by Marlowe's daughter Angela (played by May), who has taken an instant romantic interest in him. When her leading man in their current play quits as David first arrives at the theater, Angela hovers next to her father during auditions and here, in her first moments in a feature film as a speaking character, it is instantly revealed how central body language and gesture are in May's performance toolkit. As she speaks to each man auditioning, she adopts a hyper-feminine affection that is simultaneously coy and flirtatious as she gently touches her chest and throat, drawing their attention deliberately away from her face to her body. Her hand movements are slow, languid, and fluid, and when she decides on David, it is clear through her physical gestures that she has already made up her mind. When she tells her father "Daddy, I want the cute one," it merely verifies what May's body has already made perfectly clear.

The exaggerated and comically excessive femininity that marks Angela's character in *Enter Laughing* appears to be precisely why May accepted the role, the first film acting job she accepted despite having been offered many. Until *Enter Laughing*, May had turned all of these offers down, explaining to Thompson that "they were all female Tony Randall parts."[23] For Reiner, May was the perfect person for the role because they needed an actor who understood the need for excess: "We had tried to make the dame a little more than two-dimensional, but she didn't come out that way in the script," he said. "We needed an actress who was bigger than life, who could make something out of it. I just sort of thought of Elaine right away."[24] Although the film marked important debuts in both their careers—Reiner as director and May as actor—as Reiner noted, May was much greener than he was but paid close attention to the task of learning the mechanics of movie-making: "Elaine didn't know a damn thing about making movies at first," he said. "But she was deathly serious about learning. She stood around the set and soaked up everything."[25] Establishing the strong professional relationship between May and Reiner, Thompson evokes May's earlier comedy background as the cause for what made their working together so productive when he underscored the importance of Reiner encouraging her to improvise in her performance wherever she could.[26] While Angela is certainly not the most sophisticated character May would play on screen, it was clear that she was in her comfort zone and Reiner's appreciation of her improvisational talents was no doubt a key reason for this.

So positive was May's experience making *Enter Laughing* with Reiner that she quickly followed it up with *Luv*, adapted from Murray Schisgal's stage play, which Nichols himself had previously directed but handed the screen adaptation duties over to director Clive Donner.[27] Despite his excitement when she was cast in the role, Jack Lemmon was not her only colleague to marvel at her skillset. Said Donner:

> The devastating thing about Elaine . . . is that she's better at everything—writing, acting, directing—than almost anyone else I know. Her range in the movies is wide. But not so wide that you could put her in, say, a western. Essentially, she's a product of our urban, bright, liberal world. Within that typing, she could play anything.[28]

Less positively framed, however, were the early traces of what would become May's almost signature supposed perfectionism. Thompson describes an episode during the making of *Luv* where May felt that she and co-star Peter Falk had failed to properly capture a key scene. Requesting it be reshot, both Donner and the film's producer refused, resulting in a scenario where production staff who began trying to convince her that the scene they had already shot was perfect ended up, at one point, with one of them suggesting that May was "behaving childishly." According to Thompson, May—who had offered to pay for the retake herself—responded to this with unflinching clarity: "We all go down the drain together . . . This is a great way to get a comedy—fill everyone with enormous rage." Finally, it was decided the scene would be reshot, but Thompson remains unclear whether this was simply to give in to May's demands or that there was a realization that her issues with the scene were valid.[29] Considering the almost effusively positive manner in which both Donner and Lemmon speak about her in Thompson's article and that she would later work with Falk on her 1976 film *Mikey and Nicky*, it is tempting to perhaps assume that the latter was the case.

In *Luv*, May plays Ellen Manville, the unhappy, sexually unfulfilled wife of Falk's fast-talking con-man Milt. The film begins as Milt discovers his luckless, depressed old college friend Harry Berlin (Lemmon) about to jump off a bridge to end his own life. Inviting him back to his suburban house for dinner, Milt's scheme is suddenly clear: wanting to leave sour, sharp Ellen for the bouncy young Linda (Nina Wayne) with whom he is having an affair, he tries (and succeeds) to set Harry and Ellen up. Harry and Ellen marry—as do Milt and Linda—until Milt realizes he in fact does love Ellen and attempts to restore the relationships to their original condition. Again, while Ellen is a distinctly different character from Angela in *Enter Laughing*, May brings an extraordinary depth to what on paper is a relatively simple character. When Milt and Harry turn up for dinner, Ellen is cold—she moves slowly, carefully, and with what appears as strategic decisiveness. As she presents Milt with a graph of his sexual disinterest, May's physical gestures too are restrained; quite literally repressed. This stands in striking contrast to the swift, fluttery motions of her hands as she drives Lemmon back to the city in her red Volkswagen: the joke is here that her hands flit about enthusiastically as she tells Harry of her troubled childhood, resulting in terrible driving and escalating Harry's anxiety. One of the most memorable and beautifully shot scenes in the film appears in the Tunnel of Love at Coney Island: with her hands limp in her lap as she tells him "there's so little for me to believe in," May plays the scene as if Ellen's hands come to life as she talks about love's potential, and her emotions are made visible through her gestures in other ways. Here, her hands claw when she voices her suspicions that Milt is having an affair. As they ride the ferris wheel, Ellen discovers she has feelings for Harry and paws at him in a way highly reminiscent of the Nichols and May *Teenagers in a Car* comedy sketch in its revisiting of the physical awkwardness of courtship rituals.

The comic romantic ineptitude of *Teenagers in a Car* is likewise recalled in the honeymoon scene of May's directorial debut, *A New Leaf*, where a supposedly romantic scenario is hilariously subverted via an emphasis on comic awkwardness. Also marking her feature film screenwriting debut, *A New Leaf* follows Walter Matthau's Henry Graham, a cold, snooty man born into money who finds himself in desperate need of a wealthy wife with the discovery that he has squandered his entire fortune. Hurriedly wooing Elaine May's wealthy botanist Henrietta Lowell, he marries her with plans to murder her and inherit her fortune. On their wedding night, Henrietta enters the bridal chamber with a clumsily attached, flaccid red flower in her hair, preparing herself for what she clearly assumes will be the consummation of the marriage. She wears a light robe, one sleeve of which contains no arm, for reasons that form the basis for the scene's central gag. Humming as she enters the room in an uncomfortable attempt at seduction, Henrietta inelegantly removes her robe revealing a delicate, flimsy floor-length white gown underneath. Attempting to remain courteous, Henry realizes that she is unable to use one of her arms, missing as it is underneath the layers of fabric. "It's a Grecian-style nightgown," Henrietta explains, gesturing towards its single armhole and asymmetrical design. "It's very uncomfortable." More out of politeness than kindness, Henry gently tells her "I think you have your head through the armhole," and what follows is a lengthy sequence where he instructs her in simple, clear language how she can maneuver the garment into its correct position. Surrendering wholly to his manipulation of her limbs as he moves her into increasingly comical positions—at one point the entire outer layer covers her head completely—like *Teenagers in a Car*, the comedy of the scene arises out of the contrast between the standard romantic scenario and the inescapable awkwardness of the encounter between the two central players. May's physicality is crucial here—her ability to surrender to Matthau completely is less the sensual yielding of one lover to another, but rather a desperately unguarded capitulation to his ability to take control of a situation she has inadvertently rendered challenging through her character's signature gracelessness. The humor stems, of course, from the fact that Henry is just as clueless about the mechanics of the nightgown as Henrietta is; it is only between them after many minutes of fumbling that the garment is properly positioned.

Here and elsewhere in the film, May's performance style is marked by with what Jonathan Rosenbaum has identified as "its calculated power to embarrass [that] recalls the physical comedy of Jerry Lewis."[30] This is a useful point of comparison in the cringe-inducing results, but May's style is altogether less cartoon-like and over-the-top than Lewis's (although hardly seeking verisimilitude). In terms of May's performative gestures, an earlier scene where

Henry and Henrietta first meet at a high society gathering at the stately home of Mrs Gloria Cunliffe (Rose Arrick) is worthy of mention. As Henrietta, May first appears in the background of a scene over twenty-five minutes into the film, sitting awkwardly near a door at the back of the shot. She is smiling, but consciously opting out of the social clusters that have formed in the scene, the only character sitting alone. As far as May's directorial skills are concerned, this is an immaculately constructed shot: as groups of people dominate Henrietta across the frame, she is isolated, and effectively placed in the background like an ungainly ornament. When Henry and Henrietta are first introduced, she drops her glove, and Henry picks it up for her in a seemingly automatic gesture. As he moves towards the front of the frame to engage in a conversation in the foreground, May's Henrietta reaches out seemingly unconsciously towards him as he drifts away. It is a small gesture but an important one, and attempting to recover from having to engage in what is for her clearly awkward social contact, she returns to her tea. Sticking her little finger out to the side in a clumsy attempt at proper social etiquette is again a tiny gesture that speaks volumes as it emphasizes Henrietta's lack of confidence, underscored through contrast with the casual smoking and chatting of all those around her. Almost frozen with social dysfunction, she keeps up appearances, smiling, yet looking either at the ceiling, or off screen, desperate to avoid eye contact. The scene's climax is reached when Henrietta, very slowly, drops her teacup on the floor, and her self-consciousness explodes in a gawky, inelegant scrambling to return order, each action rendering things even more catastrophic. When she drops her second cup, her hostess cannot bear it and nastily confronts Henrietta about her "nerves": May is standing at an angle with her back to the camera so her face is not seen, and therefore her entire response to this almost unbearable attack is expressed through her rigid arms and fidgeting fingers. Coming to her rescue (for purely selfish reasons of course, commencing his courtship), Henry whisks Henrietta from the scene of her social humiliation. Here and elsewhere in the film, scenes of Henrietta's excruciating social awkwardness and clumsiness stand in striking contrast to the calm self-assuredness with which she talks about her great passion: her work as a botanist. She maintains eye contact more steadily, she speaks more slowly—still nervous, she is in these moments more confident and engaged.

In 1978, May's next screen acting role would see her again playing the wife of a flawed character played by Walter Matthau. Herbert Ross's film adaptation of Neil Simon's *California Suite* is a comedy anthology where four separate stories play out in the same Los Angeles hotel. In the storyline of "Visitors from Philadelphia," Matthau plays Marvin Michaels whose sleazy brother Harry (Herb Edelman) "gifts" him with a surprise evening with a prostitute the night before his wife Millie (May) is to arrive for them to attend the bar mitzvah of one of Marvin's young relatives. Awakening to find the young woman with whom he has no memory of spending the evening with, he is shocked that he would do something so out of keeping with his own vision of his morality. The comedy of this segment largely stems from the slapstick attempts of Marvin to thwart Millie's discovery of the comatose, passed-out body of the woman he has cheated on her with. Inevitably, the girl is discovered, and the comedy is replaced by Millie's decision-making process as she tries to both comprehend what has happened, and reach a resolution as to what action she should take. As Chuck Stephens has noted, this segment in *California Suite* demonstrates that "repression was never a necessity in May's movies, and if anything, she always seemed a little too eager for the most painful sorts of memories to make their inevitable return."[31] The casting of Matthau and May certainly seems a conscious provocation to evoke associations with the characters they played in *A New Leaf*, and again the story at its heart finds deeply flawed individuals somehow working out a relationship seemingly despite themselves.

While the film itself is largely pedestrian in tone, it is the physical comedy in the "Visitors from Philadelphia" segment that marks it a standout in this otherwise perfunctory and broadly forgotten portmanteau movie. Often literally across the body of the passed-out young woman, Matthau and May move between the hotel suite's living room and bedroom with the nuanced, choreographed precision of dancers (perhaps reflecting Ross's earlier career as a choreographer), and their slapstick is a carefully and consciously constructed one that is designed to look improvised and spontaneous. Again, a number of May's signature physical gestures and movements appear in *California Suite*: when she first appears at the front desk of the hotel, her now-familiar claw-like hands clutch bird-like at her handbag, but here it is to show firmness and control, rather than anxious desperation. Indeed, Millie is a notably different character from Amanda, May and Henrietta: she is deep-voiced, focused, and sensible. In contrast, it is Matthau's Marvin who is the sketchy, nervous one. May moves Millie's hands with careful, strong movements, and again she uses gestures almost as a kind of physical punctuation system to emphasize the meaning of her spoken dialogue: at one moment when Marvin's desperate behavior surprises her, she spreads her hands out, fingers stretched, mimicking small explosions to accentuate the immediacy of her astonishment. After the young woman is discovered, May changes Millie's body language completely—with her hands folded in front of her chest she sets up a literal barrier between Millie and Marvin, her slightly nervous fingertips the only things betraying her shock and anxiety. Again, May utilizes the dual languages of verbal dialogue and gestural communication to execute simultaneous, contradictory performances: here, of the explicitly in-control dominant betrayed woman and, more subtly, a heartbroken, confused one.

May would not act on film again until 1990 when she co-starred with her daughter Jeannie Berlin in Sandra Seacat's comedy *In the Spirit*. With a screenplay co-written by Berlin, as Rosenbaum has noted there have been rumors that May herself was involved to some degree in both direction and writing, adding that "*In the Spirit* is certainly eccentric enough to suggest May's creative input."[32] *In the Spirit* is a female buddy movie between two middle-aged women of different backgrounds, May's Marianne Flan and Marlo Thomas's Reva Prosky. Again reuniting with Falk, this time on screen as the wife of his character, Roger Flan, a well-to-do New York businessman who has relocated to Los Angeles and whose unexpected firing finds Marianne forced to endure a series of major upheavals in her until-then comfortable life. While May's performance in *In the Spirit* is wholly serviceable, there appears to be little in the film that adheres to the nuanced approach to performance and gesture more typical of her other on-screen performances. With very few central male characters in the film, it is notable how the physical dynamics of interpersonal relationships change for May: far subtler and more frank, the complex and often contradictory aspects that marked so many of her previous roles are here all but absent.

May's final two film appearances to date have been in projects written and directed by Woody Allen. With her performance as May Sloane in *Small Time Crooks* (2000), Elaine May won a Best Supporting Actress citation at that year's National Society of Film Critics Awards, a notable achievement if only based on the limited screen time her character has. The film follows brash working-class New Yorkers Frenchy (Tracey Ullman) and Ray (Allen) who open a cookie store so they can use the location to tunnel into a bank. While the robbery attempt fails, they find themselves immensely wealthy and successful when the cookie business blossoms. Frenchy's aspirations to be accepted by high society draw her increasingly apart from Ray, who in turn finds himself turning towards May for companionship. For Todd McCarthy, May's performance is "endearingly odd,"[33] while Stephen Holden describes her character in his glowing review of Elaine May's performance, as "the kind of stubbornly eager dullard who sends guests running at a swank Manhattan party by enthusiastically burbling out the day's weather to anyone who will listen."[34]

May Sloane first appears in the film when she is invited by Frenchy to help with her cookie store, and due to her lack of perceived intellectual prowess (she is at one time called "blithering"), Frenchy and Ray decide not to tell her about their burglary plans. In front of a policeman customer, the unaware Ms Sloane openly reveals the drilling at the back of the property, gesturing to the sound she is complaining about with her hands raised and clawing, pointing in a seemingly subconscious manner towards the areas she perceives the loud noises coming from. In this performance, hands are vital—the character's hands are often pointing or bunched up, mirroring on a minute scale the binary extremes of the character herself (either rigid with self-consciousness or relaxed to the point where she appears to contain no ability whatsoever to keep a secret or maintain confidentiality). Indeed, May Sloane's hands and the power within them are the source of one of their own jokes: as the cookie shop grows into a major franchise, she becomes the company's vice president, in charge of both public relations and physical therapy (the latter requiring her to do "deep massage"). Again, as an actor May's hands speak as much about her characterizations as her dialogue: in one scene when she hovers in the background where the men are playing poker, she clasps her hands in front of her body quite formally, suggesting both a protective move but also simultaneously one that denotes some kind of awareness that she and her behavior are potentially being scrutinized. Like Millie in *California Suite*, May highlights specific words by making what are effectively punctuation marks with her hands, underscoring the word "elegant" when she talks about Hugh Grant's character David by repeating a similar gesture where her fingers suddenly stretch out, almost forming physical asterisks with her hands.

In *Small Time Crooks*, May's hands barely stop moving, and when they do it is almost in itself an excessive gesture emphasizing her character's *non-performativity* (such as when Ray attempts to flirt with her: she is so paralyzed with social awkwardness because she does not reciprocate his romantic interest that her hands appear to freeze). Like so many other Elaine May characters, May Sloane's hands fidget, fiddle and twitch as if she is playing with an invisible object in her hands, yet it is when there is a physical object being held—such as the teacup in *A New Leaf*—that May deliberately brings attention most forcefully to that part of her body. In both *Small Time Crooks* and *Crisis in Six Scenes*, May curiously repeats a significant, almost identical action with her hands but—in the context of two different characters—the meaning communicated by this repeated movement is notably different. At a classy party near the end of *Small Time Crooks* where Ray has planned a jewel robbery, May Sloane is brought along as lookout. While Ray attempts to open a safe in an upstairs bedroom, she awkwardly (and hilariously) attempts to feign the behavior of a casual, carefree party guest. Central to this—particularly when she is approached by a soon-to-be suitor who tells her she reminds him of his dead wife—May Sloane desperately clutches her glass of champagne in an almost manic manner, clinging onto it melodramatically as if her life literally depended on it. While she verbally attempts to play it cool, her nervousness is revealed by her glass-clinging hands.

Likewise, in the first episode of *Crisis in Six Scenes* May's character Kay Munsinger also finds herself clutching a wine glass in a near-identical manner as May Sloane, but for an entirely different effect. Set in the 1960s, here she plays a marriage counsellor married to Allen's Sidney, a famous author played by Allen himself, and the scene finds her in the midst of a book club held in her living room with a number of other women around her age, all attempting to critically negotiate Franz Kafka's 1915 novella *Metamorphosis*. While many of the women voice opinions that are perhaps comically obtuse, Kay waits patiently to speak: when it is finally her turn, she clutches her glass and speaks kindly yet with clarity and authority. While the way she holds the drinking vessel here might recall the teacup in *A New Leaf* or the champagne glass in *Small Time Crooks*, the gesture speaks not of awkwardness or self-consciousness, but of a barely-restrained passion: the *intensity* of her response is communicated less by the way she verbalizes it as by the manner with which she tries to repress it, literally turning that energy towards the object she holds in her hands.

The book club ladies are recurring visitors to Kay and Sidney's house throughout the six episodes that make up the series, culminating in the final episode where Kay, the book club, and Kay and Sidney's young houseguest and would-be one-day financier Alan Brockman (John Magaro) have all been radicalized by Lennie Dale (Miley Cyrus), an activist and wanted criminal. Throughout the series, May continues to demonstrate her command over the nuance of body language and gesture, particularly in her hands: in Episode 2, for example, when she fears there is a home invader, she uses an aggressive chopping motion with her hands that is co-ordinated with the peaks and drops in her voice to emphasize the urgency of the situation to Sidney. Later in this episode, when the police arrive to investigate after she has discovered that the home invader is in fact her beloved Lennie, whom she wishes to protect, her hands opt again for a typically May-like nervous clawing gesture, repeatedly touching the tips of her thumb and forefinger of each hand in an anxious, seemingly unconscious physical action. As she is increasingly seduced by Lennie's ideological teachings, Kay's body again communicates as much about her conversion as do the narrative and dialogue: in Episode 4, she clutches her pen with a near-religious enthusiasm as she speaks with the group about the writings of Chairman Mao Zedong, her hands almost striking a pose similar to that of praying.

Unlike *Small Time Crooks*, however, *Crisis in Six Scenes* was broadly dismissed, and yet even many critics who rejected the series in general acknowledged that May's performance was a highlight.[35] May has since then not acted again on screen, although at the time of writing she continues to perform in the theater. That her last screen performance to date was as Kay, a character so notably distinct from the typical nervous, clumsy type that she had returned to so often throughout her movies is, however, a useful point from which to reflect on the sheer range of her skills as a physical performer: across her screen acting filmography, the same or similar gestures are repeated and returned to time and time again, often to revisit or rejuvenate certain character traits, but just as likely to reconfigure them completely. May's gestural vocabulary is a visual language that is just as strong a method of communication as spoken dialogue, and in the numerous collaborations that have marked her screen career as a performer, as an actor May wholly embodies the truism that actions can often speak louder than words.

NOTES

1. Thomas Thompson, "Whatever happened to Elaine May?," *LIFE* magazine, 28 July 1967: 60.
2. Thompson, p. 54b.
3. Sam Kashner, "Who's Afraid of Nichols & May?," *Vanity Fair*, January 2013 <https://www.vanityfair.com/hollywood/2013/01/nichols-and-may-reunion-exclusive> (accessed January 2019).
4. Thompson, p. 60.
5. Thompson, p. 54b. As noted in the introduction to this collection, however, May later cast doubt over the veracity of the autobiographical details of her life she has given in interviews. See Jonathan Rosenbaum, "The Mysterious Elaine May: Hiding in Plain Sight," *JonathanRosenbaum.net*, 8 August 1997 <https://www.jonathanrosenbaum.net/1997/08/21700/> (accessed January 2019).
6. David Ansen, "The $40 Million Movie Soufflé," *Bulletin*, May 1987: 128.
7. Richard Brody, "Elaine May Talks About 'Ishtar'," *The New Yorker*, 1 April 2016 <https://www.newyorker.com/culture/richard-brody/elaine-may-talks-about-ishtar> (accessed January 2019).
8. Kashner.
9. Edward Dwight Easty, *On Method Acting: The Classic Actor's Guide to the Stanislavsky Technique as Practiced at the Actor's Studio* (New York: Ivy Books, 1981), p. 145.
10. Ibid., p. 145.
11. Christopher Olsen, "Comic Gesture Using 'Viewpoints'," in Christopher Olsen (ed.), *Acting Comedy* (London: Routledge, 2016), p. 92.
12. Ibid., p. 98.
13. Ibid., p. 99.
14. Adam Kendon, *Gesture: Visible Action as Utterance* (Cambridge: Cambridge University Press, 2004), p. 15.
15. Ibid., p. 16.
16. Ibid., p. 355.
17. Linda Mizejewski, *Pretty/Funny: Women Comedians and Body Politics* (Austin: University of Texas Press, 2014), p. 5.
18. Ibid., pp. 1–2.
19. Chantal Akerman on *Jeanne Dielman*, quoted in Barbara Koenig Quart, *Women Directors: The Emergence of a New Cinema* (New York: Prager, 1988), p. xiii.
20. Judith Butler, "Performative Acts and Gender Constitution: An Essay in Phenomenology and Feminist Theory," in Sue-Ellen Case (ed.), *Performing Feminisms: Feminist Critical Theory and Theatre* (Baltimore: The Johns Hopkins University Press, 1990), p. 270.
21. May also has an impressive career as a stage actor, and at the time of writing is currently performing on Broadway in the stage play *The Waverly Gallery*.
22. Thompson, p. 60.
23. Ibid., p. 60.
24. Ibid., p. 60.

25. Ibid., p. 60.
26. Ibid., p. 60.
27. Ibid., p. 54a,
28. Ibid., p. 60.
29. Ibid., p. 60.
30. Jonathan Rosenbaum, "The Mysterious Elaine May: Hiding in Plain Sight," *JonathanRosenbaum.net*, 8 August 1997 <https://www.jonathanrosenbaum.net/1997/08/21700/> (accessed January 2019).
31. Chuck Stephens, "Chronicle of a Disappearance," *Film Comment* 42.2 (March–April 2006): 52.
32. Rosenbaum (1997).
33. Todd McCarthy, "Small Time Crooks," *Variety*, 15 May 2000 <variety.com/2000/film/reviews/small-time-crooks-1200462243/> (accessed January 2019).
34. Stephen Holden, "FILM REVIEW; Just Take the Money and Run? Nah, She Wants Class and Culcha," *New York Times*, 19 May 2000 <https://www.nytimes.com/2000/05/19/movies/film-review-just-take-the-money-and-run-nah-she-wants-class-and-culcha.html> (accessed January 2019).
35. See, for example, Sam Wollaston, "Crisis in Six Scenes—Woody Allen's TV debut is lazy, lame and badly acted. But it looks nice," *The Guardian*, 1 October 2016 <https://www.theguardian.com/tv-and-radio/2016/oct/01/crisis-in-six-scenes-woody-allens-tv-debut-is-lazy-lame-and-badly-acted-but-it-looks-nice> (accessed January 2019). Far from wanting to reduce such a serious subject to a mere footnote, while not central to the concerns of this chapter on Elaine May's skills as a screen actor, in terms of the specific point here about the decline of Allen's reputation at the time of *Crisis in Six Scenes* it would be disingenuous not to acknowledge the well-known allegations made against Allen by his daughter Dylan Farrow regarding sexual abuse in her childhood. This subject was very much in the public sphere at the time of *Crisis in Six Scenes*' release: on 1 February 2014, Farrow published an open letter to her father about her trauma in *New York Times*, while her brother, Ronan—soon to become a Pulitzer-prize-winning journalist for his role in exposing the alleged long-term sexual harassment and sexual assault allegations of one-time powerful Hollywood producer Harvey Weinstein and launching #MeToo as a widespread popular movement—wrote a highly publicized article about her plight in *The Hollywood Reporter* only months before the release of *Crisis in Six Scenes*. See: Dylan Farrow, "An Open Letter From Dylan Farrow," *New York Times*, 1 February 2014 <https://kristof.blogs.nytimes.com/2014/02/01/an-open-letter-from-dylan-farrow/> (accessed January 2019); Ronan Farrow, "My Father, Woody Allen, and the Danger of Questions Unasked," *The Hollywood Reporter*, 11 May 2016 <https://www.hollywoodreporter.com/news/my-father-woody-allen-danger-892572> (accessed January 2019).

CHAPTER 9

Otto É. May(zo)—Elaine May's Screenplay of Otto Preminger's *Such Good Friends* (1971) as Affirmation that Hell is Other People

Paul Jeffery

> "What they (existentialists) have in common is simply the fact that they believe that *existence* comes before *essence*."
> —Jean-Paul Sartre.[1]

In February 1971, while her studio-seized debut feature *A New Leaf* was being readied for an 11 March New York premiere, Elaine May took a job-for-hire—adapting Lois Gould's newly published, fictionalized semi-memoir *Such Good Friends* for director Otto Preminger.[2] Her work on the film was pseudonymously ascribed to Esther Dale, in keeping with May's general policy of not taking credit for projects for which she lacked authorial control, and has tended to be regarded as little more than a footnote in her influential career. Yet *Such Good Friends* is characterized by themes and styles which typify May's oeuvre: betrayal of a partner; the conflict between the roles we play and our "true" selves; abrupt, seemingly spontaneous, tonal shifts; a particularly intellectual, highly verbal brand of New York Jewish humor counterpointed by vulgar farce; the specter of impending death. Further, the film shows us that, even when working as intermediary between novelist Gould and director Preminger, May's outlook remains thoroughly existentialist. This philosophy, popularized by Jean-Paul Sartre, is not merely reflected in the content of her work but also shapes her entire approach to creative endeavors. Indeed, it's fascinating to see how May's inherent spontaneity, manifested as an inescapable subjectivity, merges with Preminger's highly-controlled, deliberately composed objectivity.

Most crucially, in providing arguably the most complex and nuanced female character in any of May's cinematic offerings, *Such Good Friends* offers a view into the way her existentialism impacts upon her relationship to feminism.

The movie's heroine, Julie Messinger, undergoes a journey that leads her to a new understanding of herself and her place in the world, an understanding characterized by her decision to reject any of the roles the plot has contrived for her: neither grieving widow, nor submissive daughter, nor vengeful cuckquean, nor forgiving rival, nor liberated siren. She simply walks away from all of it, all of them—*them* being the titular friends and family who have been demanding her conformance to each of their subjective realities. In the end, she takes her children and almost wordlessly disappears into Central Park. It's a resounding feminist statement, yes, a victimized woman taking a stand, taking back her life. But it's also a particularly existentialist one, not merely about a woman saying "fuck you" to a gallery of backstabbers and mansplainers (though it is also, thrillingly, that), but fundamentally about a human embracing their freedom to choose, to purely and simply be; to, in Simone de Beauvoir's words, stand up in front of the world "unique and sovereign."[3] From this viewpoint, *Such Good Friends* offers an opportunity to assess the irony of a filmmaker who is revered as a pioneer for the female auteur in New Hollywood while being simultaneously derided by some feminist critics for her stereotyped female characters and foregrounding of male relationships and perspectives.

MAY AS EXISTENTIALIST

Elsewhere in this volume, Jake Wilson discusses Elaine May's career in the context of existentialism, finding her work repeatedly returning to themes and questions congruent with a Sartrean worldview. This is hardly surprising since she has as much claim as anybody to being the inventor of that most existentialist of art forms, modern improvisational sketch comedy. After studying under profoundly influential acting teacher Maria Ouspenskaya[4] as a teenager, May in 1955 became an original member of Chicago's Compass Players, America's first purely improvisational theater. She later found national acclaim—legendary TV appearances, hit records, sold-out Broadway runs—in partnership with fellow The Compass alumnus Mike Nichols, the pair performing a signature style of improv-based sketches that would pave the way for countless subsequent performers. Infused with the contemporaneous spirit of Bebop and Beat poetry, these trailblazing improvisers harnessed the spontaneity inherent in the creative act. Exploring ways to free theatrical performance from the strictures of the predetermined, they found that the intuitive, unpredictable choices and reactions encouraged by improvisation created a theater with something of the thrill of live sport. Vital and truthful, with performers genuinely responding to each other, this new kind of comedy wasn't about jokes setting up punchlines or elaborately constructed farce—the humor lay in the unfolding of the scene, in the clash between two (or more) unique subjectivities negotiating their way through moment-to-moment existence.

> Atheistic existentialism . . . declares . . . that if God does not exist there is at least one being whose existence comes before its essence, a being which exists before it can be defined by any conception of it. That being is man or, as Heidegger has it, the human reality. What do we mean by saying that existence precedes essence? We mean that man first of all exists, encounters himself, surges up in the world—and defines himself afterwards.[5]

In comparing improvisational performance to more traditional theatrical modes, we can see how the improvised characters, even the scenes themselves, firstly exist and surge up in the world, always defining themselves post hoc. It's in this sense that we can see improvisation as profoundly existentialist and understand how May—for whom improv in various forms was the primary creative activity from her late teens into her early thirties—would imbibe the spirit and techniques of it so deeply that it would shape and define all of her subsequent creative work.

In a 1967 *New York Times* feature article, May claimed to be planning to star in an adaptation of Sartre's existentialist play *No Exit*, rewritten as a comedic thriller about three people competing to find a priceless art treasure hidden in an apartment somewhere in Chicago.[6] Though we may mourn that this project never came to fruition—it's clearly a typically Maysian gag, the article in question comprising an interview she conducted with herself under the pseudonym of Kevin Johnson—it's a revealing insight into her private worldview. As she says (to herself) "If you can give me a better definition of hell than mutual distrust, I'd like to hear it."[7] Jonathan Rosenbaum notes that May's cinema is preoccupied by the theme of betrayal by a partner.[8] We can speculate as to whether this preoccupation is related to an actual betrayal experienced by May—whether the dissolution of her long-running partnership with Nichols, the break-up of a marriage, the premature death of an idolized father (each has been lazily posited over the years as a defining trauma)—but it's of little importance and pointlessly eradicates the distinction between personal and private. Suffice it to say that anyone who's experienced genuine betrayal learns from it and carries that learning with them. And sometimes they can't help but write about it. As May said on the subject of *Mikey and Nicky*: "Nobody fingers you but your best friend: they always do it, and they never leave town."[9]

ANGUISH, ABANDONMENT, AND DESPAIR

In 1945, Sartre gave a lecture entitled "Existentialism is a Humanism" in which he defended the philosophy and defined three core concepts: anguish, referring to the realization that one's actions have consequences for the Other and that one "cannot escape the sense of complete and profound responsibility;"[10] abandonment, meaning the understanding that one alone is responsible for all morality and choices, neither God nor human nature nor genetics nor historical determinism can absolve you of your actions—"That is what 'abandonment' implies, that we ourselves decide our being. And with this abandonment goes anguish;"[11] and despair, encapsulated by the idea that all that is outside one's direct influence is necessarily unreliable, "When Descartes said, 'Conquer yourself rather than the world,' what he meant was, at bottom, the same—that we should act without hope."[12]

The popular imagination immediately characterized the philosophy as one of misery and pessimism.[13] It is, in fact, a profoundly optimistic outlook, one which grants freedom to every individual and, as a fundamental consequence, assumes that they are capable of using that freedom in creative and constructive actions, as opposed to seeing humanity as slaves to determinism or biology or a moral framework designed by a God in some form. Most importantly, this freedom extends to the realization of the self, the creation of one's self, as it were. Simone de Beauvoir reminds us that "the scope of the verb to be must be understood; bad faith means giving it a substantive value, when in fact it has the sense of the Hegelian dynamic: *to be is to have become, to have been made as one manifests oneself*" (my emphasis).[14]

The parallel between a human living in an existentialist universe and an actor performing in improv is fairly obvious. The improvising performer is alone on the stage, without a script/governing moral framework, forced to construct their character as they go. Abandoned by the director/God, they are completely responsible for the formation of their being and their actions, relying solely on the inherently unreliable feedback of scene partner and (possibly, but not always) audience. And, if they're to be successful, acting without hope—in the sense that it doesn't take long for the novice improviser to learn that the biggest factor in a failed improv is trying to force the direction of the scene towards a predetermined outcome, to try to "conquer the world" rather than oneself. Improvs have a life of their own, so to speak, and all one can really do is one's best and see how it turns out.

In addition, the dichotomy of the actor, the psycho-spiritual split that delineates actor from character, is little more than Sartre's Being and Consciousness embodied. For all actors working in the Stanislavskian tradition—often erroneously equated with "Method" acting in the popular imagination (accompanied by an array of myths and fabrications of what this entails) but more accurately seen as a particularly formalised version of what Cynthia Baron calls "Modern Acting"[15]—the fundamental goal is to achieve the elusive state of being "in the moment." Definitions of this phrase vary but they share the core idea of responding spontaneously—physically and emotionally—to the unfolding events of the scene, the behavior of your scene partners and the overall given circumstances of the fiction. It implies *becoming the character*, whatever one takes that to mean. Skeptics assert that one never literally becomes the character, just as one is never literally in the moment—actors playing murderers don't actually murder their co-stars, and so forth. It's a common conclusion, then, that actors are talking various shades of rubbish when they speak of such things, that their behavior is simply pretense and their intellectualizing of it mere pretension.

Yet it *is* possible to be both the character and not-the-character simultaneously. I assert this through having experienced it, though proof is next to impossible since I'm talking about a subjective internal state. But, from a Sartrean perspective, if we are both Being and Consciousness and the Being precedes the Consciousness—allows the Consciousness to exist—we can, at a metaphorical level, comprehend how one can hold onto one's Consciousness, as it were, while liberating one's Being to take part in the fiction. The Being—what we might call the organism, which has no Consciousness of its own, which simply exists—"believes" the truth of what's happening and behaves accordingly, while the governing Consciousness merely watches on, ready to intervene in an emergency.

There's not room here to explore this mysterious process in any but the most simplistic terms, but it's a fair conclusion that Elaine May, trained as a teenager by original First Studio member Maria Ouspenskaya, forged under Paul Sills[16] in the creative furnace that was The Compass, becoming fully mature in *An Evening with Nichols and May*'s nightly repetitions of what had once been fresh and vibrantly lived comic scenes, developed a working process thoroughly infused with a Sartrean world-view.

SUCH GOOD FRIENDS: THE NOVEL

In 1966, *New York Times* reporter Philip Benjamin died in hospital from complications after minor surgery. His widow, Lois—subsequently known as Lois Gould after marrying her psychoanalyst (like Elaine May, coincidentally)—found among his personal papers a coded diary which recorded his long history of sexual infidelity, many of the encounters with her friends and acquaintances. These events form the spine of Gould's novel, published in 1970 and spending seven weeks on the *New York Times* bestsellers list.[17]

Narrated in the first person, it tells of Julie Messinger, thirty-one-year-old

Jewish Manhattanite, full-time mother of two and sexually neglected in her marriage to successful magazine art director and part-time children's author Richard. Her husband's lack of interest in her, putatively due to his busy work life and distaste for their ever-present children, creates a void which she fills with masturbation and masochistic fantasies. Julie tells of her superficial Upper East Side life, interspersed with flashbacks to an upbringing at the hands of a judgemental, controlling, emotionally remote mother obsessed by appearances and "correct" behavior.[18] An adolescence battling obesity and a college-era lesbian relationship thwarted by mutual guilt and fear constitute further background to Julie's understandably embittered and bitingly sarcastic sense of self. This dark interior narrative is contrasted with the image she presents to the world—admittedly, the small world of her Manhattan social set—that of a happy, perfect wife and mother with everything a woman could want.

The novel begins with a call from her friend, the doctor Timmy Spector. Richard, in hospital for removal of a mole, has had an allergic reaction to the anaesthetic and lapsed into a coma. From the intensive care waiting room, Julie calls a gallery of family, friends, work colleagues and assorted acquaintances to ask them to donate blood so that Richard's blood can be exchanged. As the days pass, Richard's condition worsens—first his liver fails, followed by his kidneys—and an ever-growing array of organ specialists joins the committee of dubious carers for the lamentable patient.

Julie's main support over this time are close friends Cal—a photographer and a work colleague of Richard's—and Cal's young actress girlfriend Miranda. Julie and Miranda form a close bond which is complicated when Miranda confesses to Cal—and Cal subsequently informs Julie—that she and Richard have been conducting a year-long affair. It triggers Julie to re-examine a coded diary she'd found among Richard's papers, allowing her to crack the code and realize that Richard had been regularly screwing a wide array of her friends, going back to the beginning of their marriage. Denied the opportunity to confront her philandering spouse, Julie becomes somewhat unmoored from her sense of self. She endures abortive sexual encounters with Cal—who remains impotent in her presence—and Dr Spector in a non-consensual blowjob scene in which more time is devoted to her musings on the comparative taste of his semen than the act itself.

Julie continues attending the ICU, reluctantly welcoming Miranda's presence and forming an awkward, conflicted solidarity as *de facto* joint widows. Richard eventually dies without regaining consciousness, the funeral preparations are endured and executed. A very brief coda allows Julie to inform us that, six months on, things have found a new normality, though she still resists her children's entreaties—echoed by her mother—to "get them a new dad."

SUCH GOOD FRIENDS: SCRIPTING AND SHOOTING

Buzz about the book's impending release led to Otto Preminger securing the film rights before publication.[19] He initially engaged Gould to adapt the novel herself but reportedly decided that she lacked the "detachment and easy manner" required.[20] Make of that what you will, though Gould would hardly be the first person—or first woman—to discover that an easy manner wasn't necessarily encouraged by working with Otto Preminger. Elaine May was Preminger's next choice, but she was in the midst of her post-production battles over *A New Leaf* and unavailable. Joan Micklin Silver lasted two weeks ("She was a little more psychologically attuned to the character than Otto cared to be, and probably a little bit more of a feminist than Otto cared to be.")[21] Former *Newsweek* film reviewer (and pseudonymous author of salacious 1967 bestseller *The Exhibitionist*) David Slavitt managed to stick it out for three.[22] August and September of 1970 saw a relatively prolonged period of work with the wife/husband team of Joan Didion and John Gregory Dunne while Preminger was in Los Angeles promoting *Tell Me That You Love Me, Junie Moon* but they refused to return with him to New York so were excused from the project.[23] Playwright David Shaber gave it a shot and managed to shape the amorphous, stream-of-consciousness material sufficiently enough to earn himself an "adaptation" credit on the finished film. But an unsatisfied Preminger halted the process and began prepping another film.[24]

By February 1971, May was available and Preminger could return to his original choice. According to Preminger's son Erik, an associate producer on the film who was present for all script meetings (and who would later cameo as the "pecan pie waiter" in *The Heartbreak Kid*) May and Preminger would conference before May disappeared to write alone for two weeks, returning to allow the director to make minor alignments to conform with his vision. After a number of such sessions, May had completed a satisfactory script which, again according to Erik Preminger, "was shot basically as written."[25]

Preminger, true to his roots in theater and performance, organized an exorbitant (by Hollywood standards) three-week rehearsal period before shooting began in late June.[26] As Willy Frischauer notes, by the start of shooting Preminger "expect[ed] the stars to be word perfect and know their place in every sense."[27] His elaborately composed sequence shots left little room for looseness—spatial or temporal—from his cast, and he actively "discourage[d] individual notions or interpretations,"[28] a stark counterpoint to the free-wheeling performative approach of scriptwriter May. His notoriously confrontational approach created an irreconcilable breach with actress Dyan Cannon (playing Julie), who either: a) stood her ground and refused to be bullied;[29] or b) behaved like a prima donna and refused to take direction[30]—choose your framing of history depending on your personal stance on Hollywood power dynamics, toxic masculinity, and the fragile and little-understood politics of the actor–director relationship. What's not doubtful is that the shoot progressed in a fractious atmosphere hardly conducive to a comedy—even a jet-black one—yet, despite (or because of) this, Cannon delivered a performance that expertly balances vulnerability with opacity. She listens, she watches, she feels, she processes—neither she nor Preminger ever reduces the character to cliché. And, notably, the script's frequently cutting one-liners are generally delivered by Cannon in classic Elaine May style—semi-distracted, with her eyes elsewhere.

MINING FOR MAY'S CONTRIBUTION

Without being able to compare various drafts of the script, or have anyone publicly clarify who created what, the task of establishing May's input into the final product of *Such Good Friends* is necessarily speculative. This need not be an obstacle—nigh on seventy years of debate between auteurists and their opponents have produced little consensus on authorial divisions, which hasn't stopped libraries of film criticism routinely crediting directors for the creative work of their writers, actors, editors, and cinematographers. If we take Erik Preminger at his word and assume the film was shot as May wrote it ("basically"), there's much to be gained in our understanding of May by examining the film in relation to the novel—what was removed, what was added, what was kept but reinterpreted.

The starkest difference between Gould's *Such Good Friends* and Preminger/May's is that, unlike the film, the novel isn't really a comedy. It's mordant and sardonic, certainly, with Gould inserting a stream of Julie's inner thoughts as semi-comic asides in bracketed inserts, but the tone is more melancholic, the wounds which prompted the book's genesis clearly still too fresh to allow Gould (or us) much more than a rueful grin at the dark absurdity of the situation. The film, on the other hand, positions itself just this side of a *Carry On* movie from the opening sequence—a sequence which concludes with Julie leaving her apartment braless in a see-through top. Preminger provides a garish close-up of the doorman's bulging eyes accompanied by an intrusive xylophone riff, about as subtle as screaming "Boobs!" in voiceover. (It should be noted here that May had included a remarkably similar breast-focused moment in *A New Leaf*, during the montage of Walter Matthau's Henry dating a succession of prospective brides, lest we lazily ascribe this gag to Preminger on the basis that it feels like an outtake from *Skidoo*.)

While the film soon settles into a darker rhythm, the bravura (and, I'll readily concede, sometimes not-so-bravura) comic moments keep coming, for the most part additions to the source material. The film's centerpiece is the blood bank scene—a seven-minute ensemble sequence which intercuts and overlays fragments of conversation, all of it original, between a representative sample of the eponymous population. May's gift for dialogue, for encapsulating a character in a handful of lines—honed by years of improvising two-handers—gets full rein, the room awash with the type of pithy observation of erudite Manhattan Jewry that her devoted fan Woody Allen would one day make his own. Here we meet Jessica, who had her nose amputated then restored. Audrey, proud of turning her unsightly "acne pit into an Ilona Massey beauty mark." Aunt Harriet, who thinks venereal disease is something you catch in the tropics. Uncle Eddie who hands out his business cards to the crowd and promises to make them a terrific price on anything cotton. Aunt Addie who can't stop bragging about her son Sid, "an ear, nose and throat man." Louise Lasser's flaky New-Ager Marcy, who tells Julie that her marriage to Doug failed because they were so symbiotic that they were basically the same person—before the camera pans back to reveal Doug, a pin-stripe-suited nerd who accuses Marcy of "throwing a 139 dollar, 95 cent Ampex stereo speaker" at him. We can perhaps see Marcy and Doug as a sly homage to the old Nichols/May pairing—a kooky, mercurial woman and her strait-laced sidekick who also claimed to be so symbiotic as to be almost the same person,[31] and reputedly came to blows onstage.[32]

It's a rogues' gallery of Yiddish theater staples, kvetching, circulating, kvetching a little more. The overlapping dialogue, tentatively zooming camera and hospital setting, draw inevitable comparisons to Robert Altman's *M*A*S*H*, released a year earlier and produced by Preminger's brother Ingo. That it plays a little like Paul McCartney taking a stab at hip-hop is the kind of result that typically earns a director derision—an artist trying to keep pace with a new generation's innovations are often cause for scorn—but there's something admirable in such a major Classic Hollywood figure refusing to rest on past glories and instead trying to evolve. And, as awkward and inorganic as the sequence feels in comparison to Altman, May's sure handling of the stereotypes ensures it plays effectively.

Another interesting invention—I'm assuming from May, since the scene doesn't appear in the novel—takes place at Richard's office, immediately preceding his hospitalization. In an unbroken wide shot, Richard (Laurence Luckinbill) dismissively barks instructions to a group of assembled underlings, said instructions mostly consisting of evisceration of their creative work. It's impossible not to read it as a quiet riposte to Robert Evans, head of production at Paramount, who just months earlier had gutted May's debut feature. Notable is the moment when, looking at photos submitted by Cal (Ken Howard) for a double-page spread, he seizes on an image of Miranda (Jennifer O'Neill) seated alone in an empty amphitheater. Declaring it'll work with some cropping—removing all the "dead space that's just lying there"—Cal pointedly replies that the space is "not just lying there. I composed for that space." Parallels can clearly be found, both with Preminger's predilection for gratuitously long wide shots and with May's subsequent battles with studios over dead time in her films.[33]

But there's more to this office scene than well-aimed potshots at philistines in suits. Richard scoffing at an article about the Third World Film Festival, apart from definitively positioning him as a privileged white male cliché, preempts *Ishtar*—May's satirical foray into Middle-Eastern politics fifteen years later:

> All small countries with a predominantly white population are neutral, all small countries with a predominantly colored population are uncommitted. That's how we know which small countries to invade.

The scene concludes with the staff teasing Richard about his impending hospital visit, joking that if he doesn't excise their work they'll say nice things about him after he's dead. In response to a jibe from Doria (Rita Gam), a colleague later revealed to be one of Richard's conquests, he smarmily responds with "No one ever listens to a woman—they'll just think you were making it with me." So, in the space of less than 160 seconds of screentime, May nails Richard's racism, sexism, bullying of staff and lack of artistic sensibility, all while advancing the plot, milking the subtext and throwing in quotable one-liners. It's a dazzling display of May's verbal dexterity and sense of cinematic economy and captures why she was in such high demand as a script doctor into the 1980s and 1990s.

But the most audacious, resonant part of the scene is achieved purely through staging and framing. The scene opens on a three-shot—Richard standing in front of a wall of photos is mid-sentence, explaining to Cal and Molly (Nancy Guild) why the images suck. As he wanders away to pontificate on how he will fix their ineptitude, the camera zooms back to reveal editor Barney (William Redfield) seated at a desk, Doria standing behind Barney and a fourth man who does little but occupy some of that pesky dead space at the edge of the frame. The six are arranged horizontally across the screen in a tableau as dialogue continues. More than thirty seconds into the shot, Richard moves towards the camera, having to slightly circle Barney's desk in the process. The camera pans to keep him centered and Julie is revealed in the back corner of the frame, leaning against the wall, disengaged. It takes no more than a second for Richard to complete his move around the desk, the camera reframes the original six and Julie has vanished again. At the conclusion of the one minute and 19-second shot, Richard retraces his steps, the camera repeats its pan and we get another brief glimpse of the silent Julie before she's once more banished from the frame. The group then looks at Cal's photos projected onto a screen, a full minute of shot-reverse-shot dialogue until Julie strolls in to join the tableau, almost two-and-a-half minutes into the scene, in order to mutely appreciate Richard's wit and exit with him (three feet behind him, if we want to be pedantic). It's an eloquent statement on the ease with which women are routinely silenced—not a line of dialogue, not a clearing of the throat, not a reaction shot nor cutaway to her. She's not even present in the establishing shot. This, remember, is the indisputable center of the film, the first-person narrator of the source material, a character who is physically present in every single scene. It's a deliberate strategy which silently, elegantly illustrates Julie's status in her husband's life. It is also, we might note, another instance of May repeating a gag from *A New Leaf*, the tactic mirroring Henrietta's unobtrusive introduction to that film, seated at the back of the frame at a party for a full fifty seconds before anyone—including us—notices she's there.

However, the most fascinating example of the dramatic shift engendered by Preminger and May's interpretation of the source material is in the character of Timmy Spector. Novel-Julie describes Spector as "one part sex, two parts gin, a dash of bitters."[34] As early as page 14, we're treated to detailed fantasies about "Timmy raping me while Richard kibitzed; Timmy and Richard going 'sharesies': first one at a time, then together—front and back, top and bottom."[35] And their eventual sexual encounter involves a level of compulsion that even readers of the early 1970s could understand as actual, as opposed to fantasy, rape—Julie, woozy on a mix of Dexamyl and vodka, emerges from Timmy's bathroom after throwing up, deals with a verbal barrage that she describes in terms of a boxing match ("'I'm sorry' I said, rolling it over my smashed teeth and bits of broken mouth-piece")[36] to find Timmy's apologetic hug concluding with a hand on her shoulder pushing her downwards. After the inescapable fellatio he thoughtfully gives her a lift home.[37]

Though one might imagine hard-drinking macho types to be perfectly suited for such a character—John Cassavetes or Jason Robards, perhaps—Preminger went with balding, tubby, camp-inflected Broadway star James Coco. Coco had appeared in Preminger's previous film *Tell Me That You Love Me, Junie Moon* as well as May's just-completed *A New Leaf*, but even with those inside connections he's a puzzling casting choice—unless we factor in May's rewriting of the character to include a significant measure of disempowering buffoonery.[38] The film's version of the above scene keeps Julie sober and cool. Facing an impasse in her attempts to get information about Richard's affairs from Timmy and enduring the same verbal laceration, she calculates that the fastest way to loosen a man's tongue is to loosen his fly. Which is merely the pretext for four virtuoso minutes of unbroken farce as Coco's Timmy frantically tries to remove his hidden corset while simultaneously on the phone to a patient and directing Julie in a series of useless tasks to distract her attention. It's hideously awkward, sweating slapstick that shares an obvious lineage with

May's own head-in-the-armhole wardrobe malfunction from *A New Leaf* but changes the tone from good-natured embarrassment to deliberate humiliation. Preminger, of course, shoots in long, unbroken takes that force us to watch in an odd duality: of admiration for actor Coco's breathtaking show-stopper and simultaneous discomfort at character Spector's seemingly gratuitous torture at the hands of the filmmakers. Cannon is methodical and business-like throughout, seeming happy to cede the floor to her co-star—possibly content in the knowledge that novel-Timmy has well and truly earned the punishment inflicted on film-Timmy. The scene climaxes, in both senses, before Timmy apologises for "getting it on her nose" and the pair stagger, giggling, away from the camera.

It's a dark and discomfiting sequence—especially for a 1971 Hollywood comedy—made all the more so by the complexity introduced by May and Preminger. The novel's version is hard—arduous to read, distressing to visualize—but clear-cut. Julie is a victim, her assailant inexcusable, the unfolding scene depressingly familiar but easily comprehensible. The film makes Julie the sexual initiator, gives her full cognizance of what she's doing and a clear ulterior motive to justify her behaviour—which muddies the waters of our understanding of consent—then ramps up the cognitive dissonance by engendering empathy for the body-shamed Timmy, stranded in front of Preminger's unblinking camera, beads of sweat visibly forming on his shiny forehead. Yet, despite the complex undertones, the scene is played for laughs. And, for those of us who view fiction as what Milan Kundera has called "the realm where moral judgement is suspended,"[39] it is hilarious—definitively situated at one extreme of the mob/snob appeal spectrum, admittedly, but effectively funny nonetheless.

The sequence has implications for our view of May as an existentialist—it's clearly a scene whose existence precedes its essence or, as Sartre paraphrased that sentence, it begins from the subjective.[40] One doesn't start with the thought "how can I undermine patriarchal power dynamics while simultaneously questioning the reductive simplicity of woman as perennial victim" and finish with the image of a horny fat guy wrestling with a corset. I'd suggest the chronology more likely works in reverse. Though such chicken/egg questions of a screenwriter's process might be unavoidably conjectural, I'd contend that it's the kind of absurd, momentum-shifting segue that is synonymous with improvisational techniques—the "yes, ands" of the scene are breathtakingly plausible, yet stubbornly unpredictable—and shows the influence May's years as writer-performer and performer-as-writer had on her later work as writer-director.

MAY AND EXISTENTIAL FEMINISM

> Despite May being that rare woman in the industry, the content of her films has been criticized by feminists, particularly her unmistakable sympathy toward male protagonists, who dominate her narratives. Her unsettling ambivalence toward female characters—more a cruel, frank portrayal of how men see women as unlikeable, unflattering or weak—would likely make today's audiences uncomfortable, given our desire to see more films and series with female perspectives that endear us to their plights.[41]

This quote from Tina Hassannia summarizes a particular consensus that seems to have evolved in regard to May's cinema. As discussed elsewhere in this collection, Barbara Koenig Quart, in her comprehensive survey *Women Directors: The Emergence of a New Cinema*, is something of a flag-bearer for this viewpoint. The first paragraph of her twelve-page summary of May's directorial career searches for an explanation for the "appalling vision of women"[42] in May's work as well as her "proclivity to work through male characters' points of view,"[43] before finally asserting that May's work has "no feminist content."[44] She goes on to detail the female characters of May's films: *A New Leaf*'s "infantilized" Henrietta, an "astonishing study in incompetence" who is "stupid, passive and masochistic";[45] *The Heartbreak Kid*'s Lila, "one of the most negative images of a Jewish woman on film" and the "flat and vacuous" Kelly;[46] and *Mikey and Nicky*'s peripheral female characters who are exercises in "docile female masochism."[47]

A comparison of May to the similarly damned Lina Wertmüller leads Koenig Quart to suspect that both "reflect the wounds of an earlier and lonely generation of women directors."[48] Likewise, even in the midst of defending May, Jill Dawsey notes that "May is perhaps the wrong generation for feminism."[49] The established critical consensus either holds May to account for her failings as a feminist or makes excuses for said failings. Little, if any, acknowledgement seems to be given to the idea that depiction doesn't equal endorsement—that one of America's most accomplished satirists might be inviting audiences to read against the texts—her stereotyped female characters are, after all, blatantly stereotyped, leaving little doubt that they've been carefully constructed to make ironic points rather than mimetically represent some patriarchally skewed vision of reality.

Even were we to accept the proposition that May is condemning her women for their vapidity and masochism, isn't this a restatement of de Beauvoir's existential feminism? "If woman discovers herself as the inessential and never turns into the essential, it is because she does not bring about this transformation herself."[50] Or, as Sartre explains:

What people reproach us with is not, after all, our pessimism, but the sternness of our optimism ... the existentialist, when he portrays a coward, shows him as responsible for his cowardice. He is not like that on account of a cowardly heart or lungs or cerebrum, he has not become like that through his physiological organism; he is like that because he has made himself into a coward by actions.[51]

May's portrayals of women can be unflattering precisely because she presents them as responsible for themselves—Henrietta, Kelly, Lila don't have to be subservient, dependent, male-focused: they are because they masochistically choose to be so. Which, for contemporary ears, might read very close to victim-blaming. But it's no more so than de Beauvoir's assertion that "The man who sets the woman up as an Other will thus find in her a deep complicity."[52] *The Second Sex* devotes over 800 pages to spelling out the patriarchal causality of this complicity, lest there be any confusion regarding the origin of it, but absolving the woman of blame for her situation does not absolve her of responsibility for fighting her way out of it. When May "ambivalently" presents women in ways which make audiences uncomfortable, it's with the purpose of provoking just such a response—an agitation to audiences to examine the dynamics of the situation, to question why things are as they are—and to consider just what each of us can do, as unique and sovereign individuals, to change it.

May might have almost inadvertently snuck into the exclusive male fortress of Hollywood directors[53] but she caused a definitive breach in its barricades with the financial success of *The Heartbreak Kid* the following year. We're approaching the fiftieth anniversary of those moments and still waiting for the masses of female directors to storm through, and there are those who've claimed that May's alleged profligacy, irresponsibility, or general uncooperativeness on *Mikey and Nicky* and *Ishtar* shares some culpability for the delay (Koenig Quart, again, concluding that low-budget or independent films might be a better fit for May, because "freedom really lies in keeping the stakes smaller"[54]). As if, having achieved something that only two women in the previous forty years had managed—directing a Hollywood Studio feature—she was then expected to abandon her artistic integrity, the very protection of which had originally propelled her into the director's chair, and kowtow to the wishes of the studio at every juncture. What kind of victory would it be if we achieved gender parity in Hollywood only to find the new female filmmakers were the same mediocre company hacks as the old male ones? As Germaine Greer wrote:

In 1970, the movement was called "Women's Liberation" ... When (that name) was dropped for "Feminists" we were all relieved. What none of us noticed was that the ideal of liberation was fading out with the word. We were settling for equality.[55]

Which is a roundabout way of saying that getting women behind the camera, while necessary, isn't sufficient. Once there, they can't be on probation. They need permission to fail, to be idiosyncratic and wilful, to slowly discover and redefine the boundaries of an artform that, for more than a century, has been delimited by patriarchal strictures.

Most importantly, in the context of Elaine May's critical reception, they shouldn't be held to account for perceived failures to appropriately redress the balance of gender representation, or create female characters which serve any purpose other than the truth of the work for which they were created. An artist's primary responsibility, after all, is to themselves. Inherent in that, inextricable from it, is a responsibility to all the facets which comprise that self, that identity—including, of course, gender. So, as long as May's work is true to herself, her vision, it can't be anything but feminist. As Alexandra Heller-Nicholas puts it:

> But there is Feminism (a historical movement) and feminism—a way of being in the world, of working in the world, of seeing the world from a position gendered emphatically feminine.[56]

If only *Such Good Friends* had attained a more prominent place in May's resumé, perhaps the discussion of her cinematic feminist credentials—based, as it is, on a relatively small sample size—might have progressed somewhat differently.

Right from the top, the explicit feminist tone is set—Julie attends a rooftop soiree to launch Richard's new children's book. She's introduced to Bernard Kalman (Burgess Meredith), a Norman Mailer-esque Great Author who immediately begins to pontificate on his most recent visit to advise the White House from his position as Chairman of the Cultural Art Committee. Julie imagines him stark naked, with a copy of his latest Masterpiece (which is called Weissmann, just by the way) attached to his loin in place of genitals. The pair dance, Meredith's wizened, flabby flesh offering a sobering antidote to the myth of the white male artist whose art and penis are metaphorically one and the same, May showing little hesitancy in skewering masculinity and setting the tone for the rest of the film. Plus, it's funny as hell, Meredith's genial obliviousness to the fact that we can see right through him the punchline to a moment of Fellini-esque absurdity.

In a 2006 Lincoln Center appearance, May talks about the difficulty of directing in Hollywood for a woman, specifically relating to her debut with *A New Leaf*: "I wanted not to frighten anyone, and so people would leave me saying 'She's a nice girl' . . . and, of course, I wasn't. A nice girl. And when they found it out they hated me all the more."[57] Thirty-five years earlier, she'd scripted this simple summation of Julie Messinger's state of mind:

> You know, I thought about that—about whether or not I was a bitch. And I decided it just doesn't matter . . . all my life I've been "poor Julie," and that gets to be quite a credential after a while, "Look, there goes poor Julie—nice girl."

Her rationale continues—if showing Miranda the diary "disqualifies me as a 'nice girl' then you just go right ahead and think of me as a bitch." It's a clear statement of intent, surfing feminism's second wave on a board of righteous outrage. No more taking it on the chin.

But May takes it further. Cal mockingly responds as if scandalised "Hell hath no fury like a woman scorned" he chuckles. It stops Julie in her tracks. She pauses, considers, and does a beautiful about face. Cannon's mastery of this moment, this line, is among the highlights of her artfully constructed performance: "You're right. I don't want to be a woman who hell hath no more fury than." It's the completion of her journey through equality—responding as a man would—to liberation—responding better than a man would, abandoning a masculine, adversarial response for something kinder and less egotistical. Or, looked at another way, she has journeyed from the existentialism of Sartre to the existentialism of de Beauvoir. She doesn't forgive—her earlier confrontation with Miranda has made that clear—but she's free to be generous. To spare someone unnecessary pain, not because society expects it or to maintain the facade of being a "nice girl." Just because it's the human thing to do. And it allows us an insight into May's perspective on her supposedly unflattering portrayals of female characters. She has an actor's ability to empathize with everyone—she doesn't morally judge Miranda, nor any of the other treacherous friends. She writes them as they are, flawed people, but people nonetheless. And is there anything more fundamentally feminist than the simple assertion that women are people too?

SUCH GOOD FRIENDS: AN EXIT FROM HELL

> Everything encourages her to be invested and dominated by foreign existences: and particularly in love she disavows rather than asserts herself. Misfortune and distress are often learning experiences in this sense.[58]

Recalling this quote by Simone de Beauvoir, with May's history as an existential improviser merging into her inescapably feminist perspective, it's no surprise that *Such Good Friends* becomes, in her hands, a story of Julie's existential liberation. Abandoned by her unconscious husband, she's further abandoned upon discovery that he was not the husband she'd believed. Cast loose from her identity as wife—she has no profession, seemingly no hobbies, she has defined herself by her status as wife—she continues to exist, but must now form a new identity of her own. Several times in the film Julie repeats variations on the refrain "Take a good look, Tom, this is who I am. Do you still want me for your wife?" Said to herself in the mirror in the opening scene and intermittently throughout the film, it reveals a woman compulsively focused on how she looks, how she appears to the eyes of others, embodying the existentialist concept that all consciousness is self-consciousness.[59]

The identity of the "Tom" she addresses this question to is never clear (perhaps Dick or Harry could tell us) but there are no shortage of Others ready to define her as an object in their subjectivities. Her mother (Nina Foch) had already been instrumental in framing her cowed sense of self: "You're a plain girl—a potentially pretty girl—but, right now, you're overweight and plain" is the dismissive pronouncement to a teenaged Julie in flashback. It's symbolic of a constant stream of criticism Julie endures at the hands of a mother who treats her more like a doll than a human being, culminating in her later advice to a visibly distraught Julie—"next to prayer, good grooming is the greatest comfort a woman can have."

Cal wastes no time in trying to seduce Julie once their mutual betrayal is revealed and the clumsily contrived attempt, to the strains of a kazoo and centered around his photographic studio, a few drinks and an urging for her to strip for his camera so she can "see what she looks like as a centerfold" results in another uncomfortable sex scene—Cal struggling to get an erection and becoming so focused on the effort that Julie's prompted to ask drily, "Would you like me to leave and come back when you're finished?" The nude photo, again reducing Julie to the status of object in the eyes of another then revealing her objectness to herself, encapsulates Sartre's notion of The Look and how it's inextricably tied to Shame—shame not in the moralistic sense but shame as a mechanism for revealing our vulnerability and exposure before others.[60] The potential identity offered by Cal, of becoming a liberated woman (sexually speaking), screwing her way around her social circle as Richard had done, is clearly tempting—the glint in Julie's eye leaves us in no doubt that the prospect of realizing some of her well-practiced fantasies will not be a trial for her—but the actuality of the sex is a ridiculous disappointment. Sartre's advice to live without hope was never more appropriate.

Miranda, while not explicitly trying to impact on Julie, provides the impetus for a choice between two distinct identities—spurned, avenging wife and mature, forgiving "modern woman." The former she tries on for size in a beautifully played confrontation scene at Miranda's rehearsal of Shakespeare.

Vulnerable and exposed—emotionally, this time, rather than physically—Julie maintains her calm, well-groomed exterior as Miranda reveals plans to marry Richard. The calm façade gradually turns cold and resolute, culminating in Julie's exit line, original to the film—"If I'm ever in a position to do you any harm, I'm going to let you have it—right in your pretty, little, self-possessed, twelve-year-old teeth." The latter approach, that of the contemporary member of the sexual revolution, forgiving and understanding, is the version Gould allows in the novel. Miranda is welcomed at the hospital, a form of solidarity ensues as the women bond—awkwardly but genuinely—over their mutual fear for Richard's wellbeing.

But May/Preminger's Julie rejects all of these possible selves, all relationally dependent. As Richard goes into cardiac arrest, she takes her place in an astonishing ten-person tableau, arranged horizontally and in depth in the waiting room, all looking at her for the duration of the two-minute shot. She reaches a point where she no longer cares for the machinations of plot:

> I've never seen anyone dying before. It's such hard work. All that effort, just to live one minute longer. Just to catch one more breath. So who cares who he screwed, or how many times, or whose feelings got hurt. If he only lives.

He doesn't. Timmy enters to deliver the news, ten artfully arrayed faces watching Julie for a reaction. But there's no reaction, just acceptance. And the film dispenses with all the business of the funeral, all the mundanity of the novel's posthumous scenes. We simply get the assembled friends returning silently to Julie's apartment. She disappears as Uncle Eddie begins to offer his unbidden opinion on her real-estate options, returning with her two children and leaving the apartment without a word of explanation. To her mother's suggestion that she accompany her, the reply is a matter-of-fact "No, Mother." As she walks into Central Park and the credits roll, we realize that she's yet to choose an identity—for her, the future will be improvised.

NOTES

1. Jean-Paul Sartre, *Existentialism and Humanism*, trans. Philip Mairet (London: Methuen, 2007), p. 27.
2. Foster Hirsch, *Otto Preminger: The Man Who Would Be King* (New York: Alfred A. Knopf, 2007), p. 451.
3. Simone de Beauvoir, *The Second Sex*, trans. Constance Borde and Sheila Malovany-Chevallier (New York: Alfred A. Knopf, 2010), p. 844.
4. As discussed elsewhere in this book, Maria Ouspenskaya was a Russian actress who was

among the original members of the Moscow Art Theatre's First Studio in 1912. The Studio—a smaller-scale company within the MAT under the immediate direction of Stanislavsky disciple Leopold Sulerzhitsky—was where much of the experimentation (the "nuts-and-bolts" application and refinement of Stanislavsky's theories of acting) was accomplished, away from the commercial pressures of the main-stage company. Ouspenskaya—along with fellow Studio members including Richard Boleslawski, Michael Chekhov and Vera Soloviova—was among a wave of Stanislavksian evangelists who brought his ideas to the U.S. and Britain. Among her students in America number gurus of modern American acting such as Stella Adler, Lee Strasberg, and Harold Clurman. For a comprehensive account of Ouspenskaya's life and work, see Pamela Sue Heilman, "The American Career of Maria Ouspenskaya (1887–1949): Actress and Teacher," *LSU Historical Dissertations and Theses*, 6890 (1999) <https://digitalcommons.lsu.edu/gradschool_disstheses/6890> (accessed January 2019).

5. Sartre, pp. 29–30.
6. Kevin Johnson, "Elaine May: Do You Mind Interviewing Me in the Kitchen?" *New York Times*, 8 January 1967: 103.
7. Ibid., p. 103.
8. Jonathan Rosenbaum, *Essential Cinema: On the Necessity of Film Canons* (Baltimore: The Johns Hopkins University Press, 2008), p. 364.
9. Barbara Koenig Quart, *Women Directors: The Emergence of a New Cinema* (New York: Praeger, 1988), p. 48.
10. Sartre, p. 33.
11. Ibid., p. 44.
12. Ibid., p. 45.
13. Ibid., p. 23. As Sartre noted, "we are reproached for having underlined all that is ignominious in the human situation, for depicting what is mean, sordid or base to the neglect of certain things that possess charm and beauty and belong to the brighter side of human nature: for example, according to the Catholic critic, Mlle Mercier, we forget how an infant smiles."
14. de Beauvoir, p. 33.
15. Cynthia Baron, *Modern Acting: The Lost Chapter of American Film and Theatre* (London: MacMillan, 2016), p. 22.
16. Paul Sills (1927–2008), co-founder and director of The Compass Players, would go on to found The Second City, Game Theater, Story Theater and other projects rooted in long-form improvisational techniques he adapted from the revolutionary theater games developed by his mother, Viola Spolin. Janet Coleman's *The Compass: The Story of the Improvisational Theatre That Revolutionized the Art of Comedy in America* (Chicago: University of Chicago Press, 1990) is an in-depth study of the formation of The Compass Players and Sills' earlier work with The Playwrights' Theatre at the University of Chicago, where he first met May and Nichols.
17. Myrna Oliver, "Obituary: Lois Gould, 70; Novelist and Columnist," *Los Angeles Times*, 4 June 2002 <http://articles.latimes.com/2002/jun/04/local/me-gould4> (accessed January 2019 via keyword search).
18. Gould was the daughter of prominent New York fashion designer Jo Copeland and, by her own account—the 1998 memoir *Mommy Dressing: A Love Story, After a Fashion*—endured a childhood typified by being shut in her bedroom while the likes of Joan Crawford and Tyrone Power partied downstairs.
19. Willi Frischauer, *Behind the Scenes of Otto Preminger* (London: Michael Joseph, 1973), pp. 236–7.

20. Hirsch, p. 450.
21. Chris Fujiwara, *The World and Its Double* (New York: Faber and Faber, 2008), p. 386.
22. Hirsch, p. 450.
23. Ibid., p. 451.
24. Ibid., p. 451.
25. Fujiwara, p. 386.
26. Frischauer, p. 241.
27. Ibid., p. 241.
28. Ibid., p. 241.
29. Fujiwara, pp. 388–9.
30. Hirsch, pp. 454–5.
31. *American Masters: Mike Nichols*, DVD, dir. Elaine May (New York: Filmrise, 2016).
32. Sam Kashner, "Who's Afraid of Nichols and May?" *Vanity Fair*, December 2012 <https://www.vanityfair.com/hollywood/2013/01/nichols-and-may-reunion-exclusive> (accessed January 2019).
33. Chuck Stephens, "Chronicle of a Disappearance," *Film Comment* 42.2 (March–April 2006): 46. Stephens relates the (perhaps apocryphal) story of May admonishing Enrique Bravo, her camera operator on *Mikey and Nicky*, for calling cut when her two leads had walked out of frame, with the explanation "They might come back."
34. Gould, p. 12.
35. Ibid., p. 14.
36. Ibid., p. 184.
37. Ibid., pp. 180–4.
38. May's casting of Ned Beatty as the hitman in *Mikey and Nicky* makes for an interesting comparison.
39. Milan Kundera, *Testaments Betrayed* (London: Faber and Faber, 1995), p. 6.
40. Sartre, p. 27.
41. Tina Hassannia, "TIFF Retrospective on Elaine May Looks Beyond the Flop Ishtar to Her Underappreciated Body of Work," *Toronto Globe and Mail*, 7 June, 2018 <https://www.theglobeandmail.com/arts/film/article-elaine-may-above-and-beyond-ishtar/> (accessed January 2019).
42. Koenig Quart, p. 39.
43. Ibid., p. 39.
44. Ibid., p. 39.
45. Ibid., pp. 40–1.
46. Ibid., pp. 42–3.
47. Ibid., p. 47.
48. Ibid., p. 42.
49. Jill Dawsey in Julian Myers, "Four Dialogues 4: On Elaine May," *Open Space* <https://openspace.sfmoma.org/2009/08/four-dialogues-4-on-elaine-may/> (accessed January 2019).
50. de Beauvoir, p. 28.
51. Sartre, pp. 49–50.
52. de Beauvoir, p. 30.
53. "Elaine May in conversation with Mike Nichols," *Film Comment*, July/August 2006 <https://www.filmcomment.com/article/elaine-may-in-conversation-with-mike-nichols/> (accessed January 2019). The interview, conducted after a screening of *Ishtar* at Lincoln Center, describes how May initially had no desire to direct *A New Leaf* but took the mantle as a compromise when Paramount refused to allow her director approval—the

studio clearly believing that she would be more pliable and controllable than any "Queen's Champion" she might have chosen.
54. Koenig Quart, p. 50.
55. Germaine Greer, *The Whole Woman* (London; Sydney: Doubleday, 1999), p. 2.
56. Alexandra Heller-Nicholas, "Mainstream Obscurity: The Films of Elaine May," *4:3 Film*, 6 August 2016 <https://fourthreefilm.com/2016/08/mainstream-obscurity-the-films-of-elaine-may/> (accessed January 2019).
57. "Elaine May in conversation with Mike Nichols."
58. de Beauvoir, p. 844.
59. Jean-Paul Sartre, *Being and Nothingness; An Essay on Phenomenological Ontology*, trans. Hazel E. Barnes (London: Methuen, 1957), p. 449.
60. Sartre, *Being and Nothingness*, p. 261: "Now, shame, as we noted at the beginning of this chapter, is shame of *self*; it is the recognition of the fact that I am indeed that object which the Other is looking at and judging. I can be ashamed only as my freedom escapes me in order to become a given object. Thus originally the bond between my unreflective consciousness and my Ego, which is being looked at, is a bond not of knowing but of being. Beyond any knowledge which I can have, I am this self which another knows."

CHAPTER 10

Spectral Elaine May—The Later Mike Nichols Collaborations and the Myth of the Recluse

Tim O'Farrell

Just over a year after Mike Nichols' death in late 2014, the biographical documentary *American Masters: Mike Nichols* (2016), directed by Elaine May, was broadcast on American TV. Given their continuing collaborations over almost fifty years, it is fitting that May's first directorial assignment after a gap of almost thirty years since *Ishtar* (1987) is a tribute to Nichols. I want to analyze how May approached this assignment, against the pervasive perception of her as a singularly recessive figure, a reclusive artist licking her wounds. Another perspective is to grasp May's achievements as a prodigiously productive artist, one of the most intriguing and unorthodox creative talents of her generation, shape-shifting and moving between writing, acting, and directing. After considering her *American Masters* documentary, I will also examine how May's symbiotic connection with Nichols was reinforced by her rare acceptance of writing credits on their two final late-stage collaborations: *The Birdcage* (1996) and *Primary Colors* (1998).

"Vanishing Elaine May" articles have been staple journalistic fodder for decades. In 2013, Sam Kashner wrote: "The last in-depth interview she gave was to *LIFE* magazine in 1967 ... She has mostly held her silence ever since."[1] An *IndieWire* profile in 2013 described May as "famously publicity shy,"[2] and in his 2000 profile of Mike Nichols in *The New Yorker*, John Lahr noted that she "no longer gives interviews."[3] Many such pieces attribute May's banishment as a Hollywood director to *Ishtar*'s commercial and critical caning, but suggestions that she has hidden from the spotlight predate that film's release. Indeed, the 1967 *LIFE* magazine article referred to above now seems uncannily prescient. The article's preface read: "It's been six years since the famous comedy team of Mike Nichols and Elaine May broke up. Everybody knows what became of Mike Nichols: he is a spectacularly successful Broadway and Hollywood director. But . . .," before the title dramatically drops in: "Whatever Happened to Elaine May?"[4]

As has been canvassed in detail elsewhere in this book, Nichols and May met during their time at the University of Chicago in the early 1950s, beginning as performers at The Compass Players before launching their wildly successful comedy partnership, culminating in a smash Broadway show *An Evening with Nichols and May*, from which a best-selling comedy album of the same name was produced. Both May and Nichols had to find their feet after disbanding at the height of their fame in 1961. Fast-forward six years and Nichols' star was ascendant as director of the breakout hits *Who's Afraid of Virginia Woolf?* (1966) and *The Graduate* (1967). May's Hollywood CV at this time was relatively scant: she had directed a short entitled *Bach to Bach* in 1967 and appeared uncredited as the "Girl with note for Benjamin" in *The Graduate*. This apparent disjunction continues throughout later decades. Nichols cemented his place as a Hollywood heavy hitter by continuing to direct zeitgeisty hits such as *Working Girl* (1988), *Postcards From the Edge* (1990) and *The Birdcage* (1996), and an early entry into the HBO prestige TV canon, *Angels in America* (2003). May, by contrast, directed just four features: *A New Leaf* (1971), *The Heartbreak Kid* (1972), *Mikey and Nicky* (1976), and *Ishtar* (1987). She did, however, carve out a lucrative career as a (largely uncredited) screenwriting gun for hire, a topic I will return to with *The Birdcage* and *Primary Colors*, the two high-profile collaborations that confirmed May had not disappeared.

AMERICAN MASTERS: MIKE NICHOLS

Elaine May's final tribute to Mike Nichols is at once a curious and conventional beast. The conventional is easy: May's tribute to her lifelong comedic and professional partner is in many ways typical of the standard format for this long-running series broadcast on the American PBS network. Organized around producer Julian Schlossberg's interview, interspersed with clips from Nichols' body of work, archival photographs and footage, at one level this tribute is cookie-cutter public broadcaster TV arts documentary. A sprinkling of testimony from celebrities and artists who worked with or were inspired by Nichols (Dustin Hoffman, Robin Williams, Steven Spielberg, Meryl Streep, Alec Baldwin, Paul Simon, Matthew Broderick, Tom Hanks, Renata Adler, James L. Brooks and Bob Balaban) adds some stardust to the familiar format. This brings us to the curious: with interview duties ceded to Schlossberg, May is not visibly present for much of the program. However, as I will investigate later in this section, her perspective can be clearly divined by the selection and arrangement of content, which often suggests an uneasy relationship with the film industry and related critical apparatus.

In plotting a largely chronological course, May begins with a sequence that segues from a snippet of Mozart's Serenade No. 13 in G Major (*Eine Kleine Nachtmusik*) to footage of Adolf Hitler mid-rant in one of his trademark rally speeches, melding with Nichols' voiceover: "I was born in Berlin. I have memories of blackshirt kids taking my bike. I have memories of going to special Jewish school." Acknowledging the strongly Jewish heritage shared by Nichols and May which has been central to their writing and comedy style, this sequence also emphasizes Nichols' credentials as a refugee fleeing Hitler's Germany just as World War II was breaking out. He reflects on his difficulties forming friendships at school and his family's struggle to assimilate into the United States. This struggle prompts the first of Nichols' storehouse of vivid anecdotes, as he mimics his parents communicating in a hybrid German-inflected pidgin English: "Hast den room been gesweeped?"

After dispatching Nichols' school years and adolescence in relatively short order, May moves on to his introduction to college in Chicago, a crucially formative period. There he immediately met future luminaries such as Susan Sontag, whom he recalls encountering in line when enrolling, and Ed Asner. It was also in Chicago that both he and May joined The Compass Players improvisational theater troupe. In this space they honed their performance and writing skills, focusing on the creation and development of characters that would become the signature of their comedy partnership and later film work. Nichols' interest in performance is further underlined by reference to his enrollment in Method acting classes with Lee Strasberg.[5]

Despite playing *the* pivotal role in the Mike Nichols story, Elaine May does not place herself at the center of her work, which is far removed from the performance-driven mode of documentary epitomized by Nick Broomfield or Michael Moore. Her on-screen presence is restricted to archival footage from two industry awards nights fifty years apart, effectively bookending the May–Nichols working partnership. In the first, a comedy skit from the 1959 Emmy awards which appears early on, she professes to be honored to present the "Total Mediocrity Award" to Nichols who plays the recipient, "Lionel Klutz". A typically sardonic takedown of the captive audience of industry insiders, it kicks off with a token acknowledgement that the Emmy awards reward the artistic and the creative, before she rhetorically asks: "But what of the others in this industry? Seriously, there are men in the industry who go on, year in and year out, quietly and unassumingly producing garbage." The second clip, towards the end of the documentary, comes more than fifty years later, as she pays tribute at Nichols' AFI Life Achievement Award in 2010. Here she playfully roasts him, highlighting his capacity to weave a line between populist success and political significance: "Mike has chosen to do things that are really meaningful, and that have real impact and real relevance, but he makes them so entertaining and exciting that they're as much fun as if they were trash."

These sly critiques together suggest a creative manifesto founded on a hunger for distinctive, fresh material deviating from the mainstream, while remaining significant and entertaining. As a writer and director May has eschewed an industry built upon mediocrity, preferring to take the road less travelled, breaking conventions, courting controversy, and facing perpetual struggles for creative control. In the Schlossberg interview, Nichols reflects on how she instigated the break-up of their partnership during their highly successful, extended Broadway show run because she felt stifled by continually performing familiar material. He notes that while he was content doing this given the material rewards and adulation the pair received, ". . . it was strangely hard on Elaine; she felt like she had to do it over and over and over . . . Elaine wanted to do more." Nichols' testimony as to her integrity and moral compass is bolstered by an anecdote about her asking him to appear with her at a Civil Rights concert for marchers from Selma to Montgomery in 1965. When the producer of his debut feature *Who's Afraid of Virginia Woolf?* forbade him from going, she simply said: "It's up to you," prompting Nichol's reaction, "Oh fuck, I have to go."

The critique of the studio system continues with a sequence featuring Nichols' recollections of his struggles with Jack Warner as he was making *Who's Afraid of Virginia Woolf?*. When he first met Warner, he thought his friends in the studio had set up an elaborate ruse by getting an actor to play the studio head, because he seemed so exaggerated: "I thought that they had made him up as a cigar store Indian and that this was some guy playing the ultimate asshole . . . [it was] totally impossible that this could be a real person who owns the studio. I could never take him seriously." He managed to ward off a move by Warner to change the film from black and white to color two weeks before shooting began, only to be fired after shooting, when the film was being edited, and barred from the lot. This anecdote ends with Nichols reinstated via a savvy maneuver: realizing Warner's fear of condemnation by the Catholic Legion of Decency, he offered to get his friend Jackie Kennedy to sit behind the Legion's Monsignor at the test screening to praise the film as beautiful and say how much Jack (Kennedy) would have loved it.

Approaching the culmination of the *American Masters* portrait, May includes an extended sequence featuring Nichols' bitter denunciation of critical appraisals of his work and American cinema more generally. Beginning by rebuking critics for lazily reducing *The Graduate*'s thematics to a disproportionate focus on the "generation gap," he then dismisses all critics with a broad generalization of his own: "The people who describe all our work to us often don't know what they're talking about. They're wrong . . . they are people, literally, who think that expressing an opinion is a creative act." This is followed by an indictment of the notion of the *auteur* and French film criticism ("the Froggie conspiracy"), employing a familiar putdown by sniffing at the

French admiration for Jerry Lewis and fatuously leveling the *polemique* of the *Cahiers du Cinéma* critics: "To say it's the work of one man is to completely misunderstand a quite mysterious process."[6]

While this rant against critics is crudely superficial and unmoored from any historical context or nuance, it does take the portrait to an interesting conclusion: a paean to the work of screenwriters as Nichols celebrates the contribution of Robert Bolt's screenplays to the work of David Lean. Given this final tribute to the art of the screenplay, it's worth highlighting perhaps the most significant Elaine May absence of all in *American Masters: Mike Nichols*: no reference is made to two of Nichols' highest profile films on which she was screenwriter, *The Birdcage* and *Primary Colors*. The absence of these films is a stark omission in the documentary, which otherwise focuses on high-profile Nichols films by showing brief excerpts, reflections from Nichols or his associates or critical responses to the work. In the remainder of this chapter, I want to fill in these blanks by looking at these films in the context of Elaine May's broader career, with particular reference to her screenwriting.

ELAINE MAY: GUN FOR HIRE

May was a true pioneer in a period when female scriptwriters were a rarity, working on her own scripts as director in *A New Leaf*, *Mikey and Nicky*, and *Ishtar*, as well as chalking up credits as screenwriter on films such as *Heaven can Wait* (Warren Beatty, 1978), *The Birdcage* and *Primary Colors*.[7] Even more intriguingly, she was one of the leading script doctors of the late twentieth century, working uncredited on many scripts, including *Labyrinth* (Jim Henson, 1986), Mike Nichols' *Wolf* (1994) and *Dangerous Minds* (John N. Smith, 1995). She also contributed extensive uncredited rewrites for Warren Beatty's script for *Reds* (1981) and for *Tootsie* (Sydney Pollack, 1982), where she created Bill Murray's role as Tootsie's (Dustin Hoffman) playwright roommate.[8] Jason Bailey notes how both Hoffman and *Tootsie* director Sydney Pollack credit her with "fleshing out the female characters—particularly Terri Garr's Sandy, whose neuroticism mirrors the kind of roles May would often play herself."[9]

Mike Nichols expressed pride that May chose to take a writing credit on *The Birdcage*, noting in his foreword to her shooting script for the film that she very rarely did so.[10] Jonathan Rosenbaum distinguished May from Nichols as "too large and unwieldy a talent to accommodate herself to the entertainment industry," noting that "given the complex and tortuous skirmishes she had with studios on all four of her features, it is hardly surprising that she has worked in Hollywood chiefly as an anonymous script doctor."[11] May's battles over creative control are well documented both throughout this book and in pieces such as Jonathan Rosenbaum's article "The Mysterious Elaine May: Hiding in Plain Sight"[12] and Jessica Kiang's 2013 *IndieWire* retrospective appreciation.

May's choice to stay uncredited on many of the projects she worked on dates back to early in her writing career. She tried to get her name removed from *A New Leaf* after the studio re-edited the film and as Paul Jeffery's earlier chapter outlines in detail, she has a complicated relationship with the script for Otto Preminger's *Such Good Friends* (1972), for which she was credited under the pseudonym Esther Dale. When questioned as to why she didn't take a credit on these jobs, for May it ultimately came back to her lack of control: "You can make a deal if you're going to do the original writing. But if you're going to do the original re-writing, you can't. No matter how much you write, what you write, you're still a hired gun, and you have no control . . . The only time I really ever took credit was when I worked with Mike . . . because I knew him, and I thought probably he won't fuck it up."[13] Charles Grodin, who starred in *The Heartbreak Kid*, says: "Elaine is the exact opposite of everyone else in Hollywood. She's always fighting to get as little credit as possible, to keep her name off movies, to *not* be invited to the parties."[14]

POLITICS, "LIFESTYLE", AND "FAMILY VALUES": *THE BIRDCAGE* AND *PRIMARY COLORS*

May's two final collaborations with Mike Nichols indicate that she remained comfortable working out in the open with her most trusted partner. *The Birdcage* and *Primary Colors* share some revealing similarities in terms of Elaine May's writing "signature." Both explicitly deal with the political landscape of the U.S.A. in the late twentieth century, exploring unorthodox family values; the hazy line between authenticity, duplicity, and role-playing; partnerships; friendships, rivalries, marriages; and, hovering over all of these, the potential for deception and betrayal. The principal characters in both films are projecting or performing an idealized image that is constantly on the edge of being exposed. Jonathan Rosenbaum has described May's films as being "populated exclusively by monsters whom she adores,"[15] and both *The Birdcage* and *Primary Colors* broadly fit this template, featuring rounded characters who are appealing even as they behave monstrously at times. Each film employed A-list talent in exploring a socially progressive critique, cushioned inside comic cladding.

Both films move fluidly between social and broader societal politics, pivoting on May's superpower as a screenwriter and script doctor: uncovering the intricacies and nuances of interpersonal relationships. Her ability to expose quirks and render tensions in deceptively straightforward, organic and comic dialogue is also on display in both films. May's tangible contributions to the adaptation of *Primary Colors* are less obvious than her work on *The Birdcage*, but her characteristically subtle and perceptive handling of interpersonal relations is of a piece with her body of work more generally. The novel *Primary Colors*, adapted by May for Nichols, provided less latitude for creative input. By contrast, adapting the 1978 French film *La Cage Aux Folles* (Édouard Molinaro), which in turn was based on French playwright Jean Poiret's play of the same name, to make *The Birdcage*, involved transplanting both the time and place of the action, providing a clean slate for May to dissect contemporary American politics.

The Birdcage is set in South Beach, Miami, as opposed to the original glitzy Saint Tropez setting. Both films are structured as farces, from very similar premises. In each case a son returns home to tell his gay parents he intends to marry the daughter of a prominent ultra-conservative politician. The gay parents in the American version are Armand (Robin Williams), who owns The Birdcage, a drag nightclub, and his partner Albert (Nathan Lane), the flamboyant leading entertainer at the club. Before Armand and Albert met, a one-night stand between Armand and Katherine (Christine Baranski), resulted in a son Val (Dan Futterman), who was raised by Armand and Albert. As an adult, Val returns home to announce he is engaged to Barbara (Calista Flockhart), the daughter of ultra-conservative Senator Kevin Keeley (Gene Hackman) and his wife Louise Keeley (Dianne Wiest). Hoping to appease Barbara's parents, Val asks Armand to hide the fact that he's gay and effectively step back into the closet.

This sets up a classic farce structure, providing ample scope for conflict and absurdist comedy. May's script co-opts Sister Sledge's "We Are Family" as the opening song accompanying a sweeping shot of the South Beach scene before tracking into Armand's nightclub. The emphasis here is on an expansive definition of "family" as we see Albert and Armand bickering. We are then introduced to Senator Keeley, founder of The Coalition for Moral Order, a leading pressure group promoting "family values." Early on in the film it is revealed that his bid for re-election is being complicated by a typically American scandal: his co-founder of The Coalition for Moral Order, Senator Jackson, has suffered a fatal heart attack while sleeping with an underage black prostitute. When Barbara announces she is getting married to Val, the Keeleys' discomfiture at knowing nothing about her intended fiancé's "people" is balanced with their hope that the impending nuptials will provide a welcome, wholesome distraction, glossing over Senator Jackson's escapades.

From this starting point, May's script delves deeply into the distinct cultural and political wars whirling around the issues of sexuality and gender politics in the 1990s. In an era where serial Republican primary candidate Pat Buchanan (1992, 1996 and 2000) declared at the Houston Republican Convention in

1992 that there was a religious and cultural war "going on in our country for the soul of America," among other things denouncing "homosexual rights" and "radical feminism," May had plenty of material to work with. Other culture war hot button issues included attacks on funding for the National Endowment for the Arts and public broadcasters led by conservative politicians who had excoriated the work of artists such as Robert Mapplethorpe and Andres Serrano for their queer and religious content, and alleged left-wing bias in the media. Mike Nichols identified the "triumph" of May's script as being, in transposing the French source material, "to ask the question, 'How would it be if this happened right here, right now, in today's society?' She understood that you have to include every possible kind of prejudice in the telling of this story, because in the final reconciliation you represent everyone—not just gays and heterosexuals, but Jews and Gentiles, Democrats and Republicans . . . one hopes the whole country."[16]

May's script deftly renders this broader political climate, threading it through the personal circumstances of the characters in fleshing out their opposing "lifestyles" and "values." When we first meet the Keeleys Barbara lies about Val's parents in an attempt to make them more palatable to her parents, saying Val's father works "in the arts . . . on the Council of Cultural Arts," leading her father to ask horrified "The ones that funded the Mapplethorpe exhibit?" Barbara adamantly denies this: "No, no. Goodness, no. He's a cultural attaché to Greece." Asked about Val's mother, Barbara redeems herself by saying she's a housewife, prompting Mrs Keely to exclaim how refreshing this is. Later the Keeleys watch a dire show featuring Senator Keeley, Senator Jackson, and two hosts. The script states "All four men are shouting, incomprehensibly."[17] As these older white males rage against the world, Mrs Keeley describes it as "a wonderful show" and Senator Keely praises it as "the most intelligent show on television," just as Senator Keeley is shown on TV stating that abortion, same-sex marriage, contempt for family values, and pornography would not exist if politicians did not make laws to protect them. Immediately after this, as Senator Jackson's death leads the breaking news on TV, Mrs Keeley proposes "a big white wedding" to restore her husband's image, gushing: "a white wedding is family and morality and tradition."

Produced in a pre-same-sex marriage era, *The Birdcage* features unconventional, non-traditional family configurations. A running theme of palimony almost eclipses the ostensible central theme of marriage, highlighting the precariousness of rights for unmarried partners. Notwithstanding the formal barriers to recognition of Armand and Albert's relationship, the script makes it very clear that the idea of family values is broader than those heterosexual unions capable of being blessed by the law. In a fit of pique early on Albert angrily demands a palimony agreement. This narrative thread is picked up and resolved through a later sequence that stands out as a beacon of understatement and quietude in an otherwise conspicuously raucous film. Armand offers Albert a palimony agreement, explaining that it will make them safer if something happens to one of them. Once the agreement is signed, Armand says "There—we're partners. You own half of my life, and I own half of yours." When Albert queries his generosity, Armand responds "What does it matter? Take it all . . . There's only one place in the world I call home, and it's because you're there."

The treatment of more peripheral characters also bolsters the point that loving connections are not restricted to the nuclear family. May's script for *The Birdcage* updates the gay couple's maid in *La Cage Aux Folles* from a sardonic black man to a flamboyant Guatemalan, Agador Spartacus (Hank Azaria). In addition to providing comic relief, Agador is a reliable backstop, attending to and soothing Albert during his more histrionic outbursts.[18] Similarly, in a scene where Armand visits Val's biological mother, Katherine, and the pair dance together after decades without contact, there is a reservoir of affection and connection. The character of Katherine is only briefly sketched, but without judgement for her lack of maternal instinct, and positively, as someone who can acknowledge Val was better off raised by Albert and Armand. A lingering suggestion of flirtation, and more than a hint of sexual fluidity, pervades this understated scene.

At the core of *The Birdcage* is the corrosive impact of intolerance and the pressure to conform to a mainstream version of family values. While played for laughs with ruthless effectiveness, May's script clearly demonstrates the price paid by Armand and Albert in acceding to Val's request to deny their true selves. Armand is conflicted and angry at having to lie about who he is and pretend to be straight, but reluctantly does so out of love for his son. Albert understandably takes offence when it is suggested he absent himself for the Keeleys' visit, leave his home and vacate his parental role, to be replaced by Val's biological mother. After much handwringing Armand and Albert decide to reject this proposal, leading to the most telling sequence in the film, a masterclass in humor and sexual politics, as Armand and Val coach the effete Albert in passing as straight, journeying through the full catalog of gender stereotypes. From keeping the pinky down when drinking tea, to spreading mustard ("Men smear!") and slicing toast, Albert's posture, voice and gait are all microscopically examined. As Albert rehearses walking less swishly, the scene culminates in an analysis of John Wayne's gait. While some of this detail is taken from *La Cage Aux Folles*, in the final exchange May comically sums up the futility of their attempts to pass as straight as they enact roles as butch, football-loving dudes:

> ARMAND: Al, you old son-of-a-bitch! How you doin'? How do you feel about that call today? I mean, the Dolphins! Fourth-and-three play on their 30-yard line with only 43 seconds to go!

ALBERT: How do you think I feel? Betrayed, bewildered ... wrong response?
ARMAND: Actually, I'm not sure.

This sequence brilliantly reveals the lunacy of the socially determined phenomenon of "passing", making it clear—as in Douglas Sirk's *Imitation of Life* (1959)—that whenever passing is in play, what's at stake is a lack of authenticity that is socially and culturally enforced, turning a person against their own nature. This profound truth is embroidered into the script, not as a labored lesson to be dutifully digested by the audience, but in a joyous, carnivalesque sequence using subversive humor to turn conventional assumptions about gender roles and behavior on their head. The theme of authenticity carries through in Senator Keeley's withering assessment of Armand, whose lack of authenticity he immediately intuits (railing against his European snobbery, dubious crockery and controlling impulse leading him to take over the kitchen). Ironically, the senator is enraptured by Mrs. Coleman as played by Albert, remarking "They don't make women like that anymore" and remaining solicitous of her throughout the film. He contrasts her folksiness with Armand's urbanity: "She's a small-town girl and he's a pretentious European—the worst kind—with his Côte d' whatever and his decadent china."

May's script artfully uses its farce structure to wring humor from a series of denials of nature involving religion and sexuality. These repressive episodes sketch a major theme—the pressure to keep things nice by sweeping contentious issues under the carpet. Signposts to Armand and Albert's Jewish heritage are woven into the first act of the screenplay: Armand's surname is Goldman; in a local bakery Albert orders the German delicacy *schnecken* beloved of Jewish immigrant communities in the U.S. ("When the schnecken beckons!"); and Armand fondly rolls out the Yiddish vernacular in calling Val "a little pisher," or squirt. So when they acquiesce in disguising their religion by changing their name to the more Anglo "Coleman" for their evening with the Keeleys, it represents another turn away from nature and the authentic self. In this instance, the brittle neuroticism characteristic of so much Jewish humor[19] functions both as a major plot point and as a payoff tag at the end of the film when, echoing *Some Like it Hot* (Billy Wilder, 1959), Albert's wig is removed. Senator Keeley's shock when this happens does not initially register in relation to the gender switch, but rather through his protestation: "You can't be Jewish!" Ultimately the split between the families' Jewish and Christian faith is reconciled in the final scene of the film, when Barbara and Val marry in an inter-faith ceremony.

May's script also addresses other repressive episodes related to the culture wars around sexuality in the 1990s. Before the Keeleys arrive the homoerotic art in the Goldmans' house must be hidden, and when the families sit down to dinner the classical styled male coupling in their soup bowls must be explained away as a game of leapfrog. Highly topical when *The Birdcage* was produced, there are also numerous references to the Clinton administration's infamous compromise "Don't Ask, Don't Tell" policy in the script. This policy, introduced in 1994, allowed queer officers to serve in the military so long as they were not open about their sexuality. When Agador is asked by Armand to dress more soberly in a suit for the Keeleys' visit, he protests it will make him "look like a fag." Armand responds "But you'll look like a fag in uniform," to which Agador instantly hits back "Don't ask, don't tell." In a later discussion, Albert (dressed in drag to pass as Val's mom) opines: "Now there's an idiotic issue: gays in the military? I mean, those haircuts, those uniforms, who cares?" Senator Keeley launches into a signature rant about homosexuality being "one of the things that's weakening this country," prompting Albert's return to antiquity, musing about Alexander the Great's sexuality: "Talk about gays in the military."

The novel *Primary Colors*, adapted by Elaine May for Mike Nichols' 1998 film, was published in 1996 and originally simply attributed to "Anonymous." Months after publication, the author was revealed to be Joe Klein, who covered Bill Clinton's 1992 presidential primary campaign as a columnist for *Newsweek*. Klein's book was a thinly disguised exposé of the Democratic primaries, with protagonist John Stanton (played by John Travolta in the film) clearly a Bill Clinton proxy, and his wife Susan (Emma Thompson) a stand-in for Hillary Clinton. Stanton is a southern Democratic Governor hoping to become the first baby boomer president, plagued by what ex-Clinton Chief of Staff Betsey Wright (connected to the Libby Holden character in the novel and film) described as "bimbo eruptions" or rumors of extra-marital affairs. The novel was a *cause célèbre* when originally released due to its apparently insider account of the Clinton campaign's internal machinations, tactics and the scandals surrounding his candidacy.

It is not as simple to discern May's work in the adaptation of *Primary Colors* as in *The Birdcage*, as the film is much more closely aligned with its source, with its primary plot points largely constructed around Klein's lengthy, 366-page novel. Jack Stanton is viewed from the perspective of Henry Burton (Adrian Lester), the grandson of a revered civil rights pioneer, who is persuaded to leave his job as an aide to African-American Congressman Adam Larkin to act as Jack's campaign manager. Henry is diagnosed by chief campaign strategist Richard Jemmons (Billy Bob Thornton, channeling Clinton aide James Carville) with a case of "galloping TB," or "true-believerism." As accusations of sexual infidelity and other misbehavior mount, and his opponent Lawrence Harris launches attacks on his character, the Stantons hire ex-staffer Libby Holden (Kathy Bates) to investigate allegations against the Governor. When Stanton finally goes on the offensive against Harris after continually insisting he will not go negative, Harris suffers a heart attack and withdraws. Former Florida Governor Fred Picker (Larry Hagman), Harris's replacement, emerges as a real threat due to his virtuous image and unconventional approach. When the Stantons ask Libby and Henry to investigate Picker's past, they uncover drug use and homosexual liaisons, testing the Stantons' professed desire to play it clean. The Stantons fail this challenge, leaving the ultimate true believer, Libby, devastated. When she commits suicide, Henry must consider where he stands.

While both *Primary Colors* and *The Birdcage* feature characters who are prominent American politicians under intense media scrutiny, May's work in *Primary Colors* operates in less of an exaggerated comic register than *The Birdcage*, hewing more to its source in presenting an almost anthropological study of political processes. In fact, real life events involving the Clintons indicate how truth is stranger than fiction: just prior to the film's premiere, the Clinton–Lewinsky story broke, overshadowing *Primary Colors*' release. The salacious details of the liaison between how President Clinton and the young intern Monica Lewinsky went far beyond the film's relatively decorous handling of primary candidate Jack Stanton's extra-marital liaisons, which are never shown, but rather suggested, through media reports and campaign team dialogue.

Of necessity, the novel's content is subject to significant abridgement and rearrangement in changing format to film. The principal elements retained by May in her translation of Klein's novel are strikingly connected to her overall *oeuvre*: the sassy banter, colorful characterization, exploration of the dynamics of partnerships and the themes of betrayal and masculine bravado. Ultimately she delivers an even-handed analysis of the vision, charisma, egocentricity, political savvy, foibles and thick skin of the presidential candidate. She dispenses with some more turgid material arising out of the novel's fascination with the byzantine world of political operatives, while retaining elements of the Clinton campaign fictionalized in the book, including the claims of extra-marital affairs threatening to derail the campaign, the key role played by the candidate's wife, and central protagonists such as Jemmons and Henry Burton.

As in the novel, May's adaptation is focalized through Henry, so we view the Stantons and the conduct of the campaign from his perspective. The script deletes or downplays some of the novel's more salacious plotlines, including a scene where Henry goes to bed with Susan. It also treats the development of a relationship between Henry and campaign adviser/spokeswoman Daisy Green (Maura Tierney) in a much more cursory fashion. Libby Holden's relationship with girlfriend Jennifer (Stacy Edwards) is similarly introduced *in medias res* and in each case, any romance is downplayed thereafter. Stanton's mother, a character in the novel and listed in the credits as played by Diane Ladd, also ended up on the cutting room floor, despite the retention of the novel's showdown "mommathan" scene, where Stanton and Jemmons strive to outdo each other in recounting the sacrifices made by their respective "mommas" and professing their abiding devotion.

These departures from the novel focus the film intensely on the political process as seen through Henry's eyes. The novel features a number of leaders in the black community who meet with Henry, offering advice about his role in Stanton's campaign, including Luther Charles, who talks with Henry later in the book about his option of leaving the Stanton campaign and also introduces Henry to a black woman who says she was Stanton's girlfriend before he decided to marry Susan for political reasons. The screenplay for the film omits these figures, instead creating a girlfriend for Henry, March (Rebecca Walker), an activist who writes for the *Black Advocate*. This character suggests Henry is selling out in joining the Stanton campaign; she also reveals Stanton's draft-dodging past.

Henry's dilemma becomes the kernel of the film: the difficulty of retaining honor, principles, and a sense of idealism in the face of the pragmatic demands of realpolitik, the temptation for spin and compromise. This is highlighted after Henry burns his tongue on some tea, when Susan says the most important thing experience teaches you is how not to get burned. When Henry asks if people ever learn that, Susan's rejoinder "the best people don't," suggests an aversion to pragmatism or cynicism. The remainder of the film slickly explores the complexities of this abiding political conundrum: whether it's possible to avoid sacrificing your principles in the pursuit of political power, or whether the ends justify the means, with a degree of corruption and detachment from ideals an inevitable by-product of achieving power. Reducing Henry's contact with the black community, the focus moves more clearly to Libby as Henry's moral compass in the battle to maintain principles, idealism, and morality, and to resist pressure to sell out.

A stark choice seems to emerge between endorsing a negative, cynical, politically expedient approach or playing it clean to focus on substantive issues. Two characters crystallize this dilemma: Libby Holden and Fred Picker. The test Libby sets for the Stantons with her dirt file on Picker, and their failure to rise above playing dirty politics as they immediately discuss which media outlet they should leak the information to, become a key moment for Henry. Picker delivers a big rally speech bemoaning the emotional manipulation and spin endemic in contemporary politics, complaining that candidates prefer to employ populist sound bites rather than trust the electorate and explain issues in detail. He compares this approach to professional wrestling: "It's staged, and it's fake and it doesn't mean anything." But both Libby and Picker get "burned," to return to Susan's analysis: Libby's devastation with the Stantons' response to her "test" is directly related to her suicide, and Picker's past is exposed, leading to his withdrawal from the Primary contest.

Primary Colors foregrounds this neat dichotomy between clean hands (ethics and morality) and dirty hands (spin and negativity). It displays a rare level of ambiguity and sympathy in grappling with the messy reality of politics, where the need for negotiation and the art of compromise is ever present, where being a good guy and a bad guy are not mutually exclusive. The possibility for this type of pivot is demonstrated in a key scene, where Stanton escapes from bimbo eruptions and other scandals dogging his campaign in a Krispy Kreme donut store, chewing the fat with the night-shift employee Danny. Henry enters the store with the pair mid-conversation, and becomes irritated, snapping at Danny when he continually asks if he wants an apple fritter. Stanton takes the fritter to spare Danny's embarrassment, explaining to Henry that Danny has a disability and can't get insurance. Stanton notes their problems can't compare to Danny's. The demonstration of this kindness to an ordinary person, which is beyond Henry, demonstrates how Stanton's capacity for connection with people coexists with his more negative attributes—just as positive and negative aspects coexist in Fred Picker, Libby Holden, and Henry Burton.

This exploration of complexity and ambiguity is most evident in the film's closing scenes. While both novel and film include scenes with Stanton imploring Henry to stay on the campaign, the novel closes at this point, unlike the film. After Stanton talks about the incredible changes he could make if elected president, he asks: "Jesus Henry, you want me to get down on my knees? I can't do it without you. Don't leave me now . . . Henry, this is ridiculous—you gotta be with me." As the suspense builds through a dialogue-free shot-reverse medium close-up of both characters gazing intently at each other, a sound bridge of Ry Cooder's *Tennessee Waltz* moves us across time and space to Stanton's Inauguration Ball in a neat ellipse. The film ends with Henry, in a tuxedo, shaking the hand of newly elected President Stanton, reprising the opening scene where campaign chief Howard Ferguson's voiceover dissection of Stanton's differing handshake techniques accompanies slow motion shots of Stanton greeting supporters, just before Ferguson introduces the Governor to Henry. The key issues of the nature of ethics, loyalty, principles, and morality are left open for the audience to contemplate—has Henry abandoned his principles and sold out, or learned the necessity of compromise to political achievement?

CONCLUSION

There are no pat Hollywood conclusions with this ending, consistent with Elaine May's career. A questing, restless quality is apparent in her work, evidenced by her battles with studios threatening to derail her directorial vision. In *American Masters: Mike Nichols*, Nichols testifies about his painful split with May in the early 1960s when the world was at their feet with their stratospherically successful Broadway show. He implies that the grinding monotony of repeating the same show night after night affected May much more than him: "It wasn't hard on me at all, and it was strangely hard on Elaine . . . I kept thinking, what is she talking about? It's less than two hours out of every 24 . . . But Elaine wanted to do more." May's denunciation of the treatment of creative talent in *American Masters: Mike Nichols* also suggests her refusal to conform to industry standards.

The notion of "Vanishing Elaine", persistent in the media for decades, is undoubtedly connected to May's reluctance to play the game, and has been reinforced by her tendency to take on uncredited script doctor work. May's obsessions are revealed in the work. She is not afraid to examine entrails, circumnavigating the ragged edges of love, friendship, family, community, and work to achieve a deeper understanding, without compromising complexity for a cheap laugh. Humor is central to her work, but never at the expense of nuanced, rounded characterization as she charts social and political interactions, focusing on how people react to, accommodate and (occasionally) learn from each other. The complexity and ambiguity of motivation, and the possibility for reflection, growth, and development are at the heart of *The Birdcage* and *Primary Colors*, but not in any Hallmark card sense. To paraphrase her tribute to Nichols, Elaine May chooses material that has real impact and relevance, but disguises it within a veneer so entertaining that it never feels labored.

NOTES

1. Sam Kashner, "Who's Afraid Of Nichols & May?" *Vanity Fair*, January 2013 <https://www.vanityfair.com/hollywood/2013/01/nichols-and-may-reunion-exclusive> (accessed January 2019).
2. Jessica Kiang, "Retrospective: The Directorial Career of Elaine May," *IndieWire*, 8 August 2013 <https://www.indiewire.com/2013/08/retrospective-the-directorial-career-of-elaine-may-95011/> (accessed January 2019).
3. John Lahr, "Making it Real: How Mike Nichols re-created comedy and himself," *New Yorker*, 21 February 2000 <https://www.newyorker.com/magazine/2000/02/21/making-it-real-2> (accessed January 2019).
4. Thompson, Thomas, "Whatever Happened to Elaine May?" *LIFE* magazine, 28 July 1967: 54.
5. Nichols studied with Strasberg, while May studied with the Konstantin Stanislavsky-trained Maria Ouspenskaya. See Carrie Rickey, "Elaine May: Laughing Matters," *Sight & Sound* 28.10 (October 2018): 40.
6. Nichols may still have been smarting from Andrew Sarris's description of his work: "The suspicion persisted in shamefully skeptical circles that Nichols was more a tactician than a strategist and that he won every battle and lost every war because he was incapable of the

divine folly of a personal statement." (See Andrew Sarris, *The American Cinema. Directors and Directions 1929–1968* (New York: E. P. Dutton & Co., 1968), p. 218.) As the chief American proponent of the "auteur theory," an adapted version of *la politique des auteurs*, Sarris was always connected with the French New Wave critics.

7. For more on this, see Marsha McCreadie's *The Women Who Write the Movies: From Frances Marion to Nora Ephron* (New York: Birch Lane Press, 1994).
8. Jason Bailey, "Why 'Tootsie' is One of the Finest (and Most Important) Comedies Ever Made," *FlavorWire*, 2 January 2015 <http://flavorwire.com/496646/why-tootsie-is-one-of-the-finest-and-most-important-comedies-ever-made> (accessed January 2019).
9. Ibid.
10. Elaine May, *The Birdcage: The Shooting Script* (New York: Newmarket Press, 1997), p. xv.
11. Jonathan Rosenbaum, "Bridge Over Troubled Water [THE GRADUATE]," *Jonathan Rosenbaum.net*, 21 January 2018 <https://www.jonathanrosenbaum.net/2018/01/bridge-over-troubled-water-/> (accessed January 2019).
12. Jonathan Rosenbaum, "The Mysterious Elaine May: Hiding in Plain Sight," *Jonathan Rosenbaum.net*, 8 August 1997 <https://www.jonathanrosenbaum.net/1997/08/21700/> (accessed January 2019).
13. Kashner.
14. David Blum, "The Road to *Ishtar*," *New York Magazine*, 16 March 1987: 39.
15. Jonathan Rosenbaum, "My favorite end-of-the-year-poll (again, 2016)," *Jonathan Rosenbaum.net*, 24 December 2016 <http://www.jonathanrosenbaum.net/2016/12/50376/> (accessed January 2019).
16. May 1997, p. xvi.
17. Ibid., p. 24.
18. Mike Nichols said Agador was based on Judy Garland's dresser, telling Hank Azaria: "Judy would panic before every performance and her dresser would panic with her and he would panic more than her so that she'd have to be the one to tell him to calm down, and that was the ritual they had." Sam Kashner and Charles Maslow-Freen, "Mike Nichols's Life and Career: The Definitive Oral History," *Vanity Fair*, 11 September 2015 <https://www.vanityfair.com/hollywood/2015/09/remembering-director-mike-nichols> (accessed January 2019).
19. Gwendolyn Audrey Foster has noted May's dry Yiddish humor, arguing it "exposes societal falseness, the bleakness of relationships, and the humor of day to day life struggles." Gwendolyn Audrey Foster, *Women Film Directors: An International Bio-critical Dictionary* (Westport, CT: Greenwood Press, 1995), p. 246.

Conclusion

CHAPTER 11

When in Doubt, Seduce: An Interview with Screenwriter Allie Hagan

Alexandra Heller-Nicholas and Dean Brandum

In late 2017, the annual "Black List" was released, a high-profile list of the most promising as yet unproduced screenplays circulating in Hollywood voted for by industry executives. This list of the top yet-to-be-made films sparks widespread interest both within the industry and for cinephiles with a general interest in film, often capturing the zeitgeist by tapping into what—and who—is causing the most buzz. That they remain unproduced means these films are perhaps not in commercial terms "safe bets," but that is precisely what makes them so interesting: according to the Black List website, since 2005: "more than 400 Black List scripts have been produced, grossing over

Figure 11.1 Screenwriter Allie Hagan.

$26 billion in box office worldwide. Black List movies have won 53 Academy Awards from 262 nominations, including 4 of the last 10 Best Picture Oscars and 10 of the last 22 Best Screenplay Oscars."[1]

On 11 December 2017, Australian actor Margot Robbie announced in a statement on YouTube that Allie Hagan's screenplay *When in Doubt, Seduce* was on the 2017 Black List, which Robbie describes a "a true story about the early relationship between Elaine May and Mike Nichols. So hopefully you'll see it on the big screen one day!" As Robbie noted in her video, her recent film *I, Tonya* (Craig Gillespie, 2017) had previously made the Black List, a film that saw Robbie nominated for Best Actress at the 2018 Academy Awards, and her co-star Allison Janney winning a Best Supporting Actress Award.

Hagan's screenplay for *When in Doubt, Seduce*—now a forthcoming feature film—marks the continuing rise of an already impressive career. In 2016 she co-created the television series *Notorious* for ABC. She is also the creator of *Suri's Burn Book*, the viral Tumblr account, and the author of its 2012 companion book, *Suri's Burn Book: Well-Dressed Commentary from Hollywood's Little Sweetheart*. Hagan was named one of *Time Magazine*'s Best Bloggers of 2013. Before beginning her career as a screenwriter, Hagan was a policy consultant in Washington, DC. She holds both a Master's degree and a Bachelor's degree in public policy from George Washington University. She is now based in Los Angeles.

Hagan kindly took the time to talk to us at length about her screenplay and her own relationship—emotional and professional—to the work of Elaine May and Mike Nichols.

Alexandra Heller-Nicholas and Dean Brandum: So Allie, *why* Elaine May?
Allie Hagan: She has a singular brilliance—among some people in the film community, she's legendary. In researching her life for my screenplay, I found my heroine. I don't think I will ever care about anyone the way I care about her (especially considering I've never met her)—she's become this paragon of a brainy lady for me. You know that feeling when you remember the perfect thing to say after you've already gone home? I don't think that happens to Elaine.

AH-N & DB: Why now?
AH: She is kind of having a moment, isn't she?

I routinely search for her name on Twitter and there are definitely a lot of people talking about her work. It's been fueled by the Blu-Ray release of *A New Leaf* [by Olive Films in December 2017] and things like Wasson's *Improv Nation* and CNN's docuseries about comedy that talked about Elaine. Also, she appeared on Broadway in 2018 for the first time in almost sixty years.

But I think we're also reexamining how women have historically been treated in Hollywood, and that lends itself to a conversation about Elaine. Everyone's heard the rumors about her process, about how fraught all of her films were. She has a reputation for being a perfectionist, for being "difficult." But it's not like Mike was known as an easy-going guy. It's kind of heartbreaking to look at their careers and see that he has the EGOT and she got totally blackballed after *Ishtar*. Male directors—including Mike—get chance after chance, but Elaine just didn't. She put up with so much hot garbage from studios and actors and everybody—and they still stopped making her movies.

AH-N & DB: What were the circumstances of you discovering Elaine May and her work?
AH: I fell into a Mike Nichols Wikipedia hole one night and never really came out of it. The first night I clicked on the Nichols and May Wikipedia page, I didn't end up going to sleep. I just watched clip after clip after clip on YouTube, read every article I could find—I was immediately obsessed with them. After one weekend I knew it should be a movie.

AH-N & DB: Oh this is fabulous—the universal experience of getting forever lost in Wikipedia holes! Do you remember off-hand what the precise clips were that sucked you in? And where do May's and Nichols' film works individually fit into this—had you seen either of their films before, or was this wholly a Wiki hole "birthing?"
AH: I had seen, like, *The Graduate* and *The Birdcage*. Beginner stuff. Mike's *Angels in America* miniseries was the first adult piece of television I ever saw that really moved me. I hadn't seen any of her movies. (Obviously I have now.)

I'm not sure it was the first thing I saw, but *Teenagers in a Car* was the first piece of theirs I saw that I became obsessed with. It's still just as funny sixty years later. And I'm obsessed with the people who would invent that and do it every night. There's a story Elaine told *Vanity Fair* about that piece: "Once during 'Teenagers'—I still remember it—during the kissing, we either hit teeth or something, and we began to break [into laughter], . . . And we stayed together in the kiss until we could pull ourselves together, and then we parted and something happened, and we broke up again, and we couldn't stop."[2] It's just so weird and intimate! I would be a terrible actor, because I don't know how you have experiences that vulnerable and not be completely in love with the other person.

There's also a story that made it into my script about when Mike and Elaine lived in St. Louis, working for Compass. Mike was married, but his wife stayed in Chicago, and to save money, Mike and Elaine shared a room. Then when Pat would come to visit, Elaine would pretend to have her own room. That's messed up. It was the first scene I wrote for the movie because it was just . . . right there.

AH-N & DB: Honestly, at this stage we would be perfectly happy if our interview collapsed into a detailed breakdown of just *Teenagers in a Car*! Something Alexandra focuses on in a separate chapter in this book is the gestural precision of Elaine as a performer. One of our favorite parts of *Teenagers in a Car* is the absolutely hilarious "superfluous arm" sequence: they finally get to snogging but there's this problem of what to do with the almost "stuck" limb. We see this moment in *Teenagers in a Car* as a kind of precursor to the Grecian nightgown sequence in *A New Leaf*, too—a different scenario, yes, but still that same combination of clumsy and sexy and oh-just-so-completely understandable. Are there any other similarities like this that you have noticed from their early work together and their later films?

AH: Mike used much of *Teenagers* for *The Graduate*, specifically Mrs. Robinson blowing smoke out of her mouth after a kiss. I love that, because it's the same move but it's so tonally different in the two pieces. In *Teenagers*, it's *so* innocent—she's so caught off-guard she doesn't know what to do with this mouthful of smoke. And in *The Graduate*, it's more that she's so blasé about the situation that she doesn't even bother to exhale.

AH-N & DB: That's such a great observation, how the "gag" has evolved . . .
AH: *Teenagers* really exemplifies their perfect use of physical comedy. (I'm assuming that's why it was never recorded for their albums—you kind of need to see it.) Like you said, her awkward little movements are hilarious. I love how she fidgets with her clothes through the whole thing. That's so timeless and universal. There's a Taylor Swift lyric from fifty years later: "See me nervously pulling at my clothes and trying to look busy." But Elaine's complete stillness during that first kiss is also perfect. Everything about that scene is still so relatable, because it's just about how men and women interact.

If you want to deconstruct it some more, I think it's bizarre that he calls her "Jeannie" in most taped versions of the scene, including the one that's on YouTube, considering that's her daughter's name. *Whyyyy* did you do that?

AH-N & DB: We're playing devil's advocate here, but why *do* you think he did that?!
AH: I don't know. It would take, like, five expert psychologists to work through that one. I keep thinking I'm wrong, but I'm not wrong.

AH-N & DB: And as an aside, we adore May's cameo in *The Graduate* . . .
AH: It's so random, and I love it. And I wonder what the circumstances were? Was she just around that day, and he asked her to do it? The description of the character is just "A FAT GIRL," and I wonder if that was a joke if he knew Elaine was going to do it.

Another thing about it—Mike spoke a lot about how, after they split up professionally, they had a long period of not speaking. And the way he talks about it, you'd think they went through a war or something. But it really could only have been about six months, I think. And by 1967 they were fine enough for him to ask her to do this.

AH-N & DB: Has it been difficult tackling a biographical-based project like this with one of the subjects still alive?
AH: Only in that I keep expecting to see her in a crowded restaurant or get an angry email from her. I would really love to meet her. I keep a Google Doc of questions I'd ask her in case she ever grants me an audience. (Not holding my breath.)

I also, of course, wonder if she would dismiss it immediately as trash, the way they both dismissed Janet Coleman's 1993 book *The Compass: The Improvisational Theatre that Revolutionized American Comedy*. The script is heavily researched, but there's not a lot from her perspective (and she's an unreliable narrator when she does give interviews), and there's only so much you can ever know about a relationship that doesn't involve you.

AH-N & DB: This is a really very interesting point you raise here, and there are much broader issues at stake about the cultural value of art and artists—for each of us, in different ways, May is clearly a hugely influential and important creative presence in our respective cultural imaginations. Can you give us a bit of a background on your career that led you to this point and this screenplay? Was screenwriting always in your blood, or did another path take you here?
AH: I always wanted to be a screenwriter, but I was far too practical to pursue it from the start. I got a Master's in public policy and thought I would work in Washington forever. Right as Tumblr was becoming a thing, I started a blog for fun after work called *Suri's Burn Book*—a blog about celebrity children from the perspective of Suri Cruise. It unexpectedly took off, I got a book deal, I got a manager in L.A., and I was able to move to California and pursue writing professionally, with a little bit of a foot in the door.

AH-N & DB: This is such a great story, but an obvious question: why Suri Cruise? What did she in particular represent to you at that stage?
AH: I knew the kind of jokes I wanted to tell, and I knew I couldn't tell it from my own perspective. It would have come across as unnecessarily mean and potentially creepy. Writing as one of the kids eliminated that problem, and it felt obvious to choose Suri. She basically invented resting bitch face. It was 2011, and Tom and Katie were toting her around everywhere, dressing her in custom designer clothes. She was five. It was bananas.

AH-N & DB: It might be a stretch to start drawing direct parallels between Suri Cruise and Elaine May, but from your perspective as a comedy writer yourself, what is it about this importance of "voice" that you think works for May, through her scripts, in her performances with Nichols—and a little more abstractly—in her "performance" (the very rare ones we've had glimpses at, at least) of "Elaine May" herself in Q&As, interviews, that sort of thing? A second part to this is how did you find your own voice—as a storyteller, but also as someone who has clearly demonstrated their own comedy chops—through the story of May and Nichols?

AH: I'm not going to word this quite right, but the answer is—I'm drawn to characters that have a strong sense of self. It's something that really attracted me to Elaine's story. It took me until about my thirtieth birthday to understand myself and my perspective on the world and other people. But people talk about Elaine like she showed up in Chicago at twenty-two, by herself, having left a child behind in California, and was already a fully self-aware person. She had flaws, but she knew what they were and didn't give a shit.

If we're looking for parallels, my version of Suri Cruise also understands herself and her world and her place in it—but she was five when I started writing that blog, and it was (mostly) a joke. That's (I think) the difference between those types of writing. With the film, I was doing all kinds of research to try to figure out what Elaine was really like in those days. With satire, you're just taking the elements that are funny and heightening them.

For myself, I think I'm still finding it! Don't you feel that way? In the last year or so, I've figured out what my taste is, what I'm interested in writing, and that goes hand in hand with voice or perspective. I'm interested in millennial work experiences, platonic romance (I'm still recovering from the Canadian ice dancers at the 2018 Olympics), and people who like to talk.

AH-N & DB: This combination of platonic romance and people who like to talk alone makes May and Nichols perfect source material for you! This question of voice and perspective is an interesting one with May because in so many ways she is so brazen when in character, but in interviews—spanning from the early days to more recently the famous 2013 *Vanity Fair* "reunion" May and Nichols interview with Sam Kashner—she's so private and really tries to avert any direct attention to herself personally. We're curious how as a writer you juggle that really strong tension between May's public persona and her fiercely private nature?

AH: While I was writing it, I was conscious of the fact that the tales of their partnership were almost 100 per cent told by Mike Nichols. One of my favorite pieces about them was a chapter in Gerald Nachman's book, *Seriously Funny: The Rebel Comedians of the 1950s and 1960s* (2003). Mike was interviewed for the book and gave some of my favorite quotes and stories, and Elaine declined.

(Or, I guess, I'm assuming she declined. She wasn't interviewed for the book.) I tried very hard to be cognizant of the uneven distribution of authorship in their story and to take into account other people's bias. I'm trying to think back, and I think honestly—Mike never put the blame for their fights on her, only on himself. Later in life he would say things like, "She got married, which threw me for the loop." Or, "I was very hard on Elaine." I can't remember him saying anything mean about her. Which is just being good at doing press. Her *American Masters* doc is full of stuff like that, which must have been a weird experience to put together.

AH-N & DB: Perhaps what it comes down to here is that age-old tension/overlap between romantic love and human respect . . . while we can only speculate about the former with May and Nichols, the latter never seemed to be an issue. Is that—ultimately—the most important thing?
AH: Are they really that different? To have someone totally understand you and still totally respect you, is that not the most romantic thing? To me, so much of their romance (platonic or otherwise) is about how equal they were. I think the actual quote is, "I would respect you like *crazy*."

AH-N & DB: Did you know much about women and their role in comedy and Hollywood growing up?
AH: Not really. I was never a student of film or comedy the way a lot of my peers are. I've only really learned what a director actually does in the last few years. (I would feel guilty about that, but Elaine didn't know until after she had already started *A New Leaf*.[3])

AH-N & DB: There's a really crucial point here about the tension between formal "learning" and creative intuition. With comedy especially, there's an old cliché that explaining how a joke works is the most surefire way to make it unfunny. Is there a parallel here to be made with screenwriting in your experience—for you, how much was formal learning, and how much was just your gut instinct for what "worked"?
AH: That's interesting. For me, very little of my screenwriting education was formal. I took one playwriting class in college as an elective. When I first moved to L.A., I was introduced to two writers who became my mentors and shepherded me through the process of writing my first TV pilot. Working on a TV show in 2016 was a crash course in production.

Elaine had a mix of both. She didn't graduate from high school, and she actually ended up at the University of Chicago because it was one of the few schools in the country that would take students without a high school diploma. But she had some formal acting training; she had worked with Maria Ouspenskaya before moving to Chicago. And both Playwright's Theater Club and The Compass had educational components, like Second City does now. Viola Spolin directed at Compass and was hugely important to the development of improv.

Elaine wasn't trained in screenwriting, to my knowledge. She just worked really hard at it. There are stories about her working on the script for *Mikey and Nicky* before she and Mike even left Chicago.

AH-N & DB: We're also really interested here by your emphasis on both Ouspenskaya and Spolin—so many articles and critical assessments of May's work really go to sometimes extraordinary lengths to underscore that generationally she predated the rise of second wave feminism, a sort of coded (and I find, kind of icky) way of excluding her from discussions about gender politics. While I'm personally hesitant to label her—or anyone else, for that matter—a "feminist" (that feels like it should be an identity we should be able to claim or reject for ourselves, not have forced upon us by someone else speaking "over" or "for" us), I am really interested here by how you've highlighted these two female influences in particular. Could you perhaps talk a bit more about how you see their influence on May, and if there are any other women in her "story" that you feel are worth highlighting?

AH: Interesting. Let's talk about feminism for a second. I would bet that Elaine had no interest in the feminist movement. She did become famous before the second wave took hold, but I think it's also fair to say that she predates that mentality. I can't remember her ever bringing up gender politics in an interview. In every conversation about *Ishtar*, she never blamed its failure—or her subsequent professional struggles—on sexism, even though I'm sure you and I would agree that sexism was a factor. As far as other women in the story, there were a few younger women at Compass whom she mentored. Barbara Harris has a story about Elaine teaching her how to beg for money—it's in Janet Coleman's book, so . . . grain of salt:

> It was during rehearsals of *The Threepenny Opera* that she taught Barbara how to beg. They borrowed raincoats from the collection assembled at the theater for Mr. Peachum's Beggar's Outfit Shop. "It was very theatrical, sort of a happening," Barbara reflects. "She kept saying, 'We have to do it in Brechtian style.' I said, 'What's Brechtian style?' And she said, 'I'll show you.'"
>
> Elaine then walked up to a strange man. She said, "We're begging," as though she were looking down her nose at him, very superciliously. "We're begging, and we want some money," she said. The man was embarrassed and pulled out a quarter. "And now one for my friend," Elaine said. He gave her another quarter. The two beggars bought oranges with the fifty cents and made dinner out of them.[4]

But she and Mike survived because they were equal partners from the jump. (Fun fact: In every piece of accounting I've come across, Mike and Elaine were paid the same.) Even if pay equity and protection from sex discrimination didn't exist on the macro level, she had it in her own situation. It *was* ahead of its time, this male/female partnership that wasn't about marriage. They weren't Lucy and Ricky, doing a funny version of a traditional relationship.

AH-N & DB: This is absolutely extraordinary, it's great how May makes us really rethink how we use words like "progressive" and "strong woman" in a far more elastic way than we might frame them from a contemporary perspective.
AH: I hadn't thought about two of her primary teachers being women until just now. I don't know enough about the history of improv to wonder whether that world was more open to women than other fields, or even other areas of acting.

Nothing about her personality is performance. She's not playing the Cool Girl. One of the things that's so interesting and special about her is that she really doesn't seem to care about how others perceive her. She was brutally honest with friends and strangers. It might be part of why she has been so reluctant to do interviews—she wasn't interested in that kind of performance. She probably hates that idea of a celebrity having a "personal brand."

AH-N & DB: Do you think the fact that you and May share a kind of career-centered "intuition" on some level in terms of your creative practice made you understand her and her work in a less clinical, more organic way?
AH: Comparing myself to Elaine would be dumb. (Lena Dunham did it once and just . . . wow.) I think it's more that I admire her drive and her dedication to writing. She understands the mechanics of storytelling better than just about anyone; it's why she was hired to ghostwrite/"doctor" so many bad scripts. Have I already mentioned that I'm fairly sure she did a pass on *Working Girl?* There's a PDF of an earlier version of the script, without a lot of its best jokes. I'd bet my apartment on who wrote them.

But as a brainy lady writer, Elaine *is* the aspiration. I wish I were as quick as her, as inventive.

AH-N & DB: That is fascinating about *Working Girl:* what made you stumble across that, out of curiosity? And have you spent much time looking at scripts she has been acknowledged working on?
AH: I like to read scripts, and I think reading other, better writers' work makes you better. Oh! This is a wonderful story I haven't told you yet. An executive at Paramount told me that in the late 90s they submitted a script to Mike Nichols to direct. It's a famous movie that ended up getting made (by

someone else), and Mike's response to the script was, "Not bad. Nothing a million dollars and Elaine can't fix." So she did uncredited rewrites on at least a few of his movies, and I suspect that *Working Girl* was one of them. If I am wrong, this is a very rude assumption to make about another writer. (I don't think I'm wrong.)

Here's a quote, from his foreword to her script for *The Birdcage*: "The best scene in *Heartburn* came from Elaine asking Nora Ephron questions about her father. In the scene with her father in which he says to her, 'you want fidelity, marry a swan,' that all came from Elaine's questioning of Nora about her real father. On *Wolf*, Elaine saved my ass, it's as simple as that. She came and did a fantastic rewrite job. But she very rarely takes credit on movies, and I'm sort of proud she took a credit on *The Birdcage*, because it's so rare."

One thing about her writing is that she doesn't really follow modern conventions. Her scenes are very long, very dialogue-heavy. They don't follow the "rules" of where big moments should hit. I was surprised that *The Birdcage* script isn't like twenty pages "too long," considering how much talking there is. I haven't read the others, but I should.

AH-N & DB: The writing on these films—*Wolf* especially, but all of them really—is masterful. *Primary Colors* is the other Nichols film May took full credit for the screenplay on. Have you any thoughts on that from a writer's perspective? Again, it's an adaptation, but a very different one!

AH: I think about this all the time. I thought about it *this morning*! And I'm so annoyed because the best answer she ever gave about this was in the audio of the VF piece that is not online anymore. I hate myself every day for not figuring out how to download that. Sam Kashner asked her "Don't you like credit?" and she basically said she liked having credit on her projects with Mike, because she knew he was going to do a good job with it, and would treat her script with respect. There's a unique kind of freedom in *not* taking official WGA credit, because you get no blame if the movie tanks, but the agents and everybody know you did it if it does well. To me, it seems like she was as protective over her name ending up on movies as she was about, like, magazine profiles.

AH-N & DB: Regarding May's contribution to *Heartburn*, this was a thinly disguised treatment of Ephron's marriage to Carl Bernstein and its subsequent breakdown. As far as we can tell this would be May's only work with a writer whose screenplay is autobiographical. For that reason do you know if she approached the work differently, aware of the personal connection Ephron had to the project? Additionally, Ephron had previously worked with Nichols, writing the screenplay for *Silkwood* (1983), his first film in eight years. Ephron was not a performer, restricting herself to writing and directing, but do you see any comparison between them in those fields?

AH: Do you mean between Nora and Elaine? I love this quote from Natalie Portman: "At his American Film Institute tribute, it was all women who were toasting him. I think Buck [Henry] was there, and maybe one other man, but it was like Meryl and Emma and Nora and Elaine . . . He was like a feminist without trying." Mike Nichols' work was primarily about heterosexual sex. And I think that from the first day he met Elaine, he knew he could only really understand half of any story. And so he was drawn to creative women who were his equals, whether that was performing with Elaine or writing with Nora or directing Meryl. (Again, lord, who really knows about any of these guys? This could be a completely wrong interpretation and he could've been a total scumbag. I hope not, though. I really hope not.)

AH-N & DB: What do you think lies at the heart of the dynamic between the May and Nichols collaboration?
AH: Unparalleled intelligence and sexual tension. They were uniquely able to pinpoint funny or awkward or strange elements of being a human, and to make timeless comedy out of those moments. Someone likened their comedy to seeing something performed that you thought you had only ever felt or experienced yourself.

They basically invented this art form together—I don't know how you can go through that together and not want to marry that person. My theory is that they were totally in love—just never at the same time. There's a quote of Mike's—"We had a brief relationship, and then we decided we would be better off doing all this stuff to other people and keeping us for each other." *Kill me.* It's just the most devastatingly sexy thing ever.

AH-N & DB: And it's really beautiful and romantic, too. Devil's advocate here: do you think their work would have been as strong if they had developed a sexually intimate relationship, or was it that magnetic, unfulfilled attraction that added to their dynamic?
AH: Hmm. Good question. The only honest answer is "I don't know," because for all we know, they were totally hooking up the whole time. (The evidence does not support this.)

AH-N & DB: In the 2013 *Vanity Fair* interview, Kashner effectively chickened out of asking them about this: "Not only did I lose my nerve, but sitting there between them I thought they were entitled to keep a secret like that." Watching all that spectacular early footage, or even later public events like the 2006 Q&A session Nichols hosted with May after a screening of *Ishtar*, the trashy, tabloid parts of our brains wonder about this, almost like a compulsion. It's perhaps a bit of a guilty pleasure for us, but for you it's been the "meat" of your work on this extraordinary screenplay project. How do you separate your own curiosity on that front from the story about May and Nichols that you have found such a powerful way to tell?

AH: OK this is my favorite question. Listen . . . it's my guilty pleasure, too. The challenge for me was marrying the actual evidence about Mike and Elaine's relationship history, the timeline of their lives and marriages and cross-country moves, and the rumors. (David Shepherd said Mike and Elaine lived together for three days in 1955, for instance.) In my version, they fell in love, but having already burned through a marriage, she declared her relationship with Mike too important to lose and took sex off the table. My version of her saw her future in his eyes and decided it was the only thing worth protecting. This is what makes sense to me based on the things they've said about it. It is fun to think that there's one person in the world who knows the actual truth—I wonder if we will ever know for sure.

To answer your question about how do you separate personal curiosity from storytelling—you don't. Wondering what happened over those three days in 1955 fueled me for months. There's an unattributed quote in Coleman's book that says after they stopped hooking up, Elaine started doodling mean pictures of a hairless man in the margins of her scripts. This kept me up at night, pacing, feeling so sad for them both. I decided it probably wasn't true.

Mike disavowed the Coleman book; in Nachman's book: "Nichols refers to her as 'that awful woman who wrote that awful book.'" Mike and Elaine had both declined to be interviewed for it, and Coleman didn't acknowledge in her book that many of the people she did interview, particularly Del Close and Shelley Berman, had ongoing issues with Mike and Elaine.

Mike and Elaine would often say things like, "We have totally separate lives." Which is fine. But then there's a TV interview Mike and Elaine did—I think I sent you the audio of it, it's from *Person to Person*. Jeannie [Berlin, May's daughter] is there, and she talks about her school play, and Mike says, "Didn't Stevie play Zeus?" It's so small but telling—they didn't have totally separate lives. He knew Jeannie's friends' names and went to her school plays. Jeannie said he gave the best presents. And once you start thinking about that contradiction, you wonder what else they were being evasive about. I think it's just human nature—you shouldn't feel guilty about it!

NOTES

1. "About Us," The Black List <https://blcklst.com/about/> (accessed January 2019).
2. Sam Kashner, "Who's Afraid of Nichols & May?," *Vanity Fair*, January 2013 <https://www.vanityfair.com/hollywood/2013/01/nichols-and-may-reunion-exclusive> (accessed January 2019).
3. See "Elaine May in conversation with Mike Nichols," *Film Comment*, July/August 2006

<https://www.filmcomment.com/article/elaine-may-in-conversation-with-mike-nichols/> (accessed January 2019).

4. Janet Coleman, *The Compass: The Improvisational Theatre That Revolutionized American Comedy* (Chicago: University of Chicago Press, 1990), p. 69.

Bibliography

"About Us," The Black List <https://blcklst.com/about/> (accessed January 2019).
"Big Rental Films of 1973," *Variety*, 9 January 1974: 19.
"Big Rental Films of '86," *Variety*, 14 January 1986: 25.
"Bob Evans Pays Chips-Service to 'Writer as Star' at Paramount," *Variety*, 1 May 1968: 19.
"Columbia Signs Elaine May to Multiple-Picture Deal," *Boxoffice*, 23 May 1966: W-4.
"Elaine May in conversation with Mike Nichols," *Film Comment*, July/August 2006, <https://www.filmcomment.com/article/elaine-may-in-conversation-with-mike-nichols/> (accessed January 2019).
"Elaine May's 'Bumpy Ride' on 'Leaf': Manduke Sticks on 'Mickey [sic] & Nicky'," *Variety*, 27 August 1969: 6.
"Evans May Have Been Thinking of Her," *Variety*, 10 February 1971: 13.
"Film Reviews: The Heartbreak Kid," *Variety*, 13 December 1972: 20.
"From Columbia Pictures' 'News', Biography: Elaine May," 18 August 1966, Studio Biography for the film *Luv*, Elaine May Clipping Files, Margaret Herrick Library.
"Inter-Office Communication From A. N. Ryan to Eugene H. Frank, Re: *A New Leaf*," 3 April 1968. *A New Leaf*, Paramount Pictures Special Collection, Margaret Herrick Library.
"Inter-Office Communication From Bernard Donnenfeld to Charles Bluhdorn and Martin Davis, Re: *A New Leaf*," 26 February 1968. *A New Leaf*, Paramount Pictures Special Collection, Margaret Herrick Library.
"Inter-Office Communication from Peter Bart to Robert Evans, Subject: *A New Leaf*," 7 February 1969. *A New Leaf*, Production Files, Margaret Herrick Library: 3.
"Letter from Norman Flicker to Stanley Jaffe, Subject: *A New Leaf*," February 16, 1970. *A New Leaf*, Production Files, Margaret Herrick Library.
"Letter from Stanley Jaffe to Charles Bluhdorn, Martin Davis, Robert Evans, Bernard Donnenfeld," 7 October 1970. *A New Leaf*, Production Files, Margaret Herrick Library.
"Mikey and Nicky," *Variety*, 22 December 1976.
"Par, Elaine May Sue Each Other; Film Over-Budget And Incomplete," *Variety*, 29 October 1975.
"Paramount Pictures Corporation: Production Notes, *A New Leaf*," August 20, 1970. *A New Leaf*, Production Files, Margaret Herrick Library.

"Paramount's Bud Austin: turned on to television," *Broadcasting*, 2 December 1974: 57.
"Production Notes 'Mikey and Nicky'," Folder: *Mikey and Nicky*, Tom Miller Papers, Special Collection, Margaret Herrick Library.
"Women Calling 'Camera!' Women Calling 'Cut'!" Folder: *Mikey and Nicky*, Tom Miller Papers, Special Collection, Margaret Herrick Library.
"Worldwide Rights: Seven Pix Pact For Fox-Palomar," *The Independent Film Journal*, 3 February 1972: 6.
Abramowitz, Rachel, *Is That a Gun in Your Pocket? Women's Experience of Power in Hollywood* (New York: Random House, 2000).
Acker, Ally, *Reel Women: Pioneers of the Cinema, 1896 to the Present* (New York: Continuum, 1991).
American Masters: Take Two: Nichols and May, film, dir. Phillip Schopper, Eagle Rock Entertainment, 1996.
Ansen, David, "The $40 Million Movie Soufflé," *Bulletin*, May 1987: 128.
Austerlitz, Saul, *Another Fine Mess: A History of American Film Comedy* (Chicago: Chicago Review Press, 2010).
Austin, J. L., *How to Do Things with Words* (Oxford: Clarendon Press, 1955/1962).
Bach, Steven, *Final Cut* (New York: Onyx, 1987).
Bai, Matt, "How Gary Hart's Downfall Forever Changed American Politics," *New York Times*, 18 September 2014 <https://www.nytimes.com/2014/09/21/magazine/how-gary-harts-downfall-forever-changed-american-politics.html> (accessed January 2019).
Bailey, Jason, "Why 'Tootsie' is One of the Finest (and Most Important) Comedies Ever Made," *FlavorWire*, 2 January 2015 <http://flavorwire.com/496646/why-tootsie-is-one-of-the-finest-and-most-important-comedies-ever-made> (accessed January 2019).
Banks, Morwenna and Amanda Swift, *The Joke's On Us: Women in Comedy from Music Hall to the Present Day* (London: Pandora, 1987).
Baron, Cynthia, *Modern Acting: The Lost Chapter of American Film and Theatre* (London: Macmillan, 2016).
Barreca, Regina (ed.), *Last Laughs: Perspectives on Women and Comedy* (New York: Gordon and Breach, 1988).
Bart, Peter, *Infamous Players: A Tale of Movies, the Mob (and Sex)* (New York: Weinstein Books, 2011).
Beaupre, Lee, "Elaine May's 'Mikey' To Paramount; Palomar In Scratch When Budget Rises," *Variety*, 21 March 1973: 94.
——, "Pix Must 'Broaden Market'," *Variety*, 20 March 1968.
——, "Pic Biz Booby-Trap: 'Youth'," *Variety*, 31 July 1968.
Beckett, Samuel, *Waiting for Godot* (London: Faber and Faber, 1956).
Bernstein, Bob, "Review: Omnibus (Net)," *The Billboard*, 20 January 1958: 15.
Bernstein, Jeremy, "How About A Little Game?" *The New Yorker*, 12 November 1966 <https://www.newyorker.com/magazine/1966/11/12/how-about-a-little-game> (accessed January 2019).
Biskind, Peter, *Star: How Warren Beatty Seduced America* (London: Simon and Schuster, 2010).
Bletter, Diana K., "Letter to the Editor: Disgraced," *New York Times*, 30 September 1973: A11.
Blum, David, "The Road to *Ishtar*," *New York Magazine*, 16 March 1987: 34–43.
Bone, Larry, "Outraged at Simon," *Los Angeles Times*, 7 January 1973: O8.
Bramesco, Charles, "*Ishtar* at 30: Is It Really the Worst Movie Ever Made?," *The Guardian*, 15

May 2017 <https://www.theguardian.com/film/2017/may/15/ishtar-30th-anniversary-worst-movie-ever-elaine-may> (accessed January 2019).

Braun, Michael, "Mike and Elaine: Veracity-Cum-Boffs," *Esquire*, October 1960: 202.

Brill, Lesley, *The Hitchcock Romance: Love and Irony in Hitchcock's Films* (Princeton: Princeton University Press, 1988).

Brody, Richard, "DVD of the Week: *Mikey and Nicky*," *The New Yorker* (no date) <https://www.newyorker.com/culture/richard-brody/dvd-of-the-week-mikey-and-nicky> (accessed January 2019).

——, "May Flowers: Ishtar Tonight," *The New Yorker* (no date) <https://www.newyorker.com/culture/richard-brody/may-flowers-ishtar-tonight> (accessed January 2019).

——, "Elaine May Talks About 'Ishtar'," *The New Yorker*, 1 April 2016 <https://www.newyorker.com/culture/richard-brody/elaine-may-talks-about-ishtar> (accessed January 2019).

——, "Screening Alert: Elaine May's Masterly *The Heartbreak Kid*," *The New Yorker*, 30 January 2015 <https://www.newyorker.com/culture/richard-brody/screening-alert-elaine-mays-masterful-heartbreak-kid> (accessed January 2019).

Burnett, Colin, *The Invention of Robert Bresson: The Auteur and His Market* (Bloomington: University of Indiana, 2016).

Butler, Alison, *Women's Cinema: The Contested Screen* (London: Wallflower, 2002).

Butler, Judith, "Performative Acts and Gender Constitution: An Essay in Phenomenology and Feminist Theory," in Sue-Ellen Case (ed.), *Performing Feminisms: Feminist Critical Theory and Theatre* (Baltimore: The Johns Hopkins University Press, 1990), pp. 270–82.

Canby, Vincent, "*A New Leaf* (1971): Love Turns 'New Leaf' at Music Hall," *New York Times*, 12 March 1971.

——, "'Heartbreak Kid': Elaine May's 2nd Effort as Director Arrives," *New York Times*, 18 December 1972.

——, "Which Should You See?," *New York Times*, 24 December 1972.

——, "'Mikey and Nicky': Film on Amity," *New York Times* 22 December 1976 <https://www.nytimes.com/1976/12/22/archives/mikey-and-nicky-film-on-amity.html> (accessed January 2019).

Carney, Ray (ed.), *Cassavetes on Cassavetes* (London: Faber and Faber, 2001).

——, *The Films of John Cassavetes: Pragmaticism, Modernism, and the Movies* (Cambridge: Cambridge University Press, 1994).

Carr, Jeremy, "Great Directors: John Cassavetes," *Senses of Cinema*, Issue 79 (2016) <http://sensesofcinema.com/2016/great-directors/john-cassavetes/#fn-27065-26> (accessed January 2019).

Cassyd, Syd, "Ronald Kahn Buys Rights to 'Return of the Tiger'," *Boxoffice*, 25 March 1968: np.

Champlin, Charles, "Credible Comedy in 'Heartbreak Kid'," *Los Angeles Times*, 20 December 1972: C1.

——, "Critic at Large: Elaine May's 'A New Leaf'," *Los Angeles Times*, 2 April 1971.

Cocks, Jay, "Cinema: Impossible Dream," *Time Magazine*, 1 January 1973 <https://content.time.com/time/magazine/article/0,9171,903651,00.html> (accessed January 2019).

Cohen, Sascha, "The Day Women Went on Strike," *Time Magazine*, 26 August 2015 <http://time.com/4008060/women-strike-equality-1970/> (accessed January 2019).

Cole, Jake, "Spotlight on Fandor: Mikey and Nicky," *Movie Mezzanine* 2015 <http://moviemezzanine.com/spotlight-on-fandor-mikey-and-nicky/> (accessed January 2019).

Coleman, Janet, *The Compass: The Story of the Improvisational Theatre That Revolutionized the Art of Comedy in America* (Chicago: University of Chicago Press, 1990).

Cotkin, George, *Existential America* (Baltimore: The Johns Hopkins University Press, 2003).
Davis, Flora, *Moving the Mountain: The Women's Movement in America Since 1960* (New York: Simon and Schuster, 1991).
de Beauvoir, Simone, *The Second Sex,* trans. Constance Borde and Sheila Malovany-Chevallier (New York: Alfred A. Knopf, 2010).
Directory of Members 1969–70 (Directors Guild of America, Inc., 1969).
Dixon, Wheeler Winston, *Early Film Criticism of François Truffaut* (Bloomington and Indianapolis: Indiana University Press, 1993).
Doherty, Thomas, *Pre-Code Hollywood: Sex, Immorality, and Insurrection in American Cinema, 1930–1934* (New York: Columbia University Press, 1999).
Easty, Edward Dwight, *On Method Acting: The Classic Actor's Guide to the Stanislavsky Technique as Practiced at the Actor's Studio* (New York: Ivy Books, 1981).
Ebert, Roger, "Heartbreak Kid," *Chicago Sun-Times,* 1 January 1972.
Farmer, Shelley, "Why Aren't More Female and POC Directors Considered Auteurs?," *Paper,* 4 November 2015 <http://www.papermagcom/ava-du-vernay-sofia-coppola-elaine-may-auteurs-1438731738.html> (accessed January 2019).
Farrow, Dylan, "An Open Letter From Dylan Farrow," *New York Times,* 1 February 2014 <https://kristof.blogs.nytimes.com/2014/02/01/an-open-letter-from-dylan-farrow/> (accessed January 2019).
Farrow, Ronan, "My Father, Woody Allen, and the Danger of Questions Unasked," *The Hollywood Reporter,* 11 May 2016 <https://www.hollywoodreporter.com/news/my-father-woody-allen-danger-892572> (accessed January 2019).
Fields, Anna, *The Girl in the Show: Three Generations of Comedy, Culture and Feminism* (New York: Arcade Publishing, 2017).
Fine, Marshall, *Accidental Genius: How John Cassavetes Invented the American Independent Film* (New York: Hyperion, 2005).
Flatley, Guy, "At the Movies: Falk on 'Mikey': 'This is No Romp in the Park'," *New York Times,* 17 December 1976: 62.
Foster, Gwendolyn Audrey, *Women Film Directors: An International Bio-critical Dictionary* (Westport, CT: Greenwood Press, 1995).
Friendly, David T, "*Ishtar* Delay No Issue—Beatty" *Los Angeles Times,* 4 September 1986 <http://articles.latimes.com/1986-09-04/entertainment/ca-13860_1_warren-beatty> (accessed January 2019 via keyword search).
Frischauer, Willi, *Behind the Scenes of Otto Preminger* (London: Michael Joseph, 1973).
Fujiwara, Chris, *The World and Its Double* (New York: Faber and Faber, 2008).
Galloway, Stephen, "'Trouble Always Seemed Glamorous'," *The Hollywood Reporter,* 18 May 2012 <https://www.hollywoodreporter.com/news/trouble-seemed-glamorous-322331> (accessed January 2019).
Gehring, Wes D., *Screwball Comedy: A Genre of Madcap Romance* (Westport, CT: Praeger, 1986).
——, *Romantic vs. Screwball Comedy: Charting the Difference* (Lanham, MD: Scarecrow Press, 2008).
——, *Genre-Busting Dark Comedies of the 1970s: Twelve American Films* (Jefferson, NC: McFarland, 2016).
Gentile, Mary "Review: *Women Directors: The Emergence of a New Cinema* by Barbara Koenig Quart," *Film Quarterly* 44 (1990): 63.
Gilbey, Ryan, "Gilbey on Film: Shady Elaine," *New Statesman,* 15 February 2011 <https://www.newstatesman.com/blogs/cultural-capital/2011/02/elaine-may-film-hollywood> (accessed January 2019).

———, "Lost and found: *A New Leaf*," *Sight & Sound*, 14 January 2016 <https://www.bfi.org.uk/news-opinion/sight-sound-magazine/comment/lost-found-new-leaf> (accessed January 2019).

Goffman, Erving, *The Presentation of Self in Everyday Life* (Edinburgh: University of Edinburgh, 1956).

Goldstein, Eric L., "Elaine May," *Jewish Women's Archive* <https://jwa.org/encyclopedia/article/may-elaine> (accessed January 2019).

Greer, Germaine, *The Whole Woman* (London: Doubleday, 1999).

Guest, Haden, "Interview with Elaine May," Harvard Film Archive, 13 November 2011.

Haber, Joyce, "Very Early for May," *New York*, 22 July 1968: 50–1.

Hall, John A., *Liberalism: Politics, Ideology and the Market* (Chapel Hill, NC: University of North Carolina Press, 1988).

Haskell, Molly, "Stir Until Marriage Dissolves," *The Village Voice*, 28 December 1972.

———, "Masculine Feminine," *Film Comment*, March/April 1974.

Hassannia, Tina, "TIFF Retrospective on Elaine May Looks Beyond the Flop Ishtar to Her Underappreciated Body of Work," *Toronto Globe and Mail*, 7 June 2018 <https://www.theglobeandmail.com/arts/film/article-elaine-may-above-and-beyond-ishtar/> (accessed January 2019).

Heilman, Pamela Sue, "The American Career of Maria Ouspenskaya (1887–1949): Actress and Teacher," *LSU Historical Dissertations and Theses*, 6890 (1999) <https://digitalcommons.lsu.edu/gradschool_disstheses/6890> (accessed January 2019).

Heilpern, John, "Out to Lunch with Stanley Donen," *Vanity Fair*, March 2013 <https://www.vanityfair.com/hollywood/2013/03/stanley-donan-singin-in-the-rain> (accessed January 2019).

Heller-Nicholas, Alexandra, "Mainstream Obscurity: The Films of Elaine May," *4:3 Film*, 6 August 2016 <https://fourthreefilm.com/2016/08/mainstream-obscurity-the-films-of-elaine-may/> (accessed January 2019).

Howard, Alan R., "Social Satire in 'Heartbreak Kid'," *Hollywood Reporter*, 13 December 1972.

Hirsch, Foster, *Otto Preminger: The Man Who Would Be King* (New York: Alfred A. Knopf, 2007).

Hoberman, J, "Flaunting It: The Rise and Fall of Hollywood's Nice' Jewish (Bad) Boys," in J. Hoberman and Jeffrey Shandler (eds), *Entertaining America: Jews, Movies and Broadcasting* (Princeton: Princeton University Press, 2003).

———, "May Days," *The Village Voice*, 14 February 2006 <https://www.villagevoice.com/2006/02/14/may-days/> (accessed January 2019).

Holden, Stephen, "FILM REVIEW; Just Take the Money and Run? Nah, She Wants Class and Culcha," *New York Times*, 19 May 2000 <https://www.nytimes.com/2000/05/19/movies/film-review-just-take-the-money-and-run-nah-she-wants-class-and-culcha.html> (accessed January 2019).

Ionesco, Eugene, *The Bald Prima Donna* [1950], in *Plays vol 1*, trans. Donald Watson (London: Calder, 1958).

Jacobs, Diane, "The Heartbreak Kid," *Changes in the Arts*, Jan/Feb 1973. *The Heartbreak Kid*, Clipping Files, Margaret Herrick Library.

Johnson, Kevin, "Elaine May: Do You Mind Interviewing Me in the Kitchen?," *New York Times*, 8 January 1967.

Kashner, Sam, "Who's Afraid of Nichols & May?" *Vanity Fair*, January 2013 <https://www.vanityfair.com/hollywood/2013/01/nichols-and-may-reunion-exclusive> (accessed January 2019).

Kashner, Sam and Maslow-Freen, Charles, "Mike Nichols's Life and Career: The Definitive

Oral History," *Vanity Fair*, 11 September 2015 <https://www.vanityfair.com/hollywood/2015/09/remembering-director-mike-nichols> (accessed January 2019).
Keller, Craig, *Elaine's*, film essay (2016), available at <https://vimeo.com/194607579> (accessed January 2019).
Kendon, Adam, *Gesture: Visible Action as Utterance* (Cambridge: Cambridge University Press, 2004).
Kercher, Stephen E., *Revel with a Cause: Liberal Satire in Postwar America* (Chicago: University of Chicago Press, 2006).
Kiang, Jessica, "Retrospective: The Directorial Career of Elaine May," *IndieWire*, 8 August 2013 <https://www.indiewire.com/2013/08/retrospective-the-directorial-career-of-elaine-may-95011/> (accessed January 2019).
King, Geoff, *Film Comedy* (London: Wallflower, 2002).
Kissel, Howard, "Films: 'The Heartbreak Kid'," *Women's Wear Daily*, 18 December 1972: 18.
Klawans, Stuart, *Film Follies: The Cinema Out of Order* (London: Cassell, 1999).
Klein, Jesse Noah, "Why I Keep Returning to Mikey and Nicky," *Talkhouse* 2017 <http://www.talkhouse.com/keep-returning-mikey-nicky/> (last accessed 14 April 2018).
Koenig Quart, Barbara, *Women Directors: The Emergence of a New Cinema* (New York: Praeger, 1988).
Kouvaros, George, *Where Does it Happen? John Cassavetes and Cinema at the Breaking Point* (Minneapolis: University of Minnesota Press, 2004).
Krasner, David (ed.), *Method Acting Reconsidered* (New York: St. Martin's, 2000).
Kristeva, Julia, *Powers of Horror: An Essay on Abjection* (New York: Columbia University Press, 1982).
Kundera, Milan, *Testaments Betrayed* (London: Faber and Faber, 1995).
Lahr, John, "Making it Real: How Mike Nichols re-created comedy and himself," *New Yorker*, 21 February 2000 <https://www.newyorker.com/magazine/2000/02/21/making-it-real-2> (accessed January 2019).
Larson, Gary, *The Complete Far Side: 1987–1994* (Kansas City: Andrews McMeel Publishing 2003), p. 351.
Larsen, Josh, "Mikey and Nicky," *Larsen on Film*, no date (http://www.larsenonfilm.com/mikey-and-nicky> (accessed January 2019).
Lemon, Dick, "How to Succeed in Interviewing Elaine May (Try, Really Try)," *New York Times*, 4 January 1970.
Lethem, Jonathan, "*Unfaithfully Yours*: Zeno, Achilles, and Sir Alfred," *Criterion Collection*, 12 July 2005 <https://www.criterion.com/current/posts/772-unfaithfully-yours-zeno-achilles-and-sir-alfred> (accessed January 2019).
Limon, John, *Stand-Up Comedy in Theory, or Abjection in America* (Durham, NC and London: Duke University Press, 2000).
Markel, Helen, "Mike Nichols & Elaine May," *Redbook Magazine*, February 1961: 99–100.
Maslin, Janet, "Film: Hoffman and Beatty in Elaine May's *Ishtar*", *New York Times*, 15 May 1987 <https://www.nytimes.com/1987/05/15/movies/film-hoffman-and-beatty-in-elaine-may-s-ishtar.html> (accessed January 2019).
Marsh, Calum, "Track Down this Film: A New Leaf, Elaine May's Unfinished Jewel," *The Village Voice*, 22 July 2013 <https://www.villagevoice.com/2013/07/22/track-down-this-film-a-new-leaf-elaine-mays-unfinished-jewel/> (accessed January 2019).
May, Elaine, *Mikey and Nicky*, DVD (Homevision Entertainment, 2004 (original film 1976)).
——, *The Birdcage: The Shooting Script* (New York: Newmarket Press, 1997).
——, *American Masters: Mike Nichols*, DVD (New York: Filmrise, 2016).

May, Elaine and Mike Nichols, *An Evening With Mike Nichols and Elaine May*, sound recording produced by Arthur Penn (Mercury Records, 1960).
——, *Improvisations to Music*, sound recording, with pianist Marty Rubenstein, produced by Jack Tracy (Mercury Records, 1958).
McCarthy, Todd, "Small Time Crooks," *Variety*, 15 May 2000 <variety.com/2000/film/reviews/small-time-crooks-1200462243/> (accessed January 2019).
McCreadie, Marsha, *The Women Who Write the Movies: From Frances Marion to Nora Ephron* (New York: Birch Lane Press, 1994).
McGowan, Todd, "Hitchcock's Ethics of Suspense: Psychoanalysis and the Devaluation of the Object," in Thomas Leitch and Leland Poague (eds), *A Companion to Alfred Hitchcock* (Oxford: Wiley-Blackwell, 2011), pp. 508–28.
McDonald, Tamar Jeffers, *Romantic Comedy: Boy Meets Girl Meets Genre* (New York: Wallflower, 2007).
Meehan, Thomas, "What the OTB Bettor Can Learn from Walter Matthau: A Lesson From . . .," *New York Times*, 4 July 1971: SM6.
Menand, Louis, "Some Frames for Goffman," *Social Psychology Quarterly* 72.4 (December 2009): 296–9.
Mizejewski, Linda, *Pretty/Funny: Women Comedians and Body Politics* (Austin: University of Texas Press, 2014).
Moskowitz, Gene, "Film Review: *A New Leaf*," *Variety*, 10 March 1971.
Moss, Robert F., "'Blume' and 'Heartbreak Kid'—What Kind of Jews Are They?" *New York Times*, 9 September 1973.
Mulvey, Laura, "Visual Pleasure and Narrative Cinema," *Screen*, 16.3 (1975): 6–18.
Murphy, Art, "Tele Follow-Up Comment: Omnibus," *Variety*, 22 January 1958: 46.
Myers, Julian, "Four Dialogues 4: On Elaine May," *Open Space*, 28 August 2009 <https://openspace.sfmoma.org/2009/08/four-dialogues-4-on-elaine-may> (accessed January 2019).
Nachman, Gerald, *Seriously Funny: The Rebel Comedians of the 1950s and 1960s* (New York: Pantheon Books 2003).
Naremore, James, *Acting in the Cinema* (Berkeley: University of California Press, 1998).
Natale, Richard, "Eye View: Please, Mrs. Worthington, DO . . .," *Women's Wear Daily*, 21 December 1972.
Oliver, Myrna, "Obituary: Lois Gould, 70; Novelist and Columnist," *Los Angeles Times*, 4 June <http://articles.latimes.com/2002/jun/04/local/me-gould4> (accessed January 2019 via keyword search).
Olsen, Christopher, "Comic Gesture Using 'Viewpoints'," in Christopher Olsen (ed.), *Acting Comedy* (London: Routledge, 2016), pp. 89–104.
Parish, James Robert, *Fiasco: A History of Hollywood's Iconic Flops* (Hoboken: John Wiley & Sons, 2006).
Penn, Stanley, "Focusing on Young: A New Breed of Movie Attracts the Young, Shakes Up Hollywood," *The Wall Street Journal*, 4 November 1969.
Phelan, Peggy, "Survey: Art and Feminism," in Helena Reckitt (ed.), *Art and Feminism* (London: Phaidon, 2012), pp. 14–49.
Pirandello, Luigi, *Six Characters in Search of an Author*, trans. Edward Storer (New York: Dover, 1922/1998).
Plato, *Symposium or Drinking Party*, ed. and trans. Eva Brann, Peter Kalkavage and Eric Salem (Indianapolis: Hackett, 2017).
Pogue, Mac, "Adventures in Feministory: Elaine May," *Bitch Media*, 20 December 2011 <http://www.bitchmedia.org/post/adventures-in-feministory-elaine-may-feminist-film-history> (accessed January 2019).

Powers, James, "Dialogue on Film: Neil Simon," *American Film* 3.5 (March 1978): 33–48.
Price, Sam (2011), "Films that you probably haven't seen but definitely should #8—Mikey and Nicky," *Permanent Plastic Helmet*, 24 July 2011 <https://permanentplastichelmet.com/2011/07/24/films-that-you-probably-haven%E2%80%99t-seen-but-definitely-should-8-mikey-and-nicky-1976-dir-elaine-may/> (accessed January 2019).
Rabin, Nathan, "Interview: Charles Grodin," *The AV Club*, 20 May 2009 <https://www.avclub.com/charles-grodin-1798216629> (accessed January 2019).
——, "Unpacking the short but prickly filmography of Elaine May," *The AV Club*, 24 January 2013 <https://film.avclub.com/unpacking-the-short-but-prickly-filmography-of-elaine-m-1798235875> (accessed January 2019).
Renzi, Thomas C., *Screwball Comedy and Film Noir: Unexpected Connections* (Jefferson, NC: McFarland, 2012).
Rice, Robert, "A Tilted Insight," *The New Yorker*, 15 April 1961, <https://www.newyorker.com/magazine/1961/04/15/a-tilted-insight> (accessed January 2019).
Rickey, Carrie, "Elaine May: Laughing Matters," *Sight & Sound* 28.10, October 2018: 40–4.
Riesman, David, Nathan Glazer and Reuel Denney, *The Lonely Crowd* (New Haven: Yale University Press, 1951/1961).
Rivlin, Michael, "Elaine May: Too Tough for Hollywood," *Millimeter* 3.10 (1975): 16.
Rosen, Marjorie, "Isn't it About Time to Bring on The Girls?," *New York Times*, 15 December 1974.
Rosenbaum, Jonathan, "Elaine and Erich: Two Peas in a Pod?" *Los Angeles Times Calendar*, 14 June 1987 <https://www.jonathanrosenbaum.net/1987/06/elaine-and-erich-two-peas-in-a-pod-tk> (accessed January 2019).
——, *Placing Movies: The Practice of Film Criticism* (Berkeley: University of California Press, 1995).
——, "The Mysterious Elaine May: Hiding in Plain Sight," *Jonathan Rosenbaum.net*, 8 August 1997 <https://www.jonathanrosenbaum.net/1997/08/21700/> (accessed January 2019).
——, "Mikey and Nicky", DVD essay, *Jonathan Rosenbaum.net*, October 2003 <https://www.jonathanrosenbaum.net/2003/10/mikey-and-nicky-liner-notes> (accessed January 2019).
——, *Essential Cinema: On the Necessity of Film Canons* (Baltimore: The Johns Hopkins University Press, 2008).
——, "My favorite end-of-the-year-poll (again, 2016)," *Jonathan Rosenbaum.net*, 24 December 2016 <http://www.jonathanrosenbaum.net/2016/12/50376/> (accessed January 2019).
——, "Bridge Over Troubled Water [THE GRADUATE]," *Jonathan Rosenbaum.net*, 21 January 2018 <https://www.jonathanrosenbaum.net/2018/01/bridge-over-troubled-water-/> (accessed January 2019).
Ross, Steven J, *Hollywood Left and Right: How Movie Stars Shaped American Politics* (New York: Oxford University Press, 2011).
Rottenberg, Dan, "Elaine May . . . or She May Not," *Chicago Tribune*, 21 October 1973: 56.
Sachs, Kathleen, "Crucial Viewing," *CINE-FILE*, 3 September 2017 <http://www.cinefile.info/?offset=1513364114709&reversePaginate=true> (accessed January 2019).
Saito, Stephen, "Elaine May on Almost Getting Away With Murder in *A New Leaf*," *Moveablefest.com*, 1 January 2014 <http://moveablefest.com/elaine-may-new-leaf> (accessed January 2019).
Sarris, Andrew, *The American Cinema. Directors and Directions 1929–1968* (New York: E. P. Dutton & Co., 1968).
Sartre, Jean-Paul, *Being and Nothingness*, trans. Hazel Barnes (New York: Philosophical Library, 1943/1956; London: Methuen, 1957).
——, *Existentialism and Humanism*, trans. Philip Mairet (London: Methuen, 2007).

Sassatelli, Roberta, "Interview With Laura Mulvey: Gender, Gaze and Technology in Film Culture," *Theory, Culture & Society* 28.5 (2011): 123–43.
Seham, Amy, *Whose Improv Is It, Anyway?* (Jackson: University Press of Mississippi, 2001).
Shevey, Sandra, "Playgirl Interview: Neil Simon," *Playgirl* 3.1 (June 1976): 56–141.
Silverman, Kaja, *The Acoustic Mirror: The Female Voice in Psychoanalysis And Cinema* (Bloomington: Indiana University Press, 1988).
Smith, Gavin, "Of Metaphors and Purpose," *Film Comment* 35.3 (May–June 1999): 12–30.
Smukler, Maya Montañez, *Liberating Hollywood: Women Directors and the Feminist Reform of 1970s American Cinema* (New Brunswick, NJ: Rutgers University Press, 2018).
Soloway, Jill, "The Female Gaze—TIFF: Master Class," *Topple Productions*, 11 September 2016 <https://www.toppleproductions.com/the-female-gaze> (accessed January 2019).
Spolin, Viola, *Improvisation for the Theatre* (Evanston, IL: Northwestern University Press, 1963).
Spoto, Donald, *The Art of Alfred Hitchcock: Fifty Years of His Motion Pictures* (New York: Anchor Books, 1992).
Steiger, Paul E., "Movie Makers No Longer Sure What Sparkle Is," *Los Angeles Times*, 17 November 1969.
Stephens, Chuck, "Chronicle of a Disappearance," *Film Comment* 42.2 (March–April 2006): 46–8, 50–3.
Stevens, Brad, "Male Narrative/Female Narration: Elaine May's *Mikey and Nicky*," *CineAction*, 31 April 1993: 74–83.
Stevens, Kyle, "Tossing Truths: Improvisation and the Performative Utterances of Nichols and May," *Critical Quarterly* 52.3 (2010): 23–46.
Stradley, Don L. (2016), "This Dazzling Time, *Mikey and Nicky*," Don L. Stradley blog, March 2016 <http://donstradley.blogspot.com/2016/03/mikey-and-nicky-1976.html> (accessed January 2019).
Sweet, Jeffrey, *Something Wonderful Right Away: An Oral History of Second City and The Compass Players* (New York: Limelight Editions, 2003).
Thomson, David, *Have You Seen . . .? A Personal Introduction to 1,000 Films* (New York: Alfred A. Knopf, 2008).
Thompson, Howard, "Elaine May Spends Her Summer Knee-Deep in Film," *New York Times*, 26 August 1969: 36.
Thompson, Thomas, "Whatever Happened to Elaine May?" *LIFE* magazine, 28 July 1967: 54–9.
Tobias, Andrew, "For Elaine May, a New Film—But Not A New Leaf," *New West*, 6 December 1976: 59–69.
Udel, James C., *The Film Crew of Hollywood: Profiles of Grips, Cinematographers, Designers, a Gaffer, a Stuntman and a Make-Up Artist* (Jefferson, NC: McFarland and Company, 2013).
Warga, Wayne, "Falk—Many a Sinking Ship's Saving Grace," *Los Angeles Times*, 16 December 1968: G1.
Weaver Jr, Warren, "Court to Review Obscenity Case," *New York Times*, 11 December 1973 <https://www.nytimes.com/1973/12/11/archives/court-to-review-obscenity-case-carnal-knowledge-appeal-is.html> (accessed January 2019).
Wasson, Sam, *Improv Nation: How We Made a Great American Art* (New York: Houghton Mifflin Harcourt, 2017).
Whitehead, J. W., *Mike Nichols and the Cinema of Transformation* (Jefferson, NC: McFarland, 2014).
Wollaston, Sam, "Crisis in Six Scenes—Woody Allen's TV debut is lazy, lame and badly acted. But it looks nice," *The Guardian*, 1 October 2016 <https://www.theguardian.com/

tv-and-radio/2016/oct/01/crisis-in-six-scenes-woody-allens-tv-debut-is-lazy-lame-and-badly-acted-but-it-looks-nice> (accessed January 2019).
Wolcott, James, "Mort the Knife," *Vanity Fair*, August 2007 <https://www.vanityfair.com/culture/2007/08/wolcott200708> (accessed January 2019).
Wyatt, Justin, *High Concept: Movies and Marketing in Hollywood* (Austin: University of Texas Press, 1994).
Young, Kay, *Ordinary Pleasures: Couples, Conversation and Comedy* (Columbus: Ohio State University Press, 2001).
Yule, Andrew, *Fast Fade: David Puttnam, Columbia Pictures and the Battle for Hollywood* (New York: Delcorte, 1989).
Zimmerman, Paul D., "Neil Simon: Up From Success," *Newsweek*, 2 February 1970: 53.

Index

Academy Awards, 50, 51, 117n, 139, 141, 144, 146, 160, 222
Adaptation (play), 4
Adjani, Isabelle, 3, 77, 142, 143
Agatha (1979), 146
Akerman, Chantal, 169
Albert, Eddie, 51, 104
All That Jazz (1979), 97
Allen, Woody, 4, 16, 32, 54, 101, 166, 168, 169, 176, 180n, 189
Alyce Film Inc., 58
American Academy of Dramatic Arts, 119
American Film Institute (AFI), 204, 231
American Masters: Mike Nichols (2016), 16, 202–6, 215–16
Angels in America (2003), 203, 223
Annie Hall (1977), 54
Arnold, Edward, 87
Arrick, Rose, 122, 174
Arsenic and Old Lace (1944), 94
Arthur, Jean, 87
Arzner, Dorothy, 41, 46–7
Austin, J. L., 67, 73
Azaria, Hank, 201, 217n

Bach to Bach (comedy sketch), 66, 67, 68, 80, 203
Back to School (1986), 145
Ballard, Lucien, 133
La Bamba (1987), 147
Bancroft, Anne, 30, 47, 170
Baranski, Christine, 208

Bart, Peter, 43, 48, 49
Bates, Kathy, 212
Beatty, Ned, 75, 121,133, 200
Beatty, Warren, 4, 5, 53, 54, 58–9, 77, 78, 127, 139–40, 141, 142–5, 146, 147, 149–50, 151, 152, 158, 159, 160, 161n, 200n, 206
Berlin, Ida, 44
Berlin, Jack, 2, 43
Berlin, Jeannie, 8, 24, 44, 50, 73, 104, 175, 232
Bernstein, Carl, 230
Beverly Hills Cop II (1987), 147, 155
The Big Town (1987), 147
The Birdcage (1996), 4, 16, 202, 203, 206, 207–12, 213, 216, 223, 230
Black List (screenplay list), 221–2
Blazing Saddles (1974), 55
Blind Date (1987), 153
Bludhorn, Charles, 8
Bogdanovich, Peter, 97, 98
Bonnie and Clyde (1967), 98, 144
Boxcar Bertha (1972), 133
Brice, Fanny, 169
Bringing Up Baby (1938), 74, 85, 87–9, 90, 91, 97, 100
Broadway, 3, 4, 33, 34, 35–6, 44, 45, 63, 69, 120, 139, 165, 179, 182, 191, 203, 205, 216, 222
Brooks, Mel, 55, 106, 203
Bruckheimer, Jerry, 147
Buchanan, Pat, 208
Burnett, Carol, 169
Burton, Richard, 44

INDEX

Butch Cassidy and the Sundance Kid (1969), 54

Cactus Flower (1969), 7
La Cage Aux Folles (1978), 208, 210
California Suite (1978), 4, 169, 174–5, 177
Canada, 42, 51
Cannon, Dyan, 100, 187
Capra, Frank, 85, 94
Carnal Knowledge (1971), 23, 99
Carter, John, 133
Carville, James, 212
Cassavetes, John, 3, 5, 9–10, 15, 55, 56, 57, 58, 59, 70, 75, 100, 119–38, 191
Cassavetes-Lane Workshop, 120
Catholic Legion of Decency, 205
Central Intelligence Agency (CIA), 5, 78, 142, 146, 150–1, 159
Channing, Carol, 7
Charlie Wilson's War (2007), 23
Chicago 2, 4, 24, 25–6, 28, 31, 36, 44, 63, 64, 67, 120, 182, 183, 199n, 203, 204, 223, 226, 227–8
City Slickers II: The Search for Curly's Gold (1994), 160
Clarke, Shirley, 41, 47
Clinton, Bill, 212–13
Clinton, Hillary, 212–13
Coca-Cola Company, 142, 145, 158
Cocteau, Jean, 140
Cold War, 54
Columbia Pictures, 42, 44, 46, 59, 139, 142, 145–6, 152, 155, 158
Columbo (TV series), 123, 135
The Compass Players, 4, 24–9, 31–2, 33, 36, 37n, 44, 63, 64, 67, 120, 182, 185, 199n, 203, 204, 223, 225, 228
Compton, Juleen, 47
Cooder, Ry, 215
Corman, Roger, 47
Cosby, Bill, 158, 160
Crisis in Six Scenes (2016), 4, 16, 166, 169, 177–9, 180n
Crocodile Dundee (1986), 145
Crosby, Bing, 5, 78, 141, 143
Cruise, Suri, 222, 225–6
Cruise, Tom, 145, 160
Cyrus, Miley, 178

Dale, Esther (Elaine May alias), 4, 16, 100, 181, 207
Dangerfield, Rodney, 145
Dangerous Minds (1995), 206
Darling, Joan, 47

Davenport, Dorothy, 46
A Day in the Death of Joe Egg (1972), 100
de Beauvoir, Simone, 182, 194, 193–4, 196
Deliverance (1972), 72
The Dentist (comedy sketch), 32
Didion, Joan, 100, 187
Diller, Barry, 58
Diller, Phyllis, 169
Directors Guild of America, 41
The Dirty Dozen (1967), 125
Doctor Dolittle (1967), 43
Donner, Clive, 4, 16, 165, 171–2
Dunaway, Faye, 144
Dunne, John Gregory, 187

Eastwood, Clint, 145
Easy Living (1937), 85, 87, 89
Easy Rider (1969), 42, 54
Edelman, Herb, 174
Edge of the City (1957), 119
Edwards, Stacy, 213
84 Charing Cross Road (1987), 158
Elkins, Hillard, 46, 48
Enter Laughing (1967), 4, 44, 46, 165, 169, 170–1, 172
Ephron, Nora, 101, 230
Evans, Robert, 6, 43, 46, 47, 49, 56, 189
An Evening with Mike Nichols and Elaine May (recording), 34
An Evening with Mike Nichols and Elaine May (stage show), 33–4, 36

Faces (1968), 9, 126, 128, 133, 134
Falk, Peter, 3, 4, 5, 10, 44, 55, 56, 57, 58, 75, 120, 122, 123, 124, 127, 129, 131, 133, 135, 165, 168, 172, 176
The Far Side (comic strip), 140
Farrow, Dylan, 180n
Farrow, Ronan, 180n
Ferrer, José, 170
Five Easy Pieces (1970), 139
Flashdance (1983), 147, 148
Flicker, Theodore J., 64
Flockhart, Calista, 208
Foch, Nina, 197
Fonda, Henry, 89
Fonda, Jane, 145
Fonda, Peter, 42, 54
The Fortune (1975), 139–40, 145
French New Wave, 69, 96, 217
Friedman, Bruce Jay, 52, 54, 104
Futterman, Dan, 208

Gable, Clark, 144
Gam, Rita, 190
Garland, Judy, 217n
Gazzara, Ben, 127
Generation X, 145
Germany, 25, 204
Gloria (1980), 132
The Godfather (1972), 10
Goffman, Erving, 67
Golden Globe Awards, 117
Gould, Elliott, 106
Gould, Lois, 181, 185, 187, 188, 198, 199n
Gover, Robert, 45
Grace, Carol, 75, 125
The Graduate (1967), 4, 8, 23, 30, 42, 54, 86, 97, 99, 106, 151, 165, 170, 203, 205, 223, 224
Grammy Awards, 34, 120
Grant, Cary, 88-9, 91, 94, 100
The Green Heart (short story), 45, 95
Grodin, Charles, 8, 12, 50, 51, 73, 104, 105, 142, 207
Guber, Peter, 147
Guild, Nancy, 190
Gulf and Western, 43

Hackman, Gene, 208
Hagan, Allie, 16, 221–33
Hagman, Larry, 213
Harold and Maude (1971), 54, 86, 100
Hart, Gary, 149, 161
Hawks, Howard, 85, 86, 87–90
The Hays Code, 86
The Heartbreak Kid (1972), 3, 6, 8–10, 12, 14, 15, 41, 50–5, 57, 58, 73, 75, 104–18, 120, 128, 129, 133, 136, 140–1, 187, 193, 194, 203, 207
The Heartbreak Kid (2007), 8
Heartburn (1986), 230
Heaven Can Wait (1978), 4, 51, 58, 141, 143, 206
Heaven's Gate (1980), 140, 145, 160
Hello Dolly! (1969), 7
Hellraiser (1987), 153
Hepburn, Katharine, 74, 88, 89
Hitchcock, Alfred, 27, 86, 93, 94–5
Hitler, Adolf, 71, 204
Hoffman, Dustin, 5, 30, 42, 53, 54, 59, 69, 77, 106, 127, 142, 143, 144, 145, 146, 147, 160, 170, 203, 206
Hogan, Paul, 145
Hope, Bob, 5, 78, 141, 143
Hope and Glory (1987), 147
Hopper, Dennis, 42, 54

The Hospital (1971), 100
Howard, Ken, 189
Husbands (1970), 9, 55, 126, 127, 128, 129

Improvisations to Music (recording), 3, 32, 44, 63, 64, 66
In a Lonely Place (1950), 93
In the Spirit (1990), 4, 175–6
Iran–Contra scandal, 78
Isherwood, Christopher, 44
Ishtar (1987), 3, 4–6, 10, 12, 14, 16, 42, 51, 53, 59, 76–9, 122, 125, 127, 129, 131, 135, 139–61, 167, 190, 194, 200n, 202, 203, 206, 223, 228, 231
Israel, 78, 150
It Happened One Night (1934), 85, 87, 91, 97

Jaffe, Stanley, 48–9
Jewish New Wave, 106–7

Kafka, Franz, 178
Kahn, Madeline, 97
Kahn, Sheldon, 133
Kemper, Victor J., 133
Kennedy, Jackie, 205
The Killing of a Chinese Bookie (1976), 132
The King of Comedy (1982), 109, 158–9
Klein, Joe, 212, 213
Koch, Howard, 46, 48
Kristeva, Julia, 110, 115
Kubrick, Stanley, 70

La La Land (2016), 144
Labyrinth (1986), 206
Ladd, Diane, 213
The Lady Eve (1941)
Lamour, Dorothy, 141
Lane, Burt, 119, 120
Lane, Nathan, 208
Larson, Gary, 140
The Last Emperor (1987), 147
Lavin, Linda, 53
Léaud, Jean-Pierre, 69
Leonard Part 6 (1987), 147
Lester, Adrian, 212
Lewinsky, Monica, 213
Lewis, Jerry, 158, 173, 206
Little, Cleavon, 54–5
Little Murders (1971), 86, 100
Love Streams (1984), 123
The Loved One (film), 7, 44
The Loved One (novel), 7, 44
Luckinbill, Laurence, 100, 189
Lupino, Ida, 41, 46–7

Luv (film), 4, 16, 44, 46, 55, 120, 165, 169, 171–2, 234
Luv (play), 120
Lyne, Adrian, 147

*M*A*S*H* (1970), 151, 189
McElwaine, Guy, 142, 146
McGovern, George, 149, 151
Madonna, 159, 160
Magaro, John, 178
Marion, Frances, 46
A Matter of Position (play), 35
Matthau, Walter, 7, 8, 45–6, 48, 60, 70, 71, 85, 168, 173, 174–5, 188
May, Marvin, 2, 25, 44
Meredith, Burgess, 195
Merrily We Go to Hell (1931), 46
Mesiner, Sanford, 121
Metamorphosis (novella), 178
Metro-Goldwyn-Mayer Studios (MGM), 42
Mickey One (1965), 143
Midnight Cowboy (1969), 54
Mike Nichols and Elaine May Examine Doctors (recording), 35
Mikey and Nicky (1976), 3, 5–6, 10, 14, 15, 55, 56, 58, 75–6, 77, 119–38, 140, 141, 172, 183, 193, 194, 200, 203, 206
Milland, Ray, 87
Minnie and Moskowitz (1971), 100, 125, 132
Miss Julie (play), 26
Mondale, Walter, 149
Moonlight (2016), 144
Moscow Art Theatre, 199n
Mother and Son (comedy sketch), 34–5
Mulvey, Laura, 106, 108, 109, 110, 111–12
Murphy, Eddie, 144, 146, 155
Murray, Bill, 59, 206
My Man Godfrey (1936), 85, 87, 89, 91

National Broadcasting Company (NBC), 44
National Endowment for the Arts, 209
National Society of Film Critics, 4, 51, 176
Network (1976), 100, 117
New Hollywood, 2, 11, 41, 47, 96–101, 151, 165, 170, 182
A New Leaf (1971), 3, 6–8, 12, 13, 14, 15, 41, 47–50, 51, 53, 55, 57, 70–3, 74, 76, 79, 85–103, 120, 129, 136, 140, 141, 166, 168, 169, 173, 175, 177, 178, 187, 188, 191–2, 195, 200, 203, 206, 207, 222, 224, 227
New York Film Critics Awards, 51
New York University, 25
Nichols, Mike, 1, 2, 3, 4, 6, 7, 8, 10, 11, 15, 16, 23–38, 41, 42, 44, 46, 63–9, 70, 71, 75, 76, 77, 79, 80n, 86, 96, 97, 99, 100, 106–7, 120, 123–4, 135, 139, 151, 165, 166, 167, 168, 170, 171, 173, 182, 183, 185, 189, 199, 202–17, 221–33
Nichols, Robert, 25
Nicaragua, 150
Nixon, Richard, 149, 151
No Exit (play), 183
North, Colonel Oliver, 150

O'Neal, Ryan, 97
O'Neill, Jennifer, 189
The Odd Couple (1968), 45–6
One Flew Over the Cuckoo's Nest (1975), 139
One Hundred Dollar Misunderstanding (unfinished film project), 45
The Only Game in Town (1970), 143
Opening Night (1977), 132
Ouspenskaya, Maria, 26, 37, 65, 166–7, 182, 185, 189n, 199, 216n, 227–8

Pacino, Al, 145
Palestine Liberation Organization (PLO), 78
Palomar Pictures
The Panic in Needle Park (1971)
Paramount Pictures, 50, 55, 235
The Philadelphia Story (1940), 91
Pirandello (comedy sketch), 69, 75
Pirandello, Luigi, 69
Plato, 2, 72, 74
Playwright's Theatre Club, 26
Plummer, Christopher, 7
Polanski, Roman, 75, 78, 125
Postcards From the Edge (1990), 203
Preminger, Otto, 4, 16, 100, 181–201, 207
Primary Colors (film), 202, 203, 206, 207–8, 212–14
Primary Colors (novel), 208, 212
Prince of Darkness (1987), 153
Pryor, Richard, 55
Puttnam, David, 146, 152, 158

Rafelson, Bob, 139
Rain Man (1988), 160
Reagan, President Ronald, 150, 151
Redfield, William, 190
Redford, Robert, 47, 54, 145
Reds (1980), 59, 141, 143, 146, 206
Reiner, Carl, 4, 44, 165, 170–1
Revolution (1985), 145
Reynolds, Burt, 145
Rice, Donna, 149
Riesman, David, 67, 72
Ritchie, Jack, 45, 95

The Road to Singapore (1940), 141
Robbie, Margot, 222
Roizman, Owen, 109, 117
Rollins, Jack, 32, 44
Roosevelt, President Franklin D., 149
Rose, George, 95
Rosemary's Baby (1968), 125
Roth, Philip, 12, 106, 107
Rothman, Stephanie, 47
Roxane (1987), 158
Ryan, Arthur N., 58

Sadat, President Anwar, 151
Sandinistas, 150
Santoni, Reni, 170
Sartre, Jean-Paul, 66–8, 80n, 181, 182–5, 192, 193, 196, 197
Saturday Night Live (TV series), 144
Saypol, New York Supreme Court Justice Irving H., 6
Schlossberg, Julian, 203, 205
Schneider, Bert, 42
Schwarzenegger, Arnold, 144
Scorsese, Martin, 108, 109, 132, 133, 158
Scott, Ridley, 158
Scott, Tony, 145, 147, 155
Sebastian, Beverly, 47
Second City (theatre group), 25, 33, 199, 228
The Secret of My Success (1987), 153, 155
Shaber, David, 187
Shadows (1959), 120, 123, 125
Shampoo (1975), 54, 139, 143
Shepherd, Cybill, 8, 50, 51, 52, 74, 104, 111
Shepherd, David, 26, 28, 232
Silkwood (1983), 139, 230
Sills, Paul, 26, 63, 185, 199
Silver Streak (1976), 55
Simon, Neil, 8, 41, 45, 50, 53, 73, 104, 174
Simpson, Don, 147
Sister Sledge, 208
Small Time Crooks (2000), 4, 168, 169, 176–8
Soloway, Jill, 106, 107–12, 115, 117n
Some Like it Hot (1959), 211
Someone to Watch Over Me (1987), 147
Sontag, Susan, 204
Sony Corporation, 158
The Sopranos (TV series), 10
Southern, Terry, 44
Spolin, Viola, 26–8, 30, 31, 63–4, 66, 68, 199, 228
Stanislavsky, Konstantin, 27, 28, 37n, 65, 166, 199, 216
Stanwyck, Barbara, 88
The Steve Allen Show (TV series), 32, 33

The Sting (1973), 47, 54
Strasberg, Lee, 28, 37, 65, 166–7, 199, 204, 216
Streisand, Barbra, 97, 106
Strindberg, August, 26
Sturges, Preston, 85–7, 92, 94
Such Good Friends (1971), 4, 16, 100, 130, 181–201
Sylbert, Anthea, 51
Sylbert, Richard, 51

Tati, Jacques, 148
Taylor, Elizabeth, 42, 44
Teenagers in a Car (comedy sketch), 29–31, 68–9, 172–3, 223, 224
Telephone (comedy sketch), 34, 35
Tell Me That You Love Me, Junie Moon (1970), 187, 191
The Thin Man (1934), 91
Thomas, Marlo, 176
Thompson, Emma, 212
Thornton, Billy Bob, 212
Tierney, Maura, 213
Tomlin, Lily, 169
Tonight at 8.30 (theatre group), 26
Tony Awards, 45
Too Late Blues (1961), 126
Tootsie (1982), 59, 117, 141, 145, 206
Top Gun (1986), 145, 147
Tower Commission, 150
Travolta, John, 212
Trouble with Angels (1966), 46
The Trouble with Harry (1955), 86, 94–6
20th Century Fox, 41, 42, 43, 47, 50, 55

Ullman, Tracey, 176
Unfaithfully Yours (1948), 85, 92–4, 101, 101
United Artists, 47, 55, 145
Universal Studios, 47, 72
University of Chicago, 2, 4, 25, 26, 64, 67, 120, 199n, 203, 227

Van Patten, Joyce, 122
Voight, Jon, 54
von Stroheim, Erich, 3, 70, 140

Wagner, Jane, 47
Waiting for Godot (play), 76, 82n
Walker, Rebecca, 214
Warner, Jack, 205
Warner Bros., 47, 205
The Waverly Gallery (play), 3, 179
Wayne, Nina, 172
Weber, Lois, 46

Weiland, Paul, 158, 160
Weill, Claudia, 47, 105
Weinstein, Harvey, 167, 180
Weinstein, Robert, 167
Wertmüller, Lina, 11–12, 193
What's Up, Doc? (1972), 97
When in Doubt, Seduce (screenplay), 16, 221–33
Who's Afraid of Virginia Woolf? (1966), 4, 44, 99, 203, 205
Wiest, Dianne, 208

Wilder, Billy, 3, 45, 86, 211
Wilder, Gene, 54
Williams, Paul, 144
Williams, Robin, 203, 208
Wolf (1994), 4, 206, 230
A Woman Under the Influence (1974), 123, 128
Working Girl (1988), 203, 229–30
World War II, 144, 204

Yablans, Frank, 56, 12

EU representative:
Easy Access System Europe
Mustamäe tee 50, 10621 Tallinn, Estonia
Gpsr.requests@easproject.com

www.ingramcontent.com/pod-product-compliance
Lightning Source LLC
Chambersburg PA
CBHW070324240426
43671CB00013BA/2356